NOW YOU SEE IT

NOW YOU SEE IT

Simple Visualization Techniques for Quantitative Analysis

STEPHEN FEW

Analytics Press
BURLINGAME, CALIFORNIA

Analytics Press

PO Box 1545
Burlingame, CA 94011-1545
SAN 253-5602
www.analyticspress.com
Email: info@analyticspress.com

PUBLISHER: Jonathan G. Koomey

COPY EDITOR: Nan Wishner
COMPOSITION: BookMatters and Bryan Pierce
COVER ART: Keith Stevenson
PHOTOGRAPHY: John Fernez
PRINTER AND BINDER: C&C Offset Printing Company

ISBN: 0-9706019-8-0
ISBN-13: 978-0-9706019-8-8

This book was printed on acid-free paper in China.
10 9

To those whose work with data is an
uncompromising search for truth.

ACKNOWLEDGEMENTS

First, I'd like to express deep gratitude to the many people who have attended my visual data analysis course over the past few years—in the MBA program at the University of California Berkeley, in public workshops, at conferences, and in courses that I've taught privately for many organizations—whose suggestions have helped me to more effectively craft the content of that course and, consequently, the content of this book. For me, there is no better way to hone ideas for a book than by teaching a course on the subject for awhile.

Second, I'd like to thank the following friends and colleagues (listed in alphabetical order) who graciously agreed to read a preliminary draft of this book and provide their expert feedback:

Lyn Bartram (Assistant Professor in the School of Interactive Arts and Technology at Simon Fraser University)

John Gerth (Manager of the Computer Graphics Lab at Stanford University)

Pat Hanrahan (Professor of Computer Science at Stanford University)

Marti Hearst (Professor in the School of Information at the University of California, Berkeley)

Jeffrey Heer (Assistant Professor of Computer Science at Stanford University)

Robert Kosara (Assistant Professor of Computer Science at the University of North Carolina)

Jock Mackinlay (Director of Visual Analysis at Tableau Software)

Naomi Robbins (Author of *Creating More Effective Graphs*)

John Stasko (Professor in the School of Interactive Computing at the Georgia Institute of Technology)

Hadley Wickham (Assistant Professor of Statistics at Rice University)

Although all but two of these reviewers are academics, you should not take this to mean that I wrote this book for an academic audience. I hope that many college courses will find it useful, but the contents that I cover and the language that I use were tailored for a general audience of people in organizations of all types who must make sense of quantitative data in the course of their work.

Those of you who are familiar with information visualization research no doubt recognize many of these names. The support of these experts in the field gave me confidence that I was on the right track and occasionally nudged me back in line whenever I even slightly went astray.

Third, I am especially indebted to Bryan Pierce, my colleague at Perceptual Edge, who assisted me diligently and expertly throughout the long process of writing this book with countless suggestions, eagle-eyed edits, and the tedious job of laying it out for the printer.

Finally, to my publisher, Jonathan Koomey, my copyeditor, Nan Wishner, my cover designer, Keith Stevenson, and the fine folks at BookMatters, I wish to convey my sincere appreciation, not only for playing your roles with great skill, but for doing so with the thoughtfulness and warmth that only comes from friends.

Upon this gifted age, in its dark hour
Rains from the sky a meteoric shower
Of facts…they lie, unquestioned, uncombined.
Wisdom enough to leach us of our ill
Is daily spun; but there exists no loom
To weave it into a fabric.

Huntsman, What Quarry?, Edna St. Vincent Millay, 1939 (emphasis mine)

CONTENTS

NOW YOU SEE IT

INTRODUCTION

We Have an Information Problem

We live in a data-rich world. You've no doubt heard this before, and you may have also sensed (or painfully experienced) that most of us stand on the shore of a vast sea of available data, suited up in the latest diving gear and equipped with the slickest tools and gadgets, but with hardly a clue what to do. Before long, we find ourselves drowning within a stone's throw of the shore, flailing about and wondering what went wrong.

We don't have too much information. Its quantity and rapid growth is not a problem. In fact, it represents a wealth of potential. The problem is that most of us don't know how to dive into this ocean of information, net the best of it, bring it back to shore, and sort it out—that is, understand it well enough to make good use of it. Software tools on the market vary in how effectively they can assist us in navigating the data analysis process and no matter how well designed these tools are, the results they produce will depend on how skilled we are in employing them.

Why bother to analyze data? Why strive to understand it better than we already do? Understanding alone isn't the goal. It's an important step along the journey, but our ultimate goal is to understand what the data show us about what's actually happening in our organizations so we can put that understanding to use for worthwhile ends. Whether we're part of a business working to better serve our customers, a non-profit agency trying to feed the poor, a hospital trying to reduce the number of post-operative complications, or a government trying to balance its budget, we must first understand what's actually happening in the provision of our service or product before we can act to improve what we do. Good data analysis allows us:

1. To better manage what's going on now
2. To better predict what will likely happen under particular conditions in the future, so we can create opportunities and prevent problems

We spend billions of dollars every year on technology to produce meaningful and actionable information. Unfortunately, much of that information collects in murky pools that grow larger and more stagnant by the day, even though quantitative information—the numbers that measure performance, identify opportunities, and forecast the future—is the water of life, critical to our organizations' health and success.

During the past two decades, we've seen tremendous progress in technologies that allow us to collect, store, and access data, but we've largely ignored the primary tool that makes information meaningful and useful: the human brain. While concentrating on the technologies, we've forgotten the human skills that are required to make sense of the data.

The current poor state of quantitative data analysis is a *dumbing down* that has resulted, in part, from computerization. Although some of us have resisted the temptation, most of us have become drunk on the magic potions served in logo-etched mugs by software vendors who promise spontaneous productivity if we simply buy their products.

Computers can't make sense of data; only people can. More precisely, only people who have developed the necessary data analysis skills can. Computers serve us best when we use them to more efficiently and accurately do what we already know how to do. Decision makers typically rely on information that is preprocessed for them, mostly by people who have never been trained in the fundamental skills of data analysis. These skills are rare in the workplace today, not because they're difficult to develop, but because we've been lulled into the mistaken belief that computers do this work for us, that if we have the appropriate software and know where to click with the mouse to access data and produce a report, we are data analysts by virtue of those abilities. As long as we embrace this delusion, we'll continue to produce analyses that at best barely scratch the surface and at worst lead to misinformation and costly decisions. It's time to do something about this and demand a return on investment (ROI) from the technologies that we've purchased and implemented at such great cost.

The Solution Isn't Complicated

Working with information to support decision making requires more than rudimentary analysis skills. Good decisions can't be reached through routine application of memorized or formulaic responses to predictable circumstances. Good decisions require us to creatively apply concepts and adapt skills to make sense of information. The ability to do this is not intuitive; it must be learned, and the good news is that we can learn these skills with relative ease. Ninety percent of the data analyses needed by most organizations can be performed using a simple set of skills that require only a basic and easily mastered understanding of statistics. These analyses involve a set of techniques that use graphs—visual representations of quantitative information—to explore numbers and discover meaningful patterns within them. Mastering these visual analysis techniques allows us to lift the veil that separates us from insight. Unfortunately, few people have learned these simple skills, and most who have done so followed the hard road, as I did, making individual small discoveries here and there over many years.

This book is my response to the lack of training available in visual analysis. Before deciding to write the book, I searched high and low for books and courses that taught these skills. I found that existing data analysis resources either teach sophisticated financial and statistical techniques that address relatively few problems, or they focus on a particular software product (mostly *Microsoft Excel*), taking students step by boring step through the specific mouse clicks and keystrokes needed to use the tool without explaining the underlying concepts. The basic concepts, skills, and techniques that most of us need are largely ignored.

In one of my other books, *Show Me the Numbers: Designing Tables and Graphs to Enlighten*, I teach the fundamental skills needed to present quantitative information visually to others. In *Now You See It*, I teach how to understand the message that's contained in the data because understanding is essential before anything can be presented to others. This book focuses on data exploration, leading to discovery, and data sense-making, leading to understanding. Because understanding requires that the meanings embedded in data are presented clearly and accurately, many of the principles and practices in *Show Me the Numbers* apply to this book as well. But compared to data presentation, data exploration and sense-making require extensive interaction with data and a richer set of graphs.

When we learn and begin to practice good data analysis skills, our organizations will be able to operate more intelligently. These skills, supported by well-designed software, are necessary to build a working interface between the computer and the human brain, which is the seat of true business intelligence. Without these skills, the potential of our information age and economy will remain a grand delusion. With these skills, we can transform data into a clear well of refreshing water, bringing sustenance and health to our organizations.

Traditional Software Has Hit the Wall

The methods and technologies that are supposed to support data analysis and reporting—known as *business intelligence*—have failed so far to deliver on their promise of intelligence. Despite great technical progress in data acquisition, data integration, data improvement through cleansing and transformation, and the construction of huge data warehouses that we can access at incredible speeds, the business intelligence industry has largely ignored the fact that intelligence resides in human beings, and that information only becomes valuable when it is understood, not just when it's made available.

True business intelligence relies on software that leverages the strengths of human eyes and minds and augments our cognition. Traditional business intelligence approaches to data analysis fall short. They rely primarily on tables of text, which work well for looking up individual facts but restrict thinking to one or two facts at a time. We struggle to piece these facts together into a picture of the whole that allows us to see relationships in the data. A long time ago, in 1891, the brothers Farquhar recognized this problem and proposed a solution:

> *The graphical method has considerable superiority for the exposition of statistical facts over the tabular. A heavy bank of figures is grievously wearisome to the eye, and the popular mind is as incapable of drawing any useful lessons from it as of extracting sunbeams from cucumbers.*[1]

1. *Economic and Industrial Solutions*, A. B. Farquhar and H. Farquhar, G. B. Putnam's Sons, New York NY, 1891, p. 55.

On the following page are some examples illustrating the difference in usefulness between tables and graphs for understanding information. If we wish to look up the precise amount of sales revenue, marketing expense, or profit for a specific region during a specific month (for example, the east region for the month of July), the following tables support us perfectly.

Revenue

Region	Jan	Feb	Mar	Apr	May	Jun	Jul	Aug	Sep	Oct	Nov	Dec	Total
West	28,384	30,288	34,302	32,039	32,938	34,392	33,923	33,092	34,934	30,384	33,923	37,834	396,433
Central	15,934	16,934	17,173	16,394	17,345	16,384	15,302	14,939	14,039	12,304	11,033	9,283	177,064
East	11,293	12,384	12,938	12,034	11,034	13,983	12,384	12,374	12,384	13,374	14,394	19,283	157,859
Total	55,611	59,606	64,413	60,467	61,317	64,759	61,609	60,405	61,357	56,062	59,350	66,400	731,356

Marketing Expenses

Region	Jan	Feb	Mar	Apr	May	Jun	Jul	Aug	Sep	Oct	Nov	Dec	Total
West	6,288	6,019	6,555	364	5,407	6,450	7,442	6,150	6,201	6,697	6,408	7,376	71,356
Central	4,429	5,039	4,309	4,951	5,442	4,675	4,558	5,124	5,278	4,016	5,325	5,898	59,044
East	851	1,784	1,542	1,024	1,864	1,173	1,237	1,504	714	1,152	2,620	2,501	17,966
Total	11,568	12,842	12,406	6,339	12,713	12,298	13,237	12,778	12,192	11,865	14,353	15,775	148,367

Profit Margin

Region	Jan	Feb	Mar	Apr	May	Jun	Jul	Aug	Sep	Oct	Nov	Dec	Average
West	25.11%	24.07%	25.52%	25.80%	25.93%	26.06%	25.02%	24.41%	25.13%	25.31%	25.12%	25.01%	25.13%
Central	22.13%	23.22%	22.55%	21.08%	22.54%	20.04%	27.08%	22.52%	22.31%	23.32%	21.05%	22.01%	22.38%
East	24.06%	24.80%	21.97%	18.50%	37.16%	23.02%	19.06%	20.60%	29.74%	21.41%	43.29%	19.49%	25.26%
Average	23.69%	23.93%	23.32%	21.77%	28.52%	23.01%	23.69%	22.37%	25.58%	23.24%	29.80%	22.16%	24.26%

Figure 1

If, instead, we wish to understand sales—the story that's told by patterns, trends, and exceptions in the data—the tabular displays above are not very useful. To understand the relationships within and among sales revenues, marketing expenses, and profits per region, we need pictures that make these relationships visible. The following series of line graphs gives one such picture, focusing our attention on change through time:

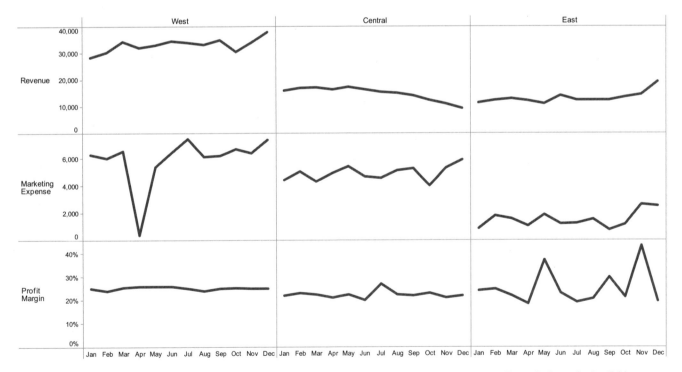

Figure 2. Created using Tableau Software

These graphs show a narrative that starts in January and ends in December, with a cast of characters who take their own journeys, sometimes related and sometimes not. Some journeys are smooth; some are jagged and volatile. Some head upward, some downward, and some traverse a flat terrain. Some scale mountains, some cross valleys, some stand alone. Notice how your eyes are powerfully drawn to the extreme dip in marketing expenses in the West region in April. The fact that there is no corresponding effect on profit margin seems odd. Also notice that, despite relatively low revenues overall, the east region has generated the highest profit margins, which occur in the months of May and November and correspond unexpectedly to increases in marketing expenses.

The following bubble plot features correlations between revenues, marketing expenses, and profit margins per region and month.

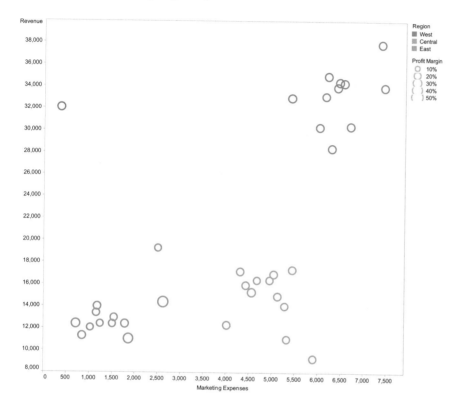

Figure 3. Created using Tableau Software

Notice that the distinct nature of each region now appears clearly as three separate clusters of green, orange, and blue values. This pattern reveals something worth investigating, for clusters as distinct as this don't occur without reasons.

Examining these graphs, however revealing, is also a bit frustrating, because other views are needed to complete our understanding. For example, it would help to see the other expenses that affect profit margins. And, in addition to profit margins, it would be useful to examine profits in dollars to see the relative effect of regional performance on the bottom line. This frustration is healthy. As answers to questions become more accessible, they naturally lead to more questions, which is a sign of growing awareness.

Well-designed pictures—visualizations—make these stories visible and bring them to life. Information visualization plays a central role in business intelligence. It provides a powerful means to net the prize fish from the vast schools of data that swim the information ocean.

We Must Use Our Eyes

Data analysis can take various forms; *visual* data analysis alone provides a simple yet illuminating window through which information can be seen, explored, and understood. Statistics can reduce large, complex data sets to a few numbers, but this reductive approach can also shear away much of the richness and subtlety in data. Statistical analysis that goes beyond the basics involves an erudite language spoken only by trained specialists, but visual analysis is accessible to a broader audience. According to the eminent 20th century statistician John Tukey: "One great virtue of good graphical representation is that it can serve to display clearly and effectively a message carried by quantities whose calculation or observation is far from simple."[2] How can visual analysis pave the way to analytical insight for the statistically uninitiated? It taps an ability that all but a few of us naturally possess: vision.

Vision is not just one of the five channels through which we sense the world; it is by far the dominant and most powerful sense. Vision provides more information than all the other senses combined, not only in terms of sheer volume but also in subtlety. More than two centuries ago, early pioneers in data visualization recognized the potential of representing quantitative information in ways that our eyes can readily perceive. When written as text, numbers must be processed one at a time, which is slow. When numbers are held and manipulated in our minds, most of us quickly become lost. Pioneering thinkers such as William Playfair (1759-1823) realized that if numbers could be accurately represented visually, they could be perceived, explored, examined, and understood quickly and to degrees that had not been possible. Playfair's early graphs, first published in 1786, were revolutionary, opening the door to previously unimaginable explorations of the meanings contained in numbers. We take this for granted today, but prior to Playfair it was difficult to comprehend quantitative patterns, trends, and exceptions. Unfortunately, we didn't begin to progress beyond Playfair's ideas until the late 1970s, and most of us are still unaware of modern visualization techniques.

When we represent quantitative information in visual form, our ability to think about it is dramatically enhanced. Visual representations not only make the patterns, trends, and exceptions in numbers visible and understandable, they also extend the capacity of our memory, making available in front of our eyes what we couldn't otherwise hold all at once in our minds. In simple terms, information visualization helps us think. The close relationship between vision and cognition has long been recognized but not understood. Today, we're beginning to better understand, appreciate, and make use of this connection through brain research.

Although visual perception is extremely powerful in itself, it can only be used effectively if we understand its rules and apply them. This book is a guide to the rules of visual perception and how they can be effectively applied to graphs to promote data exploration, analysis, and, ultimately, insight. We experience what Joseph Berkson called "*interocular traumatic impact:* a conclusion that hits us between the eyes."[3] That's the power of information visualization.

2. "Proceedings of the Symposium on Information Processing in Sight Sensory Systems", John W. Tukey and M. B. Wilk, California Institute of Technology, Pasadena CA, 1965, p. 15.

3. *Visualizing Data*, William S. Cleveland, Hobart Press, Summit NJ, 1993, p. 12.

We Must Keep Our Eyes on the Goal

When dealing with technology, it's easy to become caught up in the mechanics of the system, focusing more on using the software than the goals it was designed to help us achieve. We analyze information not for its own sake but so we can make informed decisions. Good decisions are based on understanding. Analysis is performed to arrive at clear, accurate, relevant, and thorough understanding. The connections between data and decisions are built one good question at a time until understanding bridges the gap between them.

Questions that lead to understanding fall into two camps: descriptive and predictive. Descriptive questions seek to understand what *is*:

- What is happening?
- What is causing this to happen?

That is, these questions help us understand cause and effect. On this foundation, we can ask predictive questions to extend the reach of our understanding into the future:

- What do we want to happen?
- What actions would likely lead to this desired outcome?

Answers to these questions help us shape the future. This is the goal of data analysis, from which our eyes and minds should never stray.

The Approach of this Book

Each of us plays many roles in life, some of which are more central to who we are than others. For me, the most central role is that of *teacher*. Many years ago, I discovered that I had a talent for teaching important concepts and skills that many people feared were too complicated and inaccessible. So the role of teacher is foremost in my mind as I write this book. *Now You See It* isn't a resource to pull from the shelf as a reference only when we need a particular answer. It isn't a list of best practices that we should memorize and apply as a set of rigid procedures. Rather, it is written to take us on a journey of discovery, introducing concepts and asking us to apply them in various ways so that we can take them with us and apply them effectively in our own work lives.

In this book, I sometimes ask questions before I offer answers. I do this to tap what we already know so that the new information becomes tightly and meaningfully integrated. In this way, the skills presented in this book can become an integral part of us, available at a moment's notice to be flexibly applied to new challenges in the real world. The book is filled with real examples of what works and what doesn't. These examples are included to make the concepts tangible. I've carefully sequenced the contents in a way that allows us to build our knowledge from the base up, toward greater complexity and strength. I sometimes repeat content that I've previously covered to reinforce it before expanding on it or applying it in a new way.

I wish I could work with you and a few others in a small classroom, enjoying the spontaneous interactions and insights that always erupt when people learn together. The fact that you're reading this book probably means that this opportunity isn't available to you, but I still hope our interaction can be as personal as possible. This is why I've discarded the awkward third-person perspective on which most non-fiction books rely and instead refer to myself as "I" rather than impersonally as "the author." This is also why I write about visualizations and analysis techniques that "we" can use to make sense of data. Let's take this journey together.

Don't cheat yourself. Take time to think about what you read. If you already do the work of a data analyst, you might as well work to become the best you can be; one who can make lasting difference, feel the pride of this achievement, and thoroughly enjoy your work along the way.

PART I   BUILDING CORE SKILLS OF VISUAL ANALYSIS

GENERAL CONCEPTS, PRINCIPLES, AND PRACTICES

This book is organized into three major sections: Part I covers general information that applies to all types of visual data analysis, Part II covers information that's particular to specific types, and Part III completes the book by previewing new developments in the field and my hopes for its wise use to make the world a better place. I believe that it's important, when learning something new, to become grounded in general concepts, principles, and practices in tandem with their specific applications. When teaching in a live classroom, I weave back and forth between the general and the specific with the goal of creating a rich fabric of understanding. General information tends to be a bit abstract and even boring until it is applied in ways that make it concrete, relevant, and interesting. I find it more difficult, however, when writing a book, to weave back and forth between general and specific and still produce a text that is well organized for use as a resource. So, throughout Part I, I illustrate concepts, principles, and practices with plenty of concrete examples, but I refrain from going into details on any of the specific types of visual analysis that I cover later in Part II. As a consequence, although Part I is general in nature, its content is grounded in specific examples. As you read through the whole book, you will find that the topics covered in Part I reappear in Part II, discussed in greater detail. But, don't skip Part I; learning the foundation is essential for understanding how to adapt and apply the specific visual analysis strategies in Part II to your particular situation.

Chapter 1—Information Visualization

> We begin by defining "information visualization" and briefly trace relevant highlights of its history.

Chapter 2—Prerequisites for Enlightening Analysis

> Even the best software tools and extensive training can't overcome the limitations that analysts and data often bring to the process. Even though we're not focusing on these limitations, it's worthwhile to recognize their existence and impact so we can do work to overcome them. In this chapter, we look at the attributes and attitudes that make analysts effective and the qualities that make data meaningful and useful.

Chapter 3—Thinking with Our Eyes

Information visualization is only successful when its tools and processes are aligned with the strengths of human visual perception and cognition and designed to compensate for the limits of these human attributes. In this chapter, we look at the strengths of visual perception and the limitations of memory to understand how visual analysis works and what we and our software tools must do to optimize the analysis process.

Chapter 4—Analytical Interaction and Navigation

Making sense of data relies heavily on interacting with data, which enables us to uncover and analyze the meanings that reside therein. In this chapter, we look at the 10 most common and powerful ways that we can interact with information to make sense of it. We also look at best ways to navigate through data during the sense-making process.

Chapter 5—Analytical Techniques and Practices

Some information visualization techniques and best practices apply only to specific types of analysis, such as the analysis of time series, but a few are generally useful for many types of analysis. In this chapter, we look at general techniques and practices that have a proven record of effectiveness.

Chapter 6—Analytical Patterns

Humans, equipped with powerful visual perception, are extraordinarily good at finding and making sense of patterns. Information visualization takes advantage of this ability by engaging our eyes to detect and interpret patterns that reveal the meanings in data. In this chapter, we learn the simple rules for encoding quantitative data visually to make meaningful patterns visible and understandable, both for ourselves and our audiences. Many of the patterns that are meaningful when information is visualized are specific to particular types of analysis, such as distributions or correlations, but a few patterns are common to many types of analysis. In this chapter, we look at a few of these general patterns that are worth knowing well.

1 INFORMATION VISUALIZATION

Using our eyes to explore and make sense of data isn't entirely new but it had limited application until two conditions came together in recent history to make modern information visualization possible: graphics-capable computers and lots of readily accessible data. We can analyze data represented visually on paper to some degree, but we need to interact with the data to get the answers to many important questions. We cannot dynamically interact with the printed page except to turn it around and view it from various angles. Computers running appropriate software, however, enable a dynamic dialogue between the analyst and the data. Information visualization is a relatively new approach to data analysis that is still maturing.

The Process of Data Analysis

Before fully turning our attention to information visualization, let's take a moment to consider data analysis in general. The term *data analysis* is one that is sometimes used in so broad a sense that it loses all meaning. The word *analysis* by itself refers to the process of breaking something into its elements or components. We take things apart to understand them.

When applied to data analysis, we define the term more loosely as making sense of data. Meanings reside within data, which we must find and then examine to gain understanding. Taking things apart is a big part of the process, because the meanings that we seek to understand reside in relationships between the parts. How does this part relate to that part? How are they similar and how are they different? Is one bigger than the other? How are they changing? Does one cause the other? Any activity that you engage in to directly answer these questions comprises the data analysis process.

Although information must often be prepared for analysis of it to be done effectively, such as data collection from various systems, integration, transformation, cleansing, and storing it in a database that's conveniently structured for analysis, these preparatory activities support analysis, but are not part of the data analysis process itself. Preparing data for analysis, however important, is no more a direct part of the data analysis process itself than is reading this book to prepare ourselves for more skillful analysis. This book focuses exclusively the activities of data exploration and sense-making.

Meanings and Uses of the Term "Visualization"

Visualization, as it applies to visual representations of information, can be preceded by three words, creating three terms with somewhat different meanings:

- Data visualization
- Information visualization
- Scientific visualization

I use *data visualization* as an umbrella term to cover all types of visual representations that support the exploration, examination, and communication of data. Whatever the representation, as long as it's visual, and whatever it represents, as long as it's information, this constitutes data visualization.

The terms *information visualization* and *scientific visualization* are subsets of *data visualization*. They refer to particular types of visual representations that have particular purposes. In 1999, the book *Readings in Information Visualization: Using Vision to Think* defined and differentiated the terms "information visualization" and "scientific visualization" to assist these developing areas of research. According to the authors, Stuart Card, Jock Mackinlay, and Ben Shneiderman, information visualization is "the use of computer-supported, interactive, visual representations of abstract data to amplify cognition."[1] They contrasted this with scientific visualization, which they defined as visual representation of scientific data that are usually physical in nature, rather than abstract. For example, an MRI (Magnetic Resonance Imaging) scan and its older brother the X-ray produce scientific visualizations because they display things that possess actual physical form, attempting to faithfully represent that form in a way that is easy to see, recognize, and comprehend. This book is about *information visualization*.

1. *Readings in Information Visualization: Using Vision to Think*, Stuart K. Card, Jock D. Mackinlay, and Ben Shneiderman, Academic Press, San Diego CA, 1999, p. 7.

Data Visualization		
Activities	Exploration Sense-making	➡ Communication
Technologies	Information Visualization Scientific Visualization	➡ Graphical Presentation
Immediate Goal	Understanding	
End Goal	Good Decisions	

Figure 1.1

Let's take a closer look at Card, Mackinlay, and Shneiderman's definition of *information visualization* because it describes nicely what we're concerned with in this book. Their definition features the following characteristics:

- *Computer-supported*—The visualization is displayed by a computer, usually on a screen.
- *Interactive*—The visualization can be manipulated simply and directly in a free-flowing manner, including actions such as filtering the data and drilling down to focus on details.
- *Visual representations*—The information is displayed in visual form using attributes such as location, length, shape, color, and size of objects to form a picture of the data and thereby allow us to see patterns, trends, and exceptions that might not otherwise be visible.
- *Abstract data*—Information such as quantitative data, processes, or relationships is considered abstract, in contrast to visual representations of physical objects, such as geography or the human body. Because abstract information has no natural physical form, visualizations must connect or "map" the data to visual characteristics, such as shapes and colors that represent the data in perceptible and meaningful ways.
- *Amplify cognition*—Interacting with these visualizations extends our ability to think about information by assisting memory and representing the data in ways that our brains can easily comprehend.

All of these characteristics are important to the definition, but none more so than the last: amplifying cognition. The purpose of information visualization is not to make pictures, but to help us think.

This book is about information visualization: viewing and interacting with visual representations of information to explore and make sense of it. In the chapters to come, we'll attempt to answer the question, "How can we most effectively think about data to increase our understanding and, in so doing, support the best possible decisions?"

A Brief History of Information Visualization

I won't bore you with a long and tedious journey through the corridors of time, but I would like to point out some of the historical highlights that have paved the way for today's information visualization. This brief history features events that have contributed to the visualization of quantitative data, which is our focus.

Here's the big picture, arranged along a timeline.

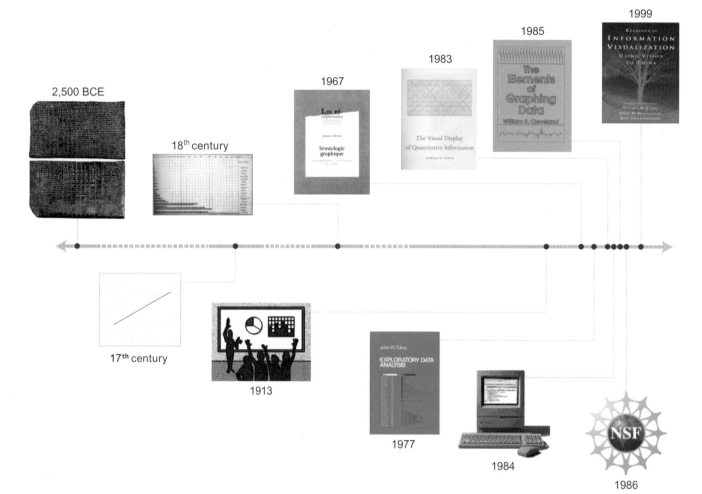

Figure 1.2

Long before methods were developed for visually displaying quantitative data, the table emerged in Babylonia at around 2,500 BCE, initially as a way to keep records of transactions and assets. A table is a simple arrangement of data into columns and rows.

Visual encodings of quantitative data didn't arise until much later, in the 17th century, when René Descartes, the French philosopher and mathematician famous for the words "Cogito, ergo sum" ("I think, therefore I am") invented the two-dimensional graph. Descartes' original purpose was not to use graphs to present data as a form of communication but to perform mathematics visually, using a system of quantitative coordinates along two-dimensional (horizontal and vertical) axes.

It wasn't until the late 18th and early 19th centuries that most of the graphs we use today were invented, applied, or dramatically improved by a Scottish social scientist named William Playfair. Playfair invented the bar graph, was the

For more extensive history of the developments that had paved the way for information visualization, see Robert Horn's wonderful book *Visual Language: Global Communication for the 21st Century*, MacroVU, Inc., Bainbridge Island WA, 1998, "Chapter 2: A Brief History of Innovations," and Michael Friendly of York University's informative website at: www.math.yorku.ca/SCS/Gallery

first to use line graphs to represent change through time, and, on one of his off days, invented the pie chart. Here's one of Playfair's original graphs.

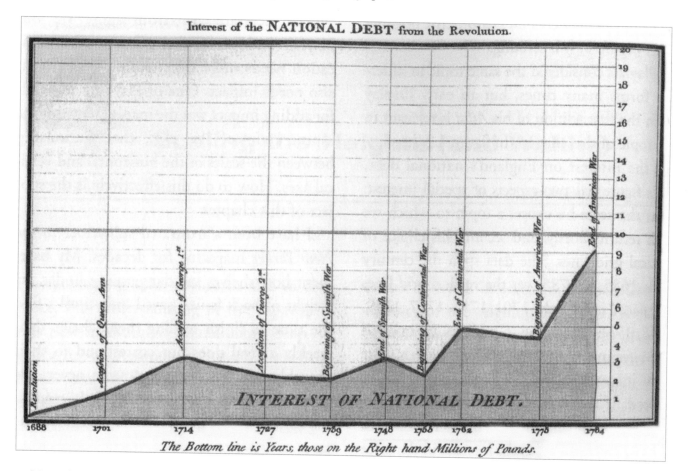

Interest of the NATIONAL DEBT from the Revolution.

INTEREST OF NATIONAL DEBT.

The Bottom line is Years, those on the Right hand Millions of Pounds.

More than a century passed after Playfair's innovations before graphs were recognized as valuable enough to warrant a college course in them. The first course was offered at Iowa State University in 1913. Sadly, few practical graphing courses have been offered since then aside from those included in programs of study in statistics.

In 1967, with the publication of his book *Sémiologie graphique* (translated into English in 1983 as *Semiology of Graphics*) Jacques Bertin introduced the notion of visual language, arguing that visual perception operated according to rules that could be followed to clearly, accurately, and efficiently express information in a visual format.

The person who really illuminated the power of visualization as a means to explore and make sense of quantitative data was Princeton statistics professor John Tukey, who, in 1977, introduced a whole new approach to statistics called *exploratory data analysis* in a book of the same name. We'll encounter Tukey later when we look at box plots, one of his wonderful inventions for examining distributions of quantitative data.

Figure 1.3. This graph was included in Playfair's *The Commercial and Political Atlas* in 1786 to make a case against England's policy of financing colonial wars through national debt.

Semiology of Graphics, Jacques Bertin, translated by William J. Berg, The University of Wisconsin Press, Mardison WI, 1983.

Semiology is the branch of knowledge that deals with the production of meanings by sign systems, in this case graphics.

A few years later, in 1983, data visualization aficionado Edward Tufte published his groundbreaking and perennially popular book *The Visual Display of Quantitative Information*, which showed us in vivid and beautiful terms that there were effective ways of displaying data visually, in sharp contrast to the ways that most of us were doing it, which weren't effective at all.

One year later, in 1984, during the Super Bowl, those of us watching the game on television were introduced by Apple to the first popular and affordable computer that offered graphics as a mode of interaction and display—the Macintosh. It featured a graphical user interface, based on one that was originally developed at Xerox's Palo Alto Research Center (Xerox PARC), from which many graphical innovations have emerged. The Macintosh opened the way for us to interact directly with data visualizations on a computer. As I mentioned earlier, this was a pivotal contribution to the advent of information visualization.

In the following year, 1985, William Cleveland, a statistician doing brilliant work at AT&T Bell Laboratories, published his book *The Elements of Graphing Data*. In the tradition of John Tukey, Cleveland greatly refined and extended the use of visualization in statistics. Today, as a statistics professor at Purdue University, Cleveland continues to contribute to the maturing field of information visualization.

A new research specialty emerged in the academic world when the National Science Foundation (NSF) launched an initiative to encourage use of computer graphics to render physical, three-dimensional phenomena, such as human anatomy, chemical interactions, and meteorological events. This effort began in 1986 with an NSF-sponsored meeting called the "Panel on Graphics, Image Processing and Workstations," which led to a 1987 report titled *Visualization in Scientific Computing*. This area of study became known as *visualization* and in time more specifically as *scientific visualization*. Out of this grew the first Institute of Electrical and Electronics Engineers (IEEE) Visualization Conference in 1990.

From the beginning, researchers also worked to display abstract (non-physical) information. Representations of abstract information eventually emerged as an area of study distinct from representations of physical phenomena. In 1999 the book *Readings in Information Visualization: Using Vision to Think* collected much of the best research to date into a single volume. Advances in information visualization have continued since then, but has produced no new milestones.

Tukey once said about data analysis:

> *As in any other science, what is done in data analysis is very much a product of each day's technology. Every external technological development of major relevance—organized tables of functions, knowledge of the mathematical consequences of the Gaussian law of error, desk calculators, stored-program electronic computers, graphical display facilities—has been accompanied by a tendency to rediscover the importance and identity of data analysis.[2]*

Several of the events on this timeline were derived from the fine book *Visual Language*, Robert E. Horn, MacroVU, Inc., 1998.

2. "Proceedings of the Symposium on Information Processing in Sight Sensory Systems", John W. Tukey and M. B. Wilk, California Institute of Technology, Pasadena CA, 1965, p. 1.

We currently live in a time when the importance of data analysis is being rediscovered and the means to perform the work, fueled by computers, are rapidly changing—sometimes for the better and sometimes not. As the flood of data threatens to drown us, it is high time that we develop the fundamental and, for the most part, simple skills that are needed to leverage these technological developments and push them in the directions that will make our data analysis easier and more effective.

2   PREREQUISITES FOR ENLIGHTENING ANALYSIS

In addition to the visual analysis practices that I cover in this book, other factors also contribute to successful analysis. Besides the analytical skills that we bring to the process, it helps if we also bring the aptitudes and attitudes that separate the best analysts from all the rest. And, independent from what we bring, the information that we analyze must also have qualities that make it suitable for enlightening analysis. In this chapter, we consider both what we and the data must bring to the process for it to be successful.

Aptitudes and Attitudes of Effective Analysts

Even with the best of intentions, not everyone is equally equipped to become a great data analyst. As in any profession, some people are simply better suited to the task. Some qualities that belong in this category are built into one's nature and are not likely to change significantly, even with effort. Take heart, however, because most of these traits can be cultivated—some easily, others with diligence. Before reading about the traits of an effective data analyst, take a moment to reflect on your own. In the margin of this page or on a separate sheet of paper, list every trait you can think of that might help people analyze data effectively.

. . . .

Chances are, you'll find many of the traits that you listed in my list as well, even though our terms might differ a little. Perhaps you'll also find a few in my list that didn't come to mind when making yours.

I believe that those who are most productive as data analysts tend to be:

- Interested
- Curious
- Self-motivated
- Open-minded and flexible
- Imaginative
- Skeptical
- Aware of what's worthwhile
- Methodical
- Capable of spotting patterns
- Analytical
- Synthetical
- Familiar with the data
- Skilled in the practices of data analysis

The more you naturally possess or work to acquire these attributes, the better you'll be at making sense of data. If data analysis is not central to your work, you can certainly improve your abilities with no need to achieve mastery. But if mastery is your goal, you might want to use this list of qualities as a benchmark for your own professional development. Let's examine each of these traits individually.

Interested

No matter how dedicated we are to our work, and how well-intentioned and disciplined, genuine interest in the data places us on a higher plane. Interest fuels the process and engages the mind. Nothing builds interest more than a sense that what we're doing is valuable and important. If we don't care about our organization's products or services or the benefits people receive from them (assuming there are benefits), then our interest in the data will be half hearted or contrived.

Interest in our work is something we can increase, but not artificially. Something might occur in the organization, in the world, or in us, which changes our level of interest, but deciding to become more interested through a mere act of will isn't likely to work.

Curious

Curiosity about the data is similar to interest in the data but not precisely the same. Even if we're not motivated by genuine interest, we can still bring a great deal of curiosity to the analysis process. When watching a movie, even if we don't care about the characters, we might still be curious about what will happen to them or wonder why they behave as they do. Curiosity is a personality trait that can be cultivated, and the more of it we acquire, the better analysts we'll become.

Do you enjoy figuring things out? Do you wonder how things work or why they happen? Do you crave information? I do, and, as a result, I'll usually keep chipping at a barrier to my understanding until it crumbles. Determination, fueled by curiosity, can make up for inadequacies in other areas, so give it full rein.

Self-Motivated

I've placed this trait immediately after curiosity because the two often go hand in hand. Good analysts don't wait around until they are told what to do and don't necessarily limit what they do to the scope of what's requested. Good analysts are driven to explore and to understand. Each step in the process leads to new questions, which they pursue without hesitation. When barriers are encountered, they don't stand still; they find a way to get through.

I suppose some types of work benefit from a lack of self-motivation. Certain tasks might be performed best by people who do precisely as they're told and do nothing when awaiting instructions. Analysis, however, is not one of them. Not only does the analysis process benefit from self-motivation, we as analysts benefit as well because it makes the process much more engaging and fulfilling.

Open-Minded and Flexible

If we approach analysis too rigidly or with a closed mind or one that is already made up, we will miss much of what might be discovered. According to the physicist Alan Sokal, science requires two fundamental attitudes:

- Willingness to accept what you find
- Willingness to discover that you are wrong

The success of data analysis depends every bit as much upon these traits.

What do we do when our usual analytical approach fails to answer questions about the data? We must be willing and able to consider new ways of looking at the information and new methods of interacting with it when the usual approach fails. Even when the usual ways work, they won't necessarily lead to all the insights that are possible. Even when it ain't broken, it pays to fix the process anyway from time to time, approaching data with fresh eyes from an unusual angle to see if it will reveal something previously unnoticed.

What happens when we decide what we'll find before looking at the data? We find only what we expect or nothing at all, despite how many revelations are scattered about the landscape. The greatest experts in any field are those who never forget how much they have yet to learn.

Imaginative

Being open to new ideas is all it takes do good work when good ideas are handed to us, but when they're not, we must tap into our imagination. It takes creativity to navigate unknown analytical territory. Much of the time, this involves asking the question "what if I try this?" over and over, circling closer to the answer with each iteration until we hit the mark. Sometimes it involves adapting approaches we've taken in other circumstances or merely heard about, even from other fields of endeavor, which just might work if the circumstances are similar. We don't have to be creative geniuses to blaze new analytical trails.

Skeptical

We should never become so sure of our data, our methods, or ourselves that we consider them to be beyond question. The obvious answer is often right but not always. We should listen to that small voice in the back of our heads that makes us uncomfortable with the results of our analysis. Even when we're confident without the slightest trace of doubt, from time to time it's worthwhile to step back and look again, perhaps from a different perspective. In so doing, from time to time we'll learn something new.

Aware of What's Worthwhile

Not all the questions that we might ask about data are of equal value. Not every scent we pick up is worth following, unless we have unlimited time. We must develop a sense of what's worthwhile versus what's likely to take a great deal of time but yield few, if any, useful results. Because time is limited, we must have priorities. For instance, some questions might lead to the discovery of a way to save money that would actually cost more to implement than it could ever save. Even if the question and the ensuing pursuit are intriguing, they wouldn't be worthwhile. As our knowledge of the data and the analytical process grows, our ability to determine what's worthy of pursuit will grow along with it.

Methodical

Sometimes it's useful to go wherever our most fleeting thoughts and whims lead us, jumping from idea to idea with little restraint. Sometimes if we follow these non-linear paths, we make discoveries. But this is the exception. Most of the time, analysis requires tried-and-true methodical practices. Most analysis involves walking a well-worn path, repeating steps that we've taken countless times, to reach a familiar goal. It is efficient and productive to learn the best set of steps and then repeat them regularly rather than reinventing the wheel over and over. Although at times it's useful to shake things up by viewing them with a skeptical eye and altering our process, most of the time a proven method works best.

Capable of Spotting Patterns

We humans are especially good at spotting patterns and deriving meaning from them. This is built into our senses and our brains. We easily spot similarities and differences. We see a collection of marks on a page holistically, not as individual marks but as an image. Our brains can stitch pieces of visual material into a coherent object and recognize, in a few pencil strokes on a page, the face of someone we know. Some of us are better at this than others, however, and all of us can hone our skills through practice. At a fundamental level, almost all of the skills that I teach in this book involve pattern detection: discerning resident patterns of meaning within visual representations of data. Learning to spot patterns that are meaningful and to ignore those that are not is a basic skill of analysis.

Analytical

To analyze something is to break it up into its parts—to decompose it. To be good data analysts, we must be able to examine something complex (that is, consisting of many parts) and to recognize the individual parts that compose it and how they connect to and affect one another to form a whole. Only in so doing can we understand how things work, the forces that cause particular conditions, and where to dig to uncover underlying causes. To make sense of a company's profits, whether large or small, rising or falling, requires that we understand the parts in the sales and operating processes that produce profits and how changes in one affect others down the line. If you were one of those kids who loved to take things apart, not to destroy them but to understand them, you're naturally analytical.

Lest I be accused of naiveté, let me confess that analysis is not as clear cut as I have just described it. There is rarely one right way to decompose something into its constituent parts. What we define as parts are often not written firmly in nature; they are arbitrary divisions that we make in one way rather than another to serve specific purposes. A firefighter, a welder, and an insurance claims adjuster will each analyze fire differently because their purposes are different. Analysis involves creativity in identifying the parts that compose some whole and the ability to revise the model when errors in understanding arise or purposes change.

Synthetical

Synthesis is the reverse of analysis. To synthesize is to put a collection of parts together into a whole. If we are synthetical, we are able to look at pieces and see how they might fit together to form a whole. Putting a jigsaw puzzle together involves synthesis. Despite the fact that we casually use the term "analysis" when describing the entire process of searching through and examining information to make sense of it, this process sometimes proceeds from focusing on individual pieces to an understanding of how they relate, how they influence one another to produce a result or form something greater. The ability to see the big picture from glimpses of its parts is often every bit as important as its opposite.

Familiar with the Data

We can be the brightest analysts in the world, but if we're not familiar with the data, we will proceed slowly and sometimes reach erroneous conclusions. We must understand the data and how the processes that produce the data work. To perform sales analysis for a company, we must not only understand the basic operations, parts, and goals of sales in general, but also the specific rules and meanings that are associated with that particular company's sales. A skilled sales manager can understand his company's sales process intimately but not necessarily know how to analyze sales data. To support this manager, we must understand both analysis and sales.

Skilled in the Practices of Data Analysis

Finally, in addition to all the traits mentioned so far, data analysts need to possess basic skills of the trade. No one starts off with these skills or acquires them without effort; they are developed through training, experience, and lots of practice. According to Derrick Niederman and David Boyum:

> *Excellence in anything is the product of practice. That's especially true of quantitative reasoning, which doesn't come naturally to any of us.*[1]

1. *What the Numbers Say: A Field Guide to Mastering Our Numerical World*, Derrick Niederman and David Boyum, Broadway Books, New York, 2003, p. 5.

Most Americans are poor quantitative thinkers. This widespread innumeracy is the father of zillions of bad decisions, and you don't need DNA testing to confirm its paternity. Numbers convey information, quantitative information. Decisions are based on information. When people are innumerate—when they do not know how to make good use of available quantitative information—they make uninformed decisions.[2]

2. *What the Numbers Say: A Field Guide to Mastering Our Numerical World*, Derrick Niederman and David Boyum, Broadway Books, New York, 2003, p. 229.

Some traits of effective analysts are interests, aptitudes, and natural inclinations that we can't pick up from a book. To some degree, we either have them or not, because they are built into our basic nature or the result of a lifetime of influences. Other traits can certainly be developed, but it's outside of the scope of this book to chart that journey. Helping you become skilled in the practices of data analysis is chief goal of this book. In the next chapters, we'll dive deep into these analytical practices.

Traits of Meaningful Data

Just as we must bring certain attributes to the process of data analysis to be successful, the data should ideally have certain characteristics; poor-quality data will yield few insights. The higher the quality of the data, the greater the potential for revelation. In the real world, we must work with the information we have even when it isn't ideal. But if we have a say in the matter, we should fight for high-quality data. Take a few minutes to compose a list of the characteristics that you think make data most useful for analysis. Think about data that you examine in your own work and the data-related problems that sometimes undermine your efforts. What are the characteristics of ideal data?

· · · · · · ·

Now compare your list to mine to come up with a comprehensive description of ideal data.

- High volume
- Historical
- Consistent
- Multivariate
- Atomic
- Clean
- Clear
- Dimensionally structured
- Richly segmented
- Of known pedigree

Let's consider each of these traits, one at a time.

High Volume

Although we won't necessarily use it all, the more information that's available to us, the more chance there is that we'll have what we need when pursuing particular questions or just looking for anything interesting.

Historical

Much insight is gained from examining how information has changed through time. Even when we focus on what's going on right now, the more historical information that's available, the more we can make sense of the present by seeing the patterns from which present conditions evolved or emerged. Historical data should be consistent or adjusted so that it is comparable over time even if record-keeping conventions have changed (see "Consistent," below).

Consistent

Things change over time, and when they do, it's helpful to keep data consistent. A good example of this is the ever-changing boundaries that define sales territories in many companies. If data such as sales revenues have not been adjusted to reflect these changes, an examination of historical revenues by territory will become muddled. It is usually best to adjust data to reflect current definitions although for some purposes it's useful to maintain separate records of the original form of the data.

Multivariate

Quantitative and categorical variables are the two types of data that we examine. A *variable* is simply an aspect of something that can change (i.e., vary). Variables are either quantitative (that is, a characteristic that is measured and expressed as a number, such as sales revenue) or categorical (also known as qualitative, representing a characteristic that's described using words rather than numbers, such as the color of a product or the geographical region of a sales order). Often, when trying to figure out why something is happening, we need to expand the number or type of variables we're examining. The more variables we have at hand when trying to make sense of data, the richer our opportunity for discovery.

Atomic

By *atomic* I mean specified down to the lowest level of detail at which something might ever need to be examined. Most analysis involves information that has been aggregated at a level much more summarized or generalized than the atomic level, but at times we need information at the finest possible level of detail. For instance, if we're sales analysts, we spend most of our time examining revenues at the product level or regional level, but there are times when we need to dive all the way down to the individual line item on a sales order to understand what's going on.

It is essential for good decision making to have the ability to see all the way down to the specific details and to be able to *slice and dice* data at various levels as needed. One of the painful lessons learned in the early days of data warehousing was that if we leave out details below a particular level of generalization because we assume they will never be needed for analysis, we will live to regret it. If we omit the details or simply cannot access them, we will bang our head against this wall again and again.

Clean

The quality of our analysis can never exceed the quality of our information. "Garbage in, garbage out." Information that is accurate, free of error, and complete is critical. This is what I mean by clean. We can't reach trustworthy conclusions if we rely on dirty data. As Danette McGilvray writes:

> *Effective business decisions and actions can only be made when based on high-quality information—the key here being effective. Yes, business decisions are based all the time on poor-quality data, but effective business decisions cannot be made with flawed, incomplete, or misleading data. People need information they can trust to be correct and current if they are to do the work that furthers business goals and objectives.[3]*

Clear

When information is expressed in cryptic codes that make no sense to us, it's meaningless. I've tried to make sense of data that's expressed in unfamiliar terms, and I assure you, it's frustrating, discouraging, and an annoying waste of time. Even if we have a data dictionary at our disposal that allows us to look up unfamiliar or difficult-to-interpret terms, we'll wear ourselves out going back and forth between the data and the dictionary. It's wonderful when someone else, like the data warehousing team, has already converted data from cryptic codes to understandable terms.

Dimensionally Structured

An analyst's time is often frittered away in attempts to extract and pull together data from complex, relationally-structured databases. Even if we're experts in constructing Structured Query Language (SQL) queries to access information that resides in multiple tables (such as in an Enterprise Resource Planning (ERP) database, which is a maze of thousands of tables), we have better things to do with our time. Writing queries to access data isn't analysis; it is simply a task that sometimes must be done before we can begin the process of analysis.

Many years ago, experts such as Ralph Kimball painstakingly developed ways of structuring data in databases so that they are much easier to access and navigate for analysis and reporting. The methodology that they developed is called *dimensional modeling*. It organizes data into two types of tables: *dimensions* and *measures* (*measures* are sometimes called *facts*). As you might have guessed, dimensions consist of categorical data and measures consist of quantitative data. Dimensions, in a typical business, consist of such things as departments, regions, products, and time (years, quarters, months, days, etc.). Measures for that same business would probably include revenues and expenses. If we wish to examine revenues by region and by date, our query would link the revenue table (a measure) to the region and date tables (dimensions). When information is structured in this manner, or if we are using software that makes it appear to be structured in this manner even if it actually resides in a complicated relational database structure, we will have a much easier time accessing it.

3. *Executing Data Quality Projects*, Danette McGilvray, Morgan Kaufmann, Burlington MA, 2008, p. 4.

Several fine books have been written about data quality and what we can do to improve it. Two of the finest authors who have written about this are Danette McGilvray and Larry English.

Richly Segmented

Analysis often benefits from sets of values that have been segmented into meaningful groups, such as customers that have been grouped by geographical region. If we are analyzing products, of which there are hundreds, perhaps many of them could be lumped together into groups that share common characteristics. For example, if we work for an office supply retailer, we might organize products into groups such as furniture, computers, and miscellaneous office supplies (paper, pencils, pens, etc.). Much analysis would rely on using these groups. Rather than having to create these groups when needed, our work will go much faster and be less prone to error if this type of segmentation has already been built into the data.

Of Known Pedigree

It is useful—sometimes critical—to know the background of our information. We need to know how it came to be, where it came from, and what calculations might have been used to create it. Knowing these details of the information's pedigree could prevent us from drawing erroneous conclusions. For instance, consider a situation involving Company A that acquired Company B five years ago; prior to the acquisition Company B defined and therefore calculated revenue differently than Company A. An analyst examining revenues for the last five years only would not be concerned with this fact, but if she needed to examine revenues from an earlier date, and especially if she wanted to compare those historical revenues to today's, she would need to take this difference into account. She could only do so if she were aware of this aspect of the data's pedigree.

In this chapter, we've considered the ideal traits that we as analysts and our data should have to produce the best results. Don't be disheartened if these ideals seem beyond your reach, especially if there are issues with data quality and you have no way to fix the problem. In the real world, we must sometimes learn to work around limitations that we can't control. We do our best, and when problems exist that affect the quality of our findings, we take them into account by tempering our conclusions and admitting an appropriate level of uncertainty.

Now that the stage has been set, it's time to turn our attention to learning the craft of visual analysis.

3   THINKING WITH OUR EYES

I cherish all five of my senses. They connect me to the world and allow me to experience beauty in inexhaustible and diverse ways. But of all our senses, vision stands out as the primary and most powerful channel of input from the world around us. Approximately 70% of the body's sense receptors reside in our eyes.

Vision is not only the fastest and most nuanced sensory portal to the world, it is also the one most intimately connected with cognition. Seeing and thinking collaborate closely to make sense of the world. It's no accident that so many words used to describe understanding are metaphors for sight, such as "insight," "illumination," and the familiar expression "I see." The title of this book, *Now You See It*, uses this metaphor to tie quantitative sense-making to the most effective means available: information visualization.

Colin Ware of the University of New Hampshire is perhaps the world's top expert in harnessing the power of visual perception to explore, make sense of, and present information. Ware makes a convincing case for the importance of visualization:

> *Why should we be interested in visualization? Because the human visual system is a pattern seeker of enormous power and subtlety. The eye and the visual cortex of the brain form a massively parallel processor that provides the highest-bandwidth channel into human cognitive centers. At higher levels of processing, perception and cognition are closely interrelated, which is the reason why the words 'understanding' and 'seeing' are synonymous. However, the visual system has its own rules. We can easily see patterns presented in certain ways, but if they are presented in other ways, they become invisible. . . . The more general point is that when data is presented in certain ways, the patterns can be readily perceived. If we can understand how perception works, our knowledge can be translated into rules for displaying information. Following perception-based rules, we can present our data in such a way that the important and informative patterns stand out. If we disobey the rules, our data will be incomprehensible or misleading.[1]*

To use visualization effectively, we must do more than simply display data graphically. We must understand how visual perception works and then present data visually in ways that follow the rules.

1. *Information Visualization: Perception for Design*, Second Edition, Colin Ware, Morgan Kaufmann Publishers, San Francisco CA, 2004, p. xxi.

The Power of Visual Perception

Traditional methods of statistics and the less sophisticated methods that are traditionally supported by business intelligence software display information in a predominantly text-based manner, usually arranged in a table. According to Edward Tufte:

> *Modern data graphics can do much more than simply substitute for small statistical tables. At their best, graphics are instruments for reasoning about quantitative information. Often the most effective way to describe, explore, and summarize a set of numbers—even a very large set—is to look at pictures of those numbers. Furthermore, of all methods for analyzing and communicating statistical information, well-designed data graphics are usually the simplest and at the same time the most powerful.[2]*

2. *The Visual Display of Quantitative Information*, Edward R. Tufte, Graphics Press: Cheshire, CT 1983, Introduction.

The table below works well if we need precise values or an easy means to look up individual values.

2007 Sales Revenue
(U.S. dollars in thousands)

	Jan	Feb	Mar	Apr	May	Jun	Jul	Aug	Sep	Oct	Nov	Dec
Domestic	1,983	2,343	2,593	2,283	2,574	2,838	2,382	2,634	2,938	2,739	2,983	3,493
International	574	636	673	593	644	679	593	139	599	583	602	690
	$2,557	$2,979	$3,266	$2,876	$3,218	$3,517	$2,975	$2,773	$3,537	$3,322	$3,585	$4,183

Figure 3.1

However, sense-making involves operations that go beyond looking up specific values in a table like the one above. For example, in this case, to understand trends in sales revenue, we need to compare revenue to other variables that might help us find relationships and patterns, which in turn would allow us to make decisions about changes in our business operation. During the process of sense-making, we only occasionally need precise values that must be expressed as text.

Most data analysis involves searching for and making sense of relationships among values and making comparisons that involve more than just two values at a time. To perform these operations and see relationships among data, which exhibit themselves as patterns, trends, and exceptions, we need a picture of the data. When information is presented visually, it is given form, which allows us to easily glean insights that would be difficult or impossible to piece together from the same data presented textually. The graph on the following page instantly brings to light several facts that weren't obvious in the table of the same data above.

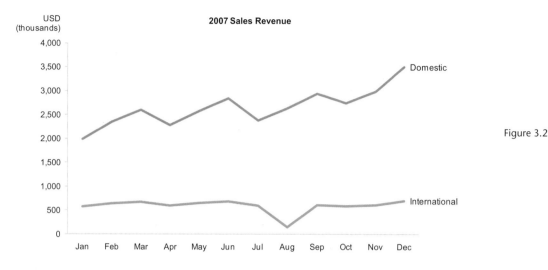

Figure 3.2

Notice aspects of the domestic versus international sales story that were not obvious in the table but pop out in the graph.

. . . .

Here are a few facts that the graph makes visible:

- Domestic sales were much higher than international sales throughout the year.
- Domestic sales trended upward during the course of the year as a whole while international sales remained relatively flat.
- The month of August was an exception to otherwise relatively consistent sales in the international market. (Perhaps most of this company's international customers are Europeans who were on vacation in August.)
- Domestic sales exhibited a monthly pattern of up, up, down, which repeated itself quarterly, with the highest sales in the last month and the lowest sales in the first month of each quarter. (This is a common pattern in sales—sometimes called the "hockey stick" pattern because of its shape—which results from sales people being paid bonuses for meeting and exceeding quarterly sales quotas so that they intensify efforts to increase their bonuses as the quarter's end draws near.)

Patterns and relationships such as these are what we strive to find and understand when we analyze data.

How Visual Perception Works

We certainly don't need to be experts in visual perception to create effective information visualization, but here are a few basic facts we should know about how visual perception works:

- Our eyes sense light that enters them after reflecting off the surfaces of objects in the world.
- What we perceive as an object is built up in our brains as a composite of several visual properties, which are the building blocks of vision.
- Even though we perceive this composite of properties as a whole object, we can still distinguish the properties that compose it.
- These individual properties, which vision is specifically tuned to sense, include two-dimensional (2-D) location, length, width, area, shape, color, and orientation, to name a few.

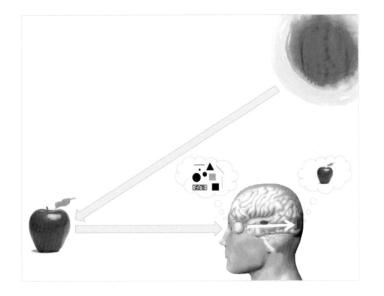

Figure 3.3

If we can use these basic and easily perceived attributes to represent data visually, we can direct much of the work that is required to view and make sense of data to simple and efficient perceptual processes in the brain. Rather than reading individual values one at a time, which is how we perceive tables of text, we can, thanks to a graph, see and potentially understand many values at once. This is because visual displays combine values into patterns that we can perceive as wholes, such as the patterns formed by lines in a line graph.

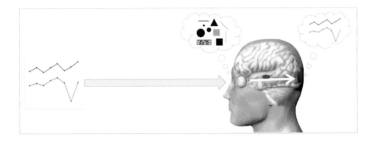

Figure 3.4

Using Knowledge of Perception to Create Effective Visualizations

We should keep a few facts in mind about how we collect and process visual information if we want to create effective information visualizations.

> Fact #1: We do not attend to everything that we see. Visual perception is selective, as it must be, for awareness of everything would overwhelm us. Our attention is often drawn to contrasts to the norm.

For this reason, to successfully see meaning in visual displays, we must encode data in ways that allow what's interesting and potentially meaningful to stand out from what's not. What stands out to you as you look at the image below?

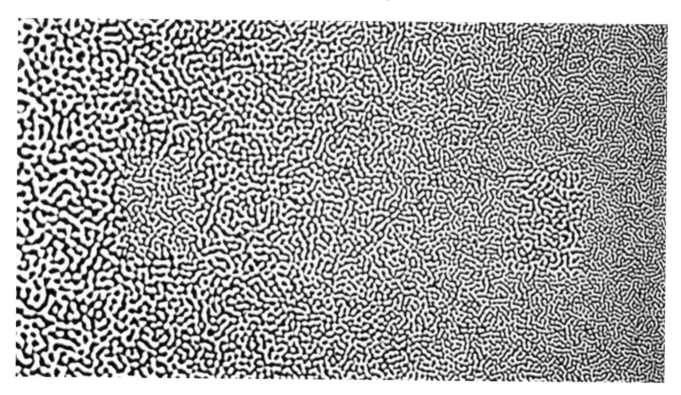

Figure 3.5. This image appears in *Information Visualization: Perception for Design*, Second Edition, Colin Ware, Morgan Kaufmann Publishers, San Francisco CA, 2004, p. 171.

Among the things you notice are probably two roughly oval-shaped areas of texture embedded within the pattern that stand out from the rest: one is in the left half and one in the right half of the image. They stand out because they differ from what surrounds them. What's not obvious is that these two regions that catch our attention are exactly the same. The area that stands out on the left is made up of lines that are less thick than those that surround them. By contrast, the area on the right is surrounded by lines that are thicker than the surrounding lines. Because the two areas that stand out are embedded in contexts that differ, our perception of them is affected so that it is difficult to see that they are made up of lines of the same thickness.

We learn from this fact that information visualizations should cause what's potentially meaningful to stand out in contrast to what's not worth our attention.

Fact #2: Our eyes are drawn to familiar patterns. We see what we know and expect.

When we look at the image below, our eyes see the familiar shape of the rose and our minds quickly categorize it as fitting a recognizable pattern that we know: a rose. However, another distinct image has been worked into the familiar image of the rose, which isn't noticeable unless we know to look for it. Take a few seconds right now to see if you can spot the image that's embedded in the rose.

Figure 3.6. This image was found at www.coolbubble.com.

. . . .

Did you spot the dolphin? Once we have been primed with the image of the dolphin (turn to page 36 to see it), we can easily spot it in the rose. This second fact teaches us that visualizations work best when they display information as patterns that are both familiar and easy to spot.

In addition to visual perception, information visualization must also be rooted in an understanding of how people think. Only then can visualizations support the cognitive operations that make sense of information.

Fact #3: Memory plays an important role in human cognition, but working memory is extremely limited.

The two photographs on the next page illustrate one of the limitations of working memory. We only remember the elements to which we attend. Imagine that you haven't seen these two photos of the sphinx side by side and hadn't noticed that the stand of trees that appears to the left of the sphinx's head on the left is missing from the photo on the right. If these two versions of the photo were rapidly alternated on a screen with an instant of blank screen in between, you wouldn't notice this rather significant difference between the two unless you specifically attended to that section of the photo just before a swap occurred.

I've used an animated version of these two images in many classes and presentations, and only a few people notice the difference even after viewing the two images swapping back and forth for a full 30 seconds.

Figure 3.7. This demonstration of "change blindness" was prepared by Ronald A. Rensink, Associate Professor of Psychology and Computer Science at the University of British Columbia. Additional examples can be found at www.psych.ubc.ca/~rensink/flicker/download/.

Stated differently, unless the specific part of the photo containing the trees was stored in working memory just before the swap, you would no longer remember it when you viewed the next photo and therefore wouldn't notice the difference. In addition to not remembering anything other than the few things that we attend to, we also don't clearly see anything that we don't focus on directly. To see something clearly, we must look at it directly because only a small area of receptors in the retina of each eye called the fovea are designed for high-resolution vision. Light that hits the retina outside of this relatively small area is perceived much less clearly. This third fact makes it clear that information visualization must serve as an external aid to augment working memory.

The gist of the three facts above is that, for information visualization to be effective, just any old display won't do. According to Stuart Card:

> *Over history, visual abstractions have been developed to aid thinking...*
> *What information visualization is really about is external cognition, that*
> *is, how resources outside the mind can be used to boost the cognitive*
> *capabilities of the mind.*[3]

Software can only support information visualization effectively if the software operates on principles that respect how visual perception and cognition work.

3. Written by Stuart Card in the foreword to *Information Visualization: Perception for Design*, Second Edition, Colin Ware, Morgan Kaufmann Publishers, San Francisco CA, 2004, p. xvii.

Making Abstract Data Visible

We'll begin this section with an illustration. Something is wrong with the following graph. Take a moment to see if you can find a problem.

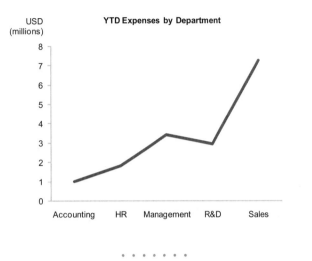

Figure 3.8

. . . .

Does anything about this graph bother you? Does any aspect of its design undermine its ability to represent data appropriately? This is a case where it doesn't make sense to encode the values as a line. The line connects values for a series of categorical items—departments in this case—that are completely independent from one another. These are discrete items in the category called "departments," which have no particular order and no close connection to one another. To connect these values with a line visually suggests a relationship that doesn't exist in the data. We are used to interpreting a line like this as indicating an increase or decrease in some variable, in this case, expenses on the vertical axis, in relation to some variable on the horizontal axis that might reasonably be expected to affect or have a comprehensible relationship to expenses, such as time. The up and down slopes of the line and the pattern formed by them are meaningless.

Lines work well for connecting values through time, such as months in a year, but are inappropriate for connecting categorical items such as departments. In the following graph, separate bars accurately encode and visually reinforce the independent nature of these departments and their expenses.

This picture of a dolphin can be found embedded in the rose in Figure 3.6.

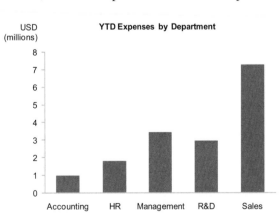

Figure 3.9

Listing departments along one of a graph's axes is an example of using a *nominal* scale. In a nominal scale, items have no particular order or close connection between one another. If we sorted these departments in order of expenses from greatest to least, this would change the scale from nominal to *ordinal* (department with the highest expenses, department with the second highest expenses, and so on), but the departments would still lack a close connection to one another. Units of time, such as years, quarters, months, or days, on the other hand, are not only ordered by their nature, they are also intimately connected one to the next. Time is an example of an *interval* scale.

An interval scale consists of a continuous range of quantitative values, divided into equal intervals. For example, if we want to count and compare sales orders of various dollar sizes, and the smallest order is 50¢ and the largest is $100, we could break order sizes into intervals of $10 each: $0.00-9.99, $10.00-19.99, and so on. This would be an interval scale. A range of time beginning at one point and ending at some later point is a quantitative range of values. Breaking time into intervals, such as years, also results in an interval scale. Because interval scales consist of ordered and intimately connected items, such as the years 2004, 2005, 2006, and 2007, it is appropriate to display values across those years using a line to connect them. It is natural and effective. Our eyes can easily trace how a set of values change through time when these values are displayed as a line, and our minds are able to easily understand the nature of this change.

The point that I'm trying to make is that there are ways to visually display data that are effective because they correspond naturally to the workings of vision and cognition, and there are ways that break the rules and consequently don't work. If we wish to display information in a way that will enable us and others to make sense of it, we must understand and follow the rules.

I'll show another example to drive this truth home. If we wish to rank and compare the sales performance of the 10 products that are displayed in each of the two graphs below, which supports this task most effectively?

Although it is true that years vary in length because of leap years and months have different numbers of days, for most analytical purposes we consider these intervals equal in size.

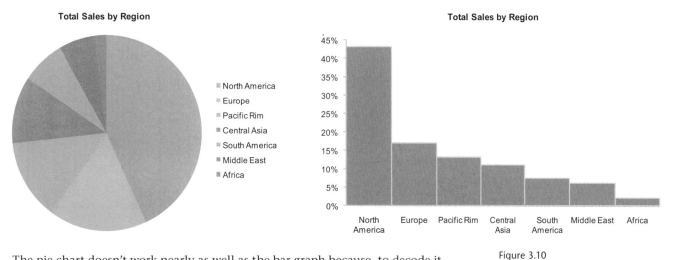

Figure 3.10

The pie chart doesn't work nearly as well as the bar graph because, to decode it, we must compare the 2-D areas or the angles formed by the slices, but visual perception doesn't accurately support either of these tasks. The graph on the right, however, superbly supports the task because we can easily compare the lengths of bars.

In 1967, with the publication of his seminal and brilliant work, *Semiologie graphique* (previously mentioned in Chapter 1) Jacques Bertin was the first person to recognize and describe the basic vocabulary of vision, that is, the attributes of visual perception that we can use to display abstract data. He teased out the basic rules of how visual perception works, which we can follow to clearly, accurately, efficiently, and intuitively represent abstract data. For any given set of information, there are effective ways to visually encode the meanings that reside within it, as well as ways to represent them poorly and perhaps even misrepresent them entirely. All those who have, since Bertin, worked to map visual properties to the meanings of abstract data have relied heavily on his work; I am among the many who owe him a debt of gratitude.

Much of Bertin's work is based on an understanding of the fundamental building blocks of visual perception. We perceive several basic attributes of visual images pre-attentively, that is, prior to and without the need for conscious awareness. For this reason, these are called *pre-attentive attributes* of visual perception. Colin Ware makes a convincing case for the importance of these pre-attentive attributes when we are creating visual representations of abstract information:

> *We can do certain things to symbols to make it much more likely that they will be visually identified even after very brief exposure. Certain simple shapes or colors 'pop out' from their surroundings. The theoretical mechanism underlying pop-out is called pre-attentive processing because logically it must occur prior to conscious attention. In essence, pre-attentive processing determines what visual objects are offered up to our attention. An understanding of what is processed pre-attentively is probably the most important contribution that vision science can make to data visualization.[4]*

4. *Information Visualization: Perception for Design*, Second Edition, Colin Ware, Morgan Kaufmann Publishers, San Francisco CA, 2004, p. 163.

Let's look at pre-attentive attributes more closely. Ware has provided a convenient list of them, organized into four groups: form, color, spatial position, and motion. The examples of each that I believe apply most directly and usefully to information visualization are:

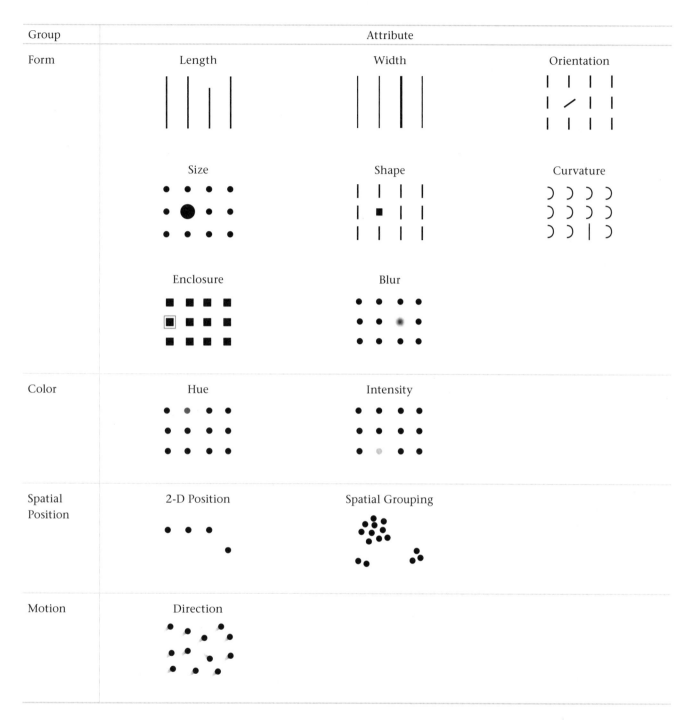

Each of these pre-attentive attributes comes in handy for one or more information visualization purposes. From time to time throughout the book, I'll point out how they can be used. A few uses, however, are so important that they deserve to be mentioned and explained before we proceed.

Some of these pre-attentive attributes are especially useful for making objects in a visualization look distinct from one another. These attributes enable us to assign various subsets of visual objects (for example, data points in a scatterplot) to categorical groups (for example, to regions, departments, products, and so on). For instance, in a scatterplot that displays the number of ads that have run for products and the resulting number of products that were sold, we might want to distinguish newspaper, television, and radio ads. The best two pre-attentive attributes for doing this are hue and shape.

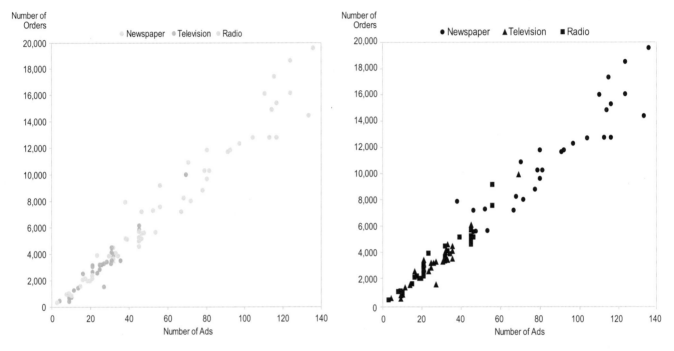

Figure 3.11

Assuming that none of us are color blind or that, if some are, we're careful to avoid using combinations of hues that we can't tell apart (for instance, red and green, which most people with color blindness have difficulty distinguishing), hues are usually a little easier to interpret than shapes (circles, squares, X's, triangles, and so on) for this purpose. Other types of graphs besides scatterplots, such as bar and line graphs, can also rely on hues to associate objects (bars or lines) with particular categories.

We can also use pre-attentive attributes to represent quantitative values. Although some attributes lend themselves to making things look different from one another (that is, to making categorical distinctions), a few naturally lend themselves to making things look greater or lesser than one another. Take a moment to examine each pre-attentive attribute in the following list to determine which ones we are able to intuitively perceive in a quantitative manner, that is, it's easy to recognize that some representations of the attribute appear greater than others:

- Length
- Width
- Orientation
- Size
- Shape
- Curvature
- Enclosure
- Spatial grouping
- Blur
- Hue
- Color intensity
- 2-D position
- Direction of motion

. . . .

Here's the list of the pre-attentive attributes that are quantitatively perceived in and of themselves, without having values arbitrarily assigned to them:

Precision of Quantitative Perception	Attribute	Example	Description
Very precise	Length	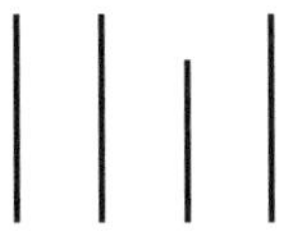	Longer = greater
	2-D Position		Higher or farther to the right = greater
Not very precise	Width	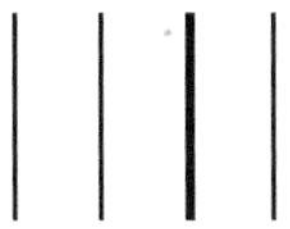	Wider = greater
	Size	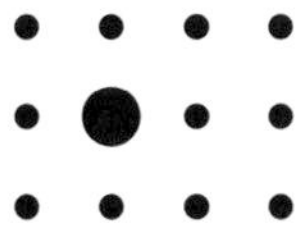	Bigger = greater
	Intensity	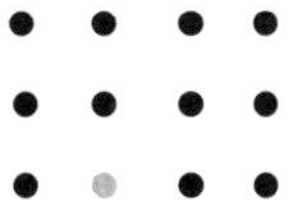	Darker = greater
	Blur	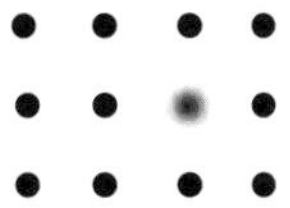	Clearer = greater

If you included "orientation" in your list, you probably did so because of your familiarity with clocks, which use different orientations to quantify hours and minutes around the dial. In this case, the quantitative meanings that we associate with various orientations of the hands (5 o'clock, 6 o'clock, and so on) have been learned and are therefore only meaningful through convention, not because we naturally think of particular orientations as representing greater or lesser values.

Only two pre-attentive attributes are perceived quantitatively with a high degree of precision: length and 2-D position. It isn't accidental that the most common ways to encode values in graphs rely on these attributes. Each of the popular graphs below uses one or both of these attributes to encode quantitative values, enabling us to compare those values with relative ease and accuracy.

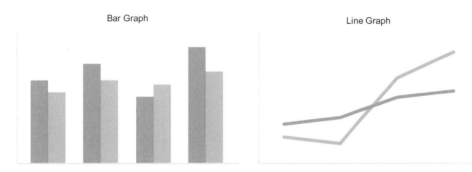

Figure 3.12

Even though information visualization relies on a broad assortment of graphs, only a few work well for typical quantitative analyses. Almost all effective *quantitative* graphs are of the 2-D, X-Y axis type.

Sometimes it's appropriate to encode quantities using one of the attributes that we can't perceive precisely, but we should usually do this only when neither length nor 2-D position is an option. For instance, each data point in the following scatterplot encodes two quantitative values: marketing expenses and sales revenues for particular products:

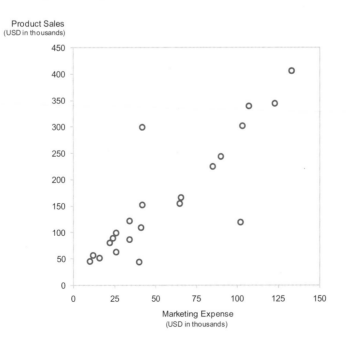

Figure 3.13

What if we needed to see the relationship of profits to both sales revenues and marketing expenses? We can't encode profits using 2-D position because we've already used the two dimensions available: horizontal position along the X-axis to encode expenses and vertical position along the Y-axis to encode revenues. What pre-attentive visual attribute could we assign to each data point to encode profit? One solution is to vary the size of each data point, with the biggest for the product with the greatest profit and the smallest for the one with the least, as illustrated below:

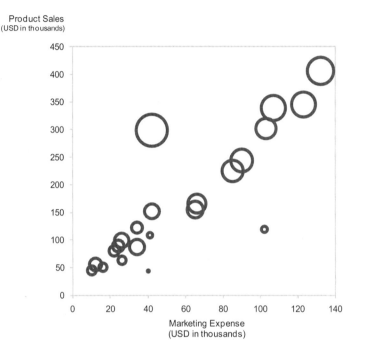

Figure 3.14

We can't compare the varying sizes of these data points precisely, but if all we need is a rough sense of how profits compare, this does the job. What if we're examining sales revenues by region, ranked from highest to lowest, using the bar graph below, but want to compare this to profits in those regions as well?

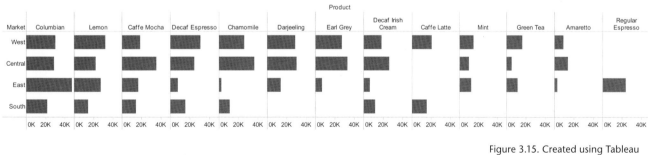

Figure 3.15. Created using Tableau Software

In this case, we could use variations in color intensity to add profits to the display, as illustrated below.

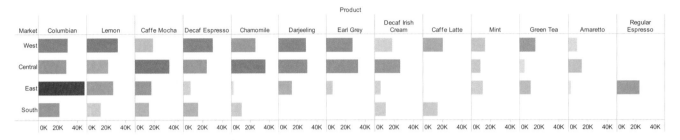

We would need a key indicating which colors signified what degree of profit, and, once again, we can't compare profits precisely when they are encoded as color intensity, but sometimes these approximate indications are all we need to make an analytical judgment.

Any time color is used the encode quantitative values, we have what's called a *heatmap*. The most familiar example of a heatmap is one that encodes values on an actual geographical map, such as a weather map where colors are used to represent variations in temperature or rainfall, as in the following example:

Figure 3.16. Created using Tableau Software

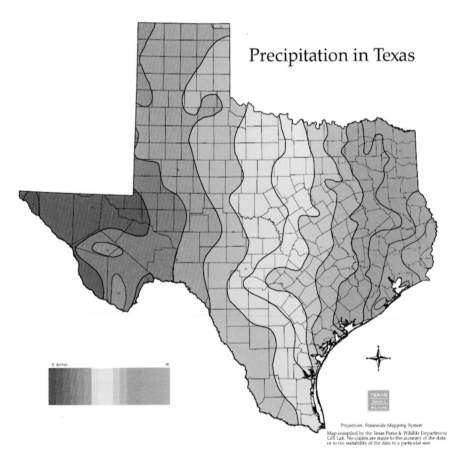

Figure 3.17. Rainfall map from the Texas Parks and Wildlife website (www.tpwd.state.tx.us/)

Heatmaps don't have to be associated with a geographical map. Another common heatmap is composed of cells (square or rectangular areas) arranged as a tabular matrix with each cell color-coded to display a quantitative value, as in the following example, which shows variations in gas mileage (miles per gallon, MPG), horsepower, and weight for several cars in the year 1982.

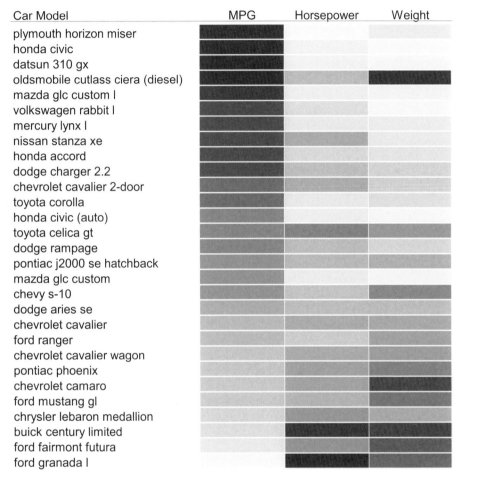

Figure 3.18

One special type of information visualization that is similar to a heatmap, called a *treemap*, uses both size and color to encode quantitative values. Treemaps were originally developed by Ben Shneiderman of the University of Maryland as a way to simultaneously display two quantitative variables for a large number of items, arranged hierarchically.

Here is an example of a treemap:

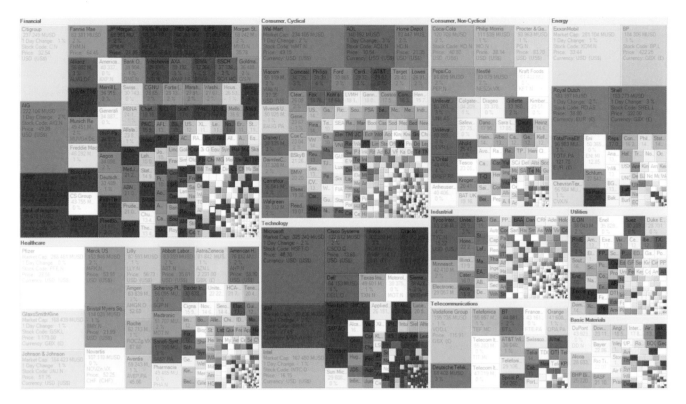

When conventional graphs, such as bar graphs, cannot be used because there are too many items to represent as bars in a single graph or even a series of graphs on a single screen, treemaps solve the problem by making optimal use of screen space. Because they rely on pre-attentive attributes to encode values (area and color) that we can't compare precisely, we reserve such methods for circumstances when other more precise visualizations cannot be used, or precision isn't necessary. We'll learn more about treemaps in *Chapter 4: Analytical Interaction and Navigation.*

Despite the usefulness of visualizations such as treemaps, most quantitative data analysis can be performed quite well with graphs that encode values using only four types of objects:

- *Points*, which use the 2-D positions of simple objects (dots, squares, triangles, and so on) to encode values
- *Lines*, which use the 2-D positions of points connected into a line to give shape to a series of values
- *Bars*, which use the heights (vertical bars) or lengths (horizontal bars) of rectangles to encode values, as well as the 2-D position of the bar's end
- *Boxes*, which are similar to bars and use lengths to encode values, but, unlike bars, are used to display the distribution of an entire set of values from lowest to highest along with meaningful points in between, such as the median (middle value)

Figure 3.19. This treemap, produced using Panopticon Explorer, displays stock market cap values as variations in the size of each rectangle and the percentage of one-day change in their values as variations in color (increases in blue and decreases in red).

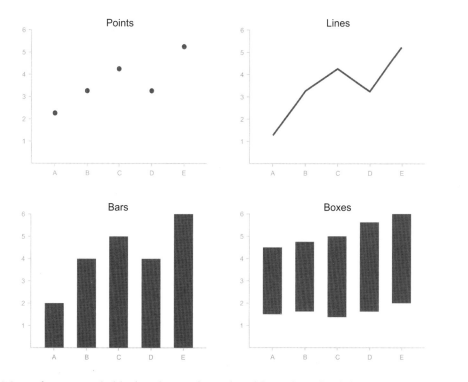

Figure 3.20

Most of us are probably familiar and comfortable with each of these ways to encode values in graphs, except perhaps for boxes, which we'll examine in detail in *Chapter 10: Distribution Analysis.* All of these methods are quite simple to decode and powerful for data analysis.

Despite similarities, visual perception does not work exactly like a camera. A camera measures the actual amount of light that comes in through the lens and shines on film or digital sensors; visual perception does not measure absolute values but instead registers differences between values. I'll illustrate what I mean. Below, you see a small rectangle colored a medium shade of gray.

Figure 3.21

Next, we have a large rectangle that is filled with a gradient of gray-scale color, ranging in luminance from fully white on the left to fully black on the right.

Figure 3.22

Now, I have placed the small gray rectangle we saw above, without altering its color, at various locations within the large rectangle. Notice how different the five small rectangles look from one another even though they are all the same color.

Figure 3.23

The reason for the apparent difference is that we perceive color not in absolute terms but as the difference between the color that we are focusing on and the color that surrounds it. In other words, we see color in the context of what surrounds it, and our perception is heavily influenced by that context. In fact, we perceive all visual attributes in this manner. Consider the lines below. The pair of lines on the left seem more different in length than the two lines on the right, but both sets differ by precisely the same amount. The difference on the left appears greater because we perceive differences as ratios (percentages) rather than as absolute values. The ratio of the lengths of the two lines on the left is 2 to 1, a difference of 100%, whereas the ratio of those on the right is 100 to 99, only a 1% difference.

———   ————————————————————

—   ————————————————————

Figure 3.24

Because visual perception works this way, when we want to use different expressions of a pre-attentive attribute, such as hue, to separate objects into different groups, we should select expressions of that attribute that vary signifi-cantly from one another. For example, the colors on the top row below are easier to discriminate than those on the bottom.

Figure 3.25

Another important fact about pre-attentive attributes that we ought to keep in mind is that our ability to perceive expressions of an attribute as distinct decreases to the extent that distractions clutter our field of vision. Ware warns:

Pre-attentive symbols become less distinct as the variety of distracters increases. It is easy to spot a single hawk in a sky full of pigeons, but if the sky contains a greater variety of birds, the hawk will be more difficult to see. A number of studies have shown that the immediacy of any pre-attentive cue declines as the variety of alternative patterns increases, even if all the distracting patterns are individually distinct from the target.[5]

5. *Information Visualization: Perception for Design*, Second Edition, Colin Ware, Morgan Kaufmann Publishers, San Francisco CA, 2004, p. 167.

As you can see in the following examples, it is much easier to focus exclusively on the red dots in a scatterplot when the only other hue is gray than when there are five other hues that are competing for our attention. Visual complexity is distracting and should therefore never be employed to a degree that exceeds the actual complexity in the data.

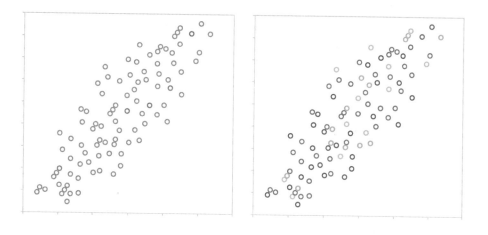

Figure 3.26

Overcoming the Limits of Memory

Memory is divided into two fundamental types: working memory and long-term memory. Long-term memory is where information is stored permanently (that is, until related brain cells die off), available for recall whenever it's needed. Long-term memory functions a bit like a computer's hard disk drive. By contrast, working memory stores information only briefly. Again using the analogy of a computer, working memory is a bit like random access memory (RAM) where information is temporarily stored while it is being processed. Information enters working memory from one of three sources: through our senses, from our imagination, or from long-term memory where it was previously stored. Working memory is where information resides while we're thinking about it; information only stays in working memory for a few seconds unless we keep it alive by continuing to think about it. If we think about it enough, it ends up being stored in long-term memory (if it wasn't already there). If we don't store it in long-term memory, it simply goes away once we cease thinking about it.

Technically, working memory consists of different sets of memory storage for different types of information. For instance, verbal information (something we've heard) and visual information (something we've seen) occupy separate repositories in working memory. Visual working memory, which is what we use when working with an information visualization, is very limited. You might think that the RAM in your computer is limited compared to the hard disk drive, but it's enormous compared to visual working memory in our brains. Research has found that visual working memory can only handle about three *chunks* (that is, storage units) of information at a time. It is hard to believe that our brains can function so powerfully with such limited capacity in working memory. If all three memory slots are already being used, the only way for a new item to get in is for one that's already there to be thrown out.

So how much is a chunk of visual information? The answer depends on the nature of the image and our expertise in handling the information that we're examining. In the following table of numbers, which we've seen before, most of us would need to store each number as a separate chunk in working memory. For instance, at any one moment, we might only be able to hold onto the three highlighted numbers.

2007 Call Volume (in thousands)

	Jan	Feb	Mar	Apr	May	Jun	Jul	Aug	Sep	Oct	Nov	Dec
United States	1,983	2,343	2,593	2,283	2,574	2,838	2,382	2,634	2,938	2,739	2,983	3,493
Europe	574	636	673	593	644	679	593	139	599	583	602	690

Figure 3.27

If this same information is displayed in a line graph, however, each line could be stored as a single chunk of visual memory, one for U.S. and one for European call volumes. The pattern formed by an entire line could constitute a single chunk.

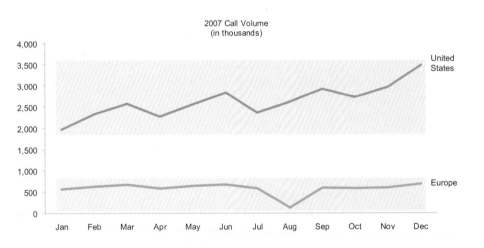

Figure 3.28

This is one of the great advantages of visualization for exploring and analyzing data. When quantitative values are displayed as visual images that exhibit meaningful patterns, more information is chunked together in these images, so we can think about a great deal more information simultaneously than if we were relying on tables of numbers alone. This greatly multiplies the number and complexity of insights that can emerge.

Getting back to the question of how much information constitutes a chunk, the amount varies depending on our expertise. Ware explains:

> *The process of grouping simple concepts into more complex ones is called chunking. A chunk can be almost anything: a mental representation of an object, a plan, a group of objects, or a method for achieving some goal. The process of becoming an expert in a particular domain is largely one of creating effective high-level concepts or chunks.*[6]

6. *Information Visualization: Perception for Design*, Second Edition, Colin Ware, Morgan Kaufmann Publishers, San Francisco CA, 2004, pp. 368 and 369.

As our expertise in analyzing particular types of data increases, so will our ability to handle bigger and bigger visual chunks of that information and to recognize characteristics of that information as meaningful.

Even when we increase the capacity of working memory by expressing data as images, the limits are still considerable, so we need additional augmentation. This brings us to another way that visualizations help us work around the limits of working memory: by providing "external storage."

Because working memory can handle so little information, data that we are exploring and analyzing should be made readily accessible through an external medium. The oldest and most common external aid to working memory is a piece of paper or other writing surface. By writing information down and keeping it on the desk in front of us, we can rapidly access that information and move it into working memory for processing as needed because it is never more than a glance away. Today, computers, especially those with reasonably high-resolution displays, can serve the same purpose. By placing as much of the information we need as possible on the screen at once, we can make the process of comparing and thinking about data a fluid experience despite our working memory's limits.

We should avoid fragmenting information that we're examining by placing it on separate screens or in locations that we can't see without scrolling. For instance, if we see a pattern in a graph and then try to compare it to a pattern in another graph that is on another screen, we will no longer remember much of what we were looking at previously once we bring up the new screen. We'll end up bouncing back and forth between separate displays, wasting time, interrupting the flow of thought, and becoming frustrated in the process.

It's difficult if not impossible while using most data analysis software to combine the information we're examining onto a single screen without the need for scrolling. In the example on the next page, however, four months of expenses for 15 separate departments are displayed together in a way that supports both easy comparisons and formulation of the big picture about expenses. This display is a powerful external aid to working memory. If we had to examine each of these departmental graphs one at a time, neither of these analytical goals could be accomplished.

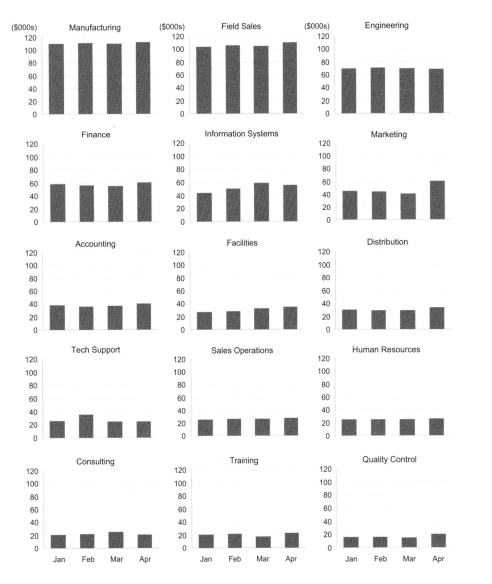

Figure 3.29

Once again, Ware states the case clearly:

> *The power of a visualization comes from the fact that it is possible to have a far more complex concept structure represented externally in a visual display than can be held in visual and verbal working memories. People with cognitive tools are far more effective thinkers than people without cognitive tools and computer-based tools with visual interfaces may be the most powerful and flexible cognitive systems. Combining a computer-based information system with flexible human cognitive capabilities, such as pattern finding, and using a visualization as the interface between the two is far more powerful than an unaided human cognitive process.[7]*

7. *Knowledge and Information Visualization*, Sigmar-Olaf Tergan and Tanja Keller, Editors, "Visual Queries: The Foundation of Visual Thinking," Colin Ware, Springer-Verlag, Berlin Heidelberg, 2005, p. 29.

In several later chapters that examine useful visualizations and techniques for specific types of analysis, we'll look at examples of how visualizations can be designed to augment working memory.

The Building Blocks of Information Visualization

To summarize the points made in this chapter, I'll describe the building blocks of quantitative information visualization. Effective information visualization is built on an understanding of how we see and think. Software that is built on this understanding can present data in ways that allow us to see what's meaningful, and it can augment our cognitive abilities in ways that allow us to make sense of what we see.

Perceptual building blocks consist of objects and the properties (such as pre-attentive attributes) that can visually represent quantitative data. It's essential that we use only objects and properties that map well to visual perception. The reasoning process that we engage in while viewing and interacting with a visualization consists of making comparisons and examining quantitative relationships (time-series, distributions, correlations, and so on). A visualization displays these relationships as visual patterns, trends, and exceptions. The goal of analyzing a visualization is to understand what these relationships mean, so we can make good decisions.

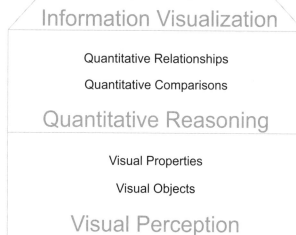

Figure 3.30

We should never forget that a picture of data is not the goal; it's only the means. Information visualization is all about gaining understanding so we can make good decisions.

4   ANALYTICAL INTERACTION AND NAVIGATION

Although at times we sit silently in thought when analyzing data, most of the process requires dynamic interaction as we navigate from a state of unknowing to one of enlightenment.

Analytical Interaction

We can only learn so much when staring at a static visualization such as a printed graph. No matter how rich and elegant the display, if it's evocative it will invite questions that it wasn't designed to answer. At that juncture, if we can't interact with the data to pursue an answer, we hit the wall. The effectiveness of information visualization hinges on two things: its ability to clearly and accurately represent information and our ability to interact with it to figure out what the information means. Several ways of interacting with data are especially useful. In this chapter, we'll examine the following 13:

- Comparing
- Sorting
- Adding variables
- Filtering
- Highlighting
- Aggregating
- Re-expressing
- Re-visualizing
- Zooming and panning
- Re-scaling
- Accessing details on demand
- Annotating
- Bookmarking

Let's look at each type of interaction in detail.

Comparing

No interaction is more frequent, useful, and central to the analytical process than comparing values and patterns. An old joke goes something like this: A therapist asks a woman "How is your husband?" to which she replies "Compared to what?" Comparison is the beating heart of data analysis. In fact, what we do when we compare data really encompasses both comparing (looking for similarities) and contrasting (looking for differences). In this book I use the term comparing loosely to cover both of these actions.

Comparing magnitudes—for example, this is greater or less than that and by what amount—is a fundamental version of this activity. The following graph supports this activity, making it easy to compare the performance of salespeople to one another.

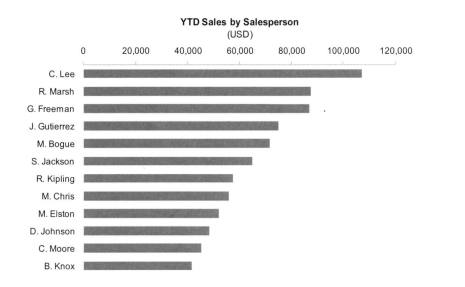

Figure 4.1

A few typical magnitude comparisons are:

Type	Description	
Nominal	Comparing values that have no particular order	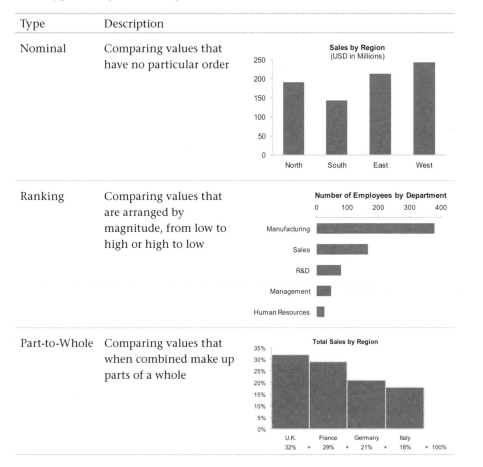
Ranking	Comparing values that are arranged by magnitude, from low to high or high to low	
Part-to-Whole	Comparing values that when combined make up parts of a whole	

Type	Description	
Deviation	Comparing the differences between two sets of values	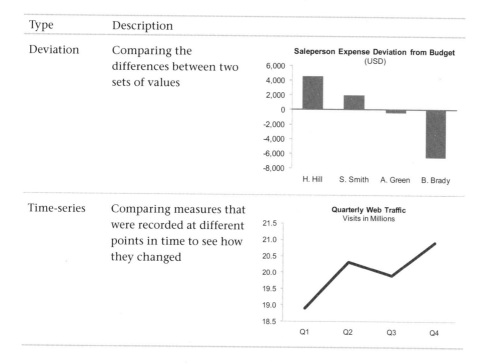
Time-series	Comparing measures that were recorded at different points in time to see how they changed	

In each of these cases, we are simply comparing the magnitudes of one value to another; in this sense, the cases are all the same. They differ, however, in the meanings that we can discover from the comparisons.

At the next level up in complexity, we compare patterns formed by entire series of values. The following graph makes it easy to compare domestic and international sales through time, exhibited in several patterns of change, including overall trends throughout the year and seasonal patterns.

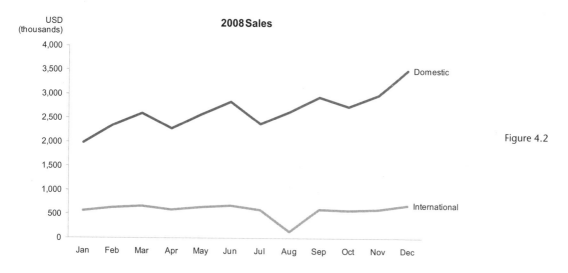

Figure 4.2

Different patterns are meaningful, depending on the nature of the data and what we're trying to understand. For instance, patterns that we might find in scatterplots while examining the correlation between two quantitative variables are usually different from patterns that might surface as meaningful while we're examining how a set of values is distributed from lowest to highest, as illustrated below:

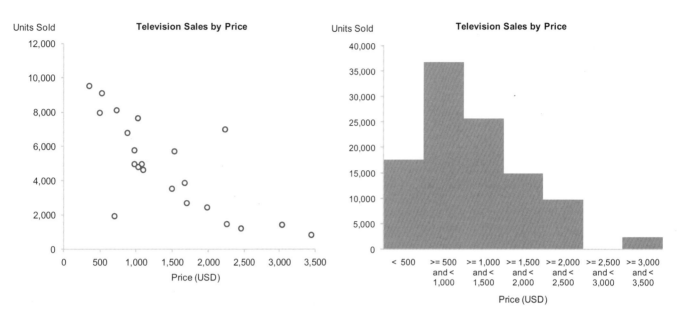

Figure 4.3

In later chapters, when we explore ways to perform particular types of analysis, such as time-series and distribution, we'll examine the particular types of comparisons and patterns that are meaningful in each.

Information visualization software should support comparisons in the following ways:

- Provide a selection of graphs that support the full spectrum of commonly needed comparisons
- Provide graphs that are designed for easy comparison of those values and relevant patterns without distraction
- Provide the means to place a great deal of information that we wish to compare on the screen at the same time, thereby avoiding the need to scroll or move from screen to screen to see the information

Many data analysis products fail to fully support comparisons of distributions because they don't provide box plots. Every general-purpose quantitative analysis product ought to include them. Another way that products often fail to support useful comparisons is by poorly rendering the objects that must be compared. Perhaps the most common example of this involves three-dimensional (3-D) graphs. Notice how difficult it is to compare the magnitudes of the values that are encoded as bars in the graph on the following page:

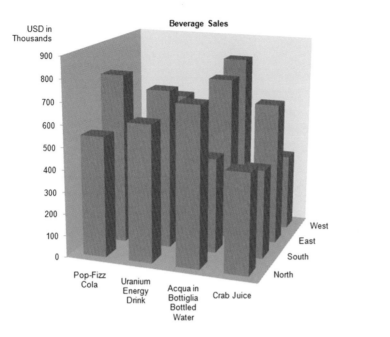

Figure 4.4

This graph suffers from occlusion: some bars are hidden behind others, which makes it impossible to compare them. When I complain about this to vendors, they often explain that this isn't a problem at all, because the graph can be rotated in a way that would allow the hidden bars to be seen. In addition to the fact that this is time-consuming and cumbersome, it undermines one of the fundamental strengths of graphs: the ability to see everything at once, which provides the big picture of relationships that we often need. Look at the 3-D graph below and try your best to interpret the values and compare the patterns of change through time.

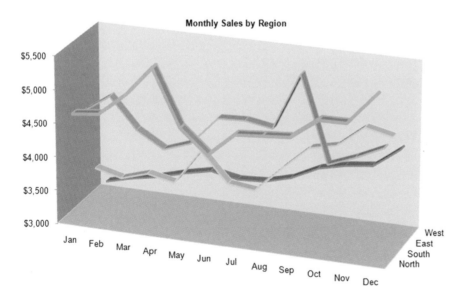

Figure 4.5. The east region is represented by the green line, but few people in my classes get this right when asked to guess.

Not only can you not interpret and compare what is going on in this graph, you probably can't tell which of the four lines represents the east region. If you don't even know which line represents which region, what good is the graph?

Even when a graph only has two axes, X and Y, if the objects that encode the data are rendered three dimensionally, the task of comparing the values is more difficult. Notice that it is easier to compare the bars in the left (2-D) graph below than those in the other two (3-D) graphs.

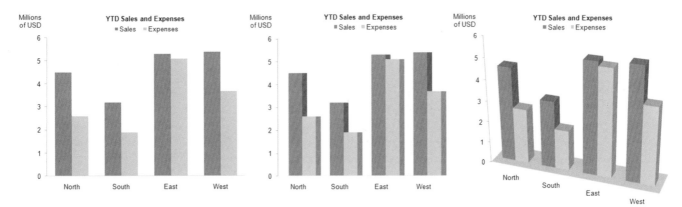

Figure 4.6

One other typical problem that undermines our ability to compare values accurately is illustrated in the next graph. How much greater is the number of "Yes" responses than "No" responses?

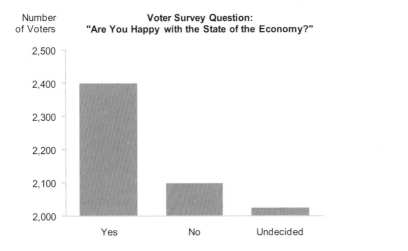

Figure 4.7

The relative heights of the bars suggests that "Yes" responses are four times greater than "No" responses, but this is not the case. When bars are used to encode values, their heights (vertical bars) or lengths (horizontal bars) will only represent the values accurately when the base of the bars begins at a value of zero. If we narrow the quantitative scale so that the bars begin at some value other than zero, their relative heights or lengths can no longer be accurately compared without first reading their values along the scale and doing math in our heads. In other words, a table of the same values could be used more efficiently to make these comparisons. There is no reason to use a graph unless its visual components can be used to make sense of the data. Software should not allow us to make the mistake illustrated above or at the very least should make it difficult to produce such a graph.

Another common comparison when analyzing data is making the distinction between values that appear normal—that is, within the quantitative range where most of the values are located—and those that appear abnormal. Values that fall outside the norm are called outliers or exceptions. When values are displayed in a well-designed visualization, it is usually easy to spot outliers and always worthwhile to examine them.

Sorting

Don't underestimate the power of a simple sort. It's amazing how much more meaning surfaces when values are sorted from low to high or high to low. Take a look at the following graph, which displays employee compensation per state:

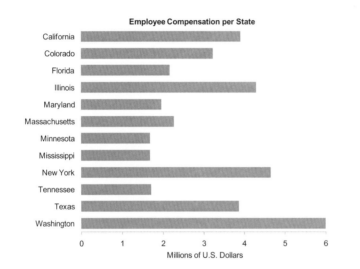

Figure 4.8

With the states in alphabetical order, the only thing we can do with ease is look up employee compensation for a particular state. It is difficult to see any meaningful relationships among the values. Now take a look at the same data, this time sorted from the state with the highest employee compensation to the one with the lowest.

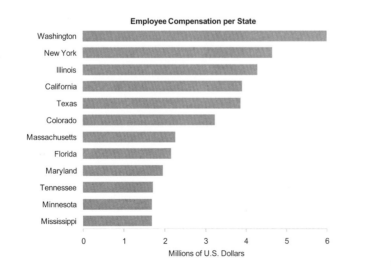

Figure 4.9

Not only is the story of how the states' compensation values relate to one another now clear, it is also easier to compare one value to another simply because values that are close to one another in magnitude are located near one another.

Let's go a step further and add another variable to the mix. In this next example, states are still sorted according to employee compensation, but a new column of bars has been added to display the number of employees for each state. Because the states are sorted by employee compensation to form a series of bars that decline in size from top to bottom, we can easily see that the related counts of employees per state do not perfectly correlate to compensation. This must be due to differences in how much employees are compensated, on average, in various states. For example, we can notice that although California and Texas pay roughly the same amount in total compensation, Texas has more employees (so presumably employees in Texas are paid less than those in California as roughly the same total amount of compensation stretches to cover more people in Texas). This graph is an illustration of how sorting can be used to examine multiple variables and analyze how the variables are correlated, if at all.

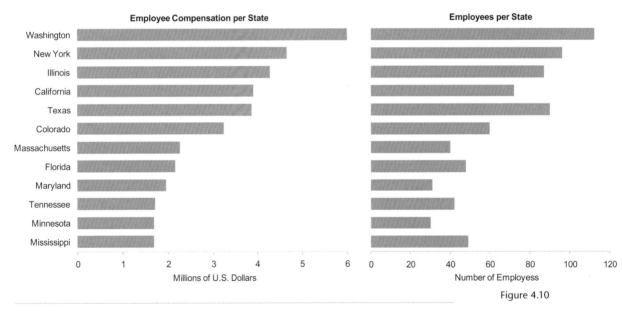

Figure 4.10

Information visualization software should support sorting in the following ways:

- Provide the means to sort items in a graph based on various values, especially the values that are featured in the graph
- Provide extremely quick and easy means to re-sort data in different ways, ideally with a single click of the mouse
- Provide the means to link multiple graphs and easily sort the data in each graph in the same way, assuming that the graphs share a common categorical variable (for example, state)

Adding Variables

We don't always know in advance every element of a data set that we'll need during the process of analyzing it. This is natural. Data analysis involves looking for interesting attributes and examining them in various ways, which always leads to questions that we didn't think to ask when we first began. This is how the process works because this is how thinking works. We might be examining sales revenues per product when we begin to wonder how profits relate to what we're seeing. We might at that point want to shift between a graph such as the one below on the left, to a richer graph such as the one on the right, which adds the profit variable.

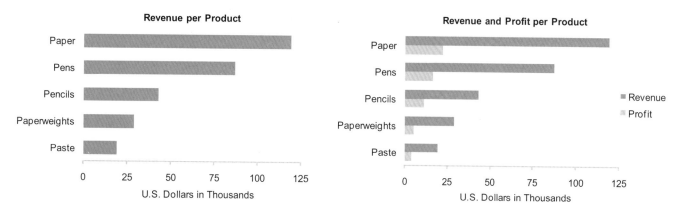

If we're examining revenue per product, sorted by product type from the best selling to worst as in the following example, we might decide to see how products are ranked by revenue without regard to product type.

Figure 4.11

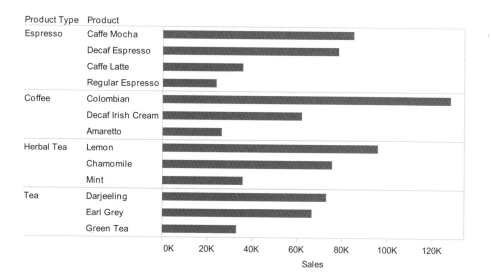

Figure 4.12. Created using Tableau Software

To do so, we would like a way to quickly remove product type from the display, switching from the view above to the one on the following page.

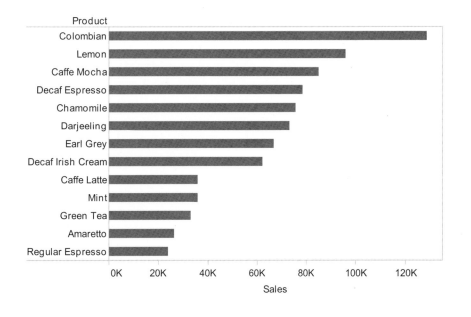

Figure 4.13. Created using Tableau
Software

Information visualization software should support adding and removing
variables in the following ways:

- Provide convenient access to every available variable that might be needed
  for analysis.
- Provide easy means to add a variable to or remove one from the display,
  such as by directly grabbing the variable and placing it or removing.

Filtering

Filtering is the act of reducing the data that we're viewing to a subset of what's
currently there. From a database perspective, this involves removing particular
data records from view. This is usually done by selecting particular items within
a categorical variable (for example, particular products or regions) or a range of
values in a quantitative variable (for example, sales orders below $20) and
indicating that they (or everything but them) should be removed from view.
Sometimes we do the opposite by restoring to view something that we previously removed. In both cases, we are working with filters, either by filtering
(removing) or unfiltering (restoring) data.

The purpose of filtering is simple: to get any information we don't need at the
moment out of the way because it is distracting us from the task at hand. On the
next page, notice how much more easily we can examine and compare sales of
shirts and pants in the right-hand graph when information regarding suits,
coats, and shoes is no longer competing for attention as it is on the left.

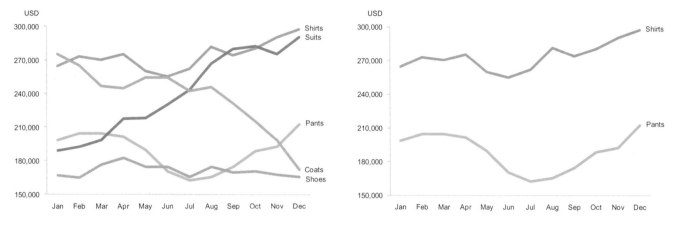

Figure 4.14

A great innovation of recent years is the development of filter controls that are so fast and easy to manipulate that we can apply a filter almost without taking our eyes off of the data. Below is a simple example of a filter control that uses radio buttons to filter regions.

Information visualization researchers refer to filters that operate in this manner as *dynamic queries*, based originally on work by Ben Shneiderman published as "Dynamic Queries for Visual Information Seeking," *IEEE Software*, 11(6), 70-77, 1994.

Figure 4.15. Filter from Spotfire

Region
⊙ (All)
○ MW
○ NE
○ SE
○ WE
○ (None)

The next example of a filter control is called a *slider*. This type of control of is especially useful for filtering ranges of quantitative values. The example below actually contains two sliders in a single control: one for the low end of the range ($1) and one for the high end ($447).

Class Sales
1   447
▶   ◀

Figure 4.16. Filter from Spotfire

This allows us to select the precise range of sales orders that we wish to view by order amount, filtering out all other orders even if the range we want to view is in the middle (illustrated below) rather than at one of the ends of the scale.

Class Sales
100   250
    ▶   ◀

Figure 4.17. Filter from Spotfire

Information visualization software should support filtering and unfiltering in the following ways:

- Allow easy filtering based on any information in the connected data sources, not just based on information that is currently being displayed. For example, even if the display only includes products, months, regions, and sales revenue, we might want to filter out all products belonging to a particular product type or all orders that were placed via the Web rather than by phone.
- Allow data to be filtered rapidly using simple controls, such as checkboxes or sliders. The lag time between issuing the filter command and seeing the results should be almost unnoticeable.
- Provide the means to directly select items in a graph (such as by using the mouse to click on them) and then remove them from display with a click or two.
- Once a filter has been applied, give some visible reminder that the filter is in effect along with an easy means to look up what has been filtered.
- Provide a means to define complex filter logic with multiple conditions (for example, remove all hardware products, except for those in the state of Colorado).
- Allow multiple graphs to be conveniently linked such that all can be filtered together in the same way in a single action.

Highlighting

Sometimes, rather than filtering out data we aren't interested in at the moment, we want to cause particular data to stand out without causing all other data to go away. Highlighting makes it possible to focus on a subset of data while still seeing it in context of the whole. At times, this involves data in a single graph only. In the following example, I have highlighted data points in red belonging to customers in their 20s who purchased products, without throwing out the other age groups. In this particular case, highlighting rather than the filtering allows us to see the relationship between the total number of purchases (along the X-axis) and the amount spent on groceries (along the Y-axis) by people in their 20s, in fairly good isolation from other age groups while still being able to see how their shopping habits compare to those of customers overall.

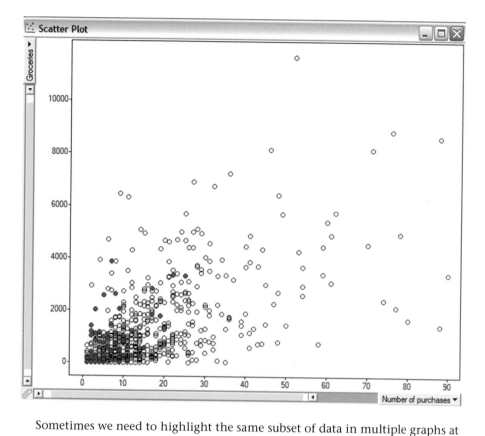

Figure 4.18. Created using Spotfire

Sometimes we need to highlight the same subset of data in multiple graphs at the same time. This is especially useful when we are simultaneously viewing several graphs, each of which displays the same set of data differently. For instance, consider the example on the following page in which we'll simultaneously view five graphs: the scatterplot from above, a bar graph with total purchases by age group, a bar graph with female vs. male purchases, a bar graph with purchases per store, and a bar graph with purchases based on the date of customers' initial purchases from the stores. We could, using this set of graphs, track the subset of customers who made their first purchases during the last three months (highlighted in red in the bottom bar graph) throughout the customer attributes featured in each of the other graphs. This technique of highlighting data in one graph, resulting in the same subset of data being highlighted in other associated graphs, is called *brushing* or *brushing and linking*. We'll look at brushing again more closely in *Chapter 5: Analytical Practices*.

Brushing was first introduced by W. S. Cleveland, R. A. Becker, and G. Weil in the paper "The Use of Brushing and Rotation for Data Analysis," originally published in *First IASC World Conference on Computational Statistics and Data Analysis*, International Statistical Institute, Voorburg, Netherlands, 1988, pp. 114–147. It later appeared in the book *Dynamic Graphics for Statistics*, edited by W. S. Cleveland and M. E. McGill, published by Wadsworth and Brooks/Cole, Pacific Grove CA, 1988.

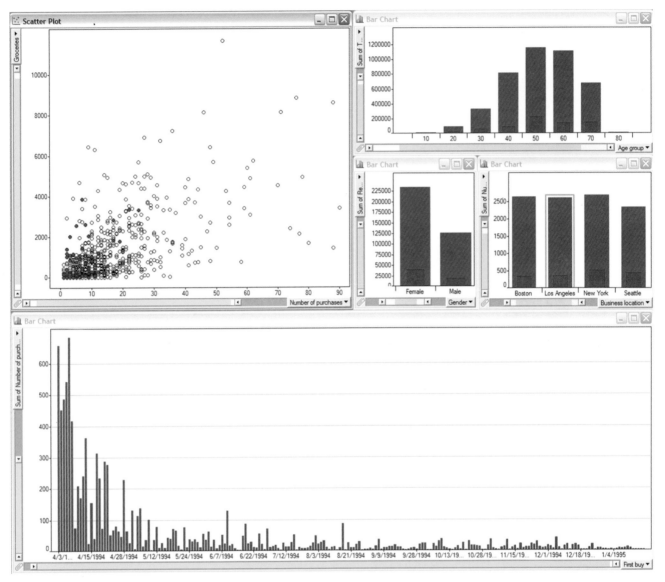

Figure 4.19. Created using Spotfire

Information visualization software should support highlighting in the following ways:

- Provide the means to highlight a subset of data by selecting from lists of categorical items (for example, departments from a list of those in the company) or from the ranges of values associated with quantitative variables (for example, expenses greater than $25,000).
- Provide the means to highlight a subset of data by directly selecting it in a graph, such as by using the mouse to draw a rectangle around the items or to click on each of the items.
- Highlight selected information so that it can be seen independently from the rest while still allowing viewers to see the entire set of data (both highlighted and not highlighted).
- Provide the means to highlight a set of items in one graph and have those same items automatically highlighted in other graphs that share the same data set.

Aggregating

When we aggregate or disaggregate information, we are not changing the amount of information but rather the level of detail at which we're viewing it. We aggregate data to view it at a higher level of summarization or generalization; we disaggregate to view it at a lower level of detail.

Consider the process of sales analysis. At its lowest level of detail, sales usually consist of line items on an order. A single order at a grocery store might consist of one wedge of pecorino cheese, three jars of the same pasta sauce, and two boxes of the same pasta. If we're analyzing sales that occurred during a particular month, most of our effort would not require knowing how many jars of the same pasta sauce were sold; we would look at the data at much higher levels than order line items. At times we might examine sales by region. At others, we might shift to sales by large groupings of products such as all pasta, grains, and rice products. Any time that a particular item looks interesting, however, we might dive down to a lower level of detail, perhaps sales per day, per individual product, or even per individual shopper. Moving up and down through various levels of generality and specificity is part and parcel of the analytical process.

Information visualization software should support aggregating in the following ways:

- Provide the means to easily aggregate quantitative data to the level of items in a categorical variable (for example, to the product type or regional level).
- Provide the means to easily aggregate data in a number of useful ways, especially summing (which should be the default), averaging (mean or median), and counting.
- Provide the means to easily aggregate data based on equal intervals of a quantitative variable. For example, if individual sales orders ranged in revenue roughly from $10 to $100, we might want to sum, average, or count the orders that fell within a series of $10 ranges ($10.00 through $19.99, $20.00 through $29.99, etc.).
- Process the transition from one level of aggregation to another without noticeable delay.
- Provide the means to create ad hoc groupings of items.

Although we usually aggregate data in conjunction with some categorical variable, resulting in a summarized value for each item that's associated with that variable (for example, for each individual product that a company sells), we sometimes want to combine particular items of a categorical variable into a single group and aggregate the data to that level. For instance, if we work for a company that groups products into firmly defined families, we might often want to aggregate values based on groups of products that belong to the same family. Let's say that our company sells hot beverages, both coffees and teas. Ordinarily, we group beverages into four families: espresso, coffee, tea, and herbal tea. However, today we want to analyze sales patterns related to caffeinated vs. decaf products. Because no such standard grouping exists, we might want to create an ad hoc grouping so we can aggregate sales based on that distinction.

A special type of aggregation and disaggregation that deserves individual attention is *drilling*. Drilling involves moving down levels of summarization (and also back up) along a defined hierarchical path. Some categorical variables relate to one another hierarchically in a multi-level arrangement of parent-to- child relationships. The hierarchical structure of any medium-to-large sales organization is a familiar example. The top of the hierarchy would be the total organization; the next level down might be several major geographical regions (such as the Americas, Europe, and Asia Pacific), followed by smaller regions (such as individual countries), followed by yet smaller regions (such as the individual states in the U.S.), followed by much smaller regions (such as counties), and ending with individual stores. Drilling during the process of analysis would involve moving from a higher to lower level, such as the country level to the state level of aggregation (drilling down) or the opposite, such as from the individual store level to the county level (drilling up).

Information visualization software should support drilling in the following ways:

- Provide the means to define hierarchical relationships among categorical variables.
- Provide the means to easily drill up or down through a hierarchy with no more than a click or two of the mouse.
- Provide the means to skip levels in a hierarchy when drilling.
- Automatically define the natural hierarchy associated with time, including years, quarters, months, days, and hours.
- Process the transition from one level of a hierarchy to another without noticeable delay.

Re-expressing

Sometimes quantitative values can be expressed in multiple ways, and each expression can lead to different insights. By the term re-expressing, I mean that we sometimes change the way we delineate quantitative values that we're examining. The most common example involves changing the unit of measure, from some natural unit, such as U.S. dollars for sales revenues, to another, such as percentages. Examining each product type's percentage of total sales might lead to insights that did not come to light when we were viewing the same values expressed as dollars.

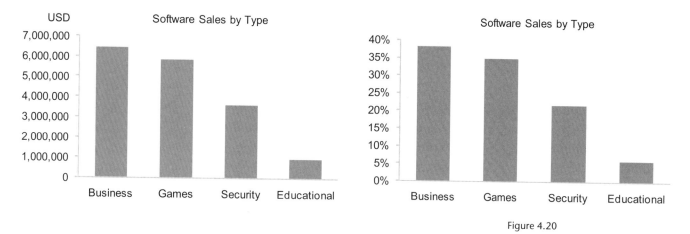

Figure 4.20

Re-expression can also take other forms. For instance, we might begin with the following graph, which paints a straightforward picture of change through time.

Figure 4.21

There might be an occasion when we would want to focus on the way that each month's sales compares to the sales in one particular month, such as January. We could use the graph above to do this, but it would take some work because this graph doesn't directly display this particular relationship between the monthly sales values. Look at the somewhat different perspective below where sales are re-expressed as the dollar amount of difference between each month and the month of January (January's sales are set at zero, and the line representing the rest of the months varies up or down in relation to January's value).

Figure 4.22

In this case, re-expression didn't involve changing the unit of measure (although it could have if we had chosen to express each month as its percentage difference from January's value). Rather, it involved a calculation that allowed us to focus on a different aspect of the year's sales data. Re-expression can take several forms, but only a few are common.

Sometimes it's useful to express time-series values as the difference between each interval's value and the value at some particular point in time, such as the month of January in the previous example. The reference value, however, could be the immediately prior period of time. The following graph displays the same data as the graph above, but this time each month is being compared to the immediately prior month and expressed as the percentage difference.

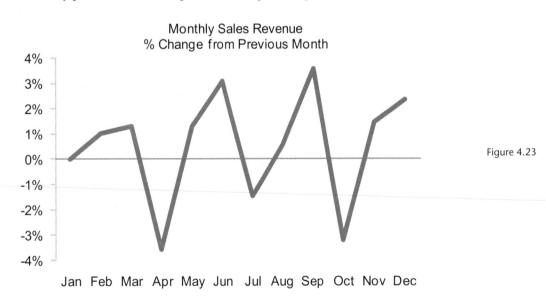

Figure 4.23

Information visualization software should support re-expression in the following ways:

- Provide an easy means to switch the current unit of measure in a graph to a percentage of the whole.
- Provide an easy means to re-express values in terms of how they compare to a reference value or as a rolling average.

At other times, especially when you wish to detect the general trend of what's happening through time, it's helpful to express values as a moving average, as in the following example that uses the same data as above but this time expresses each month's sales as the average of that month's sales and the previous two months' sales. This smoothes out some of the raggedness in the pattern, especially when values change radically from interval to interval, making it easier to see the overall trend.

Figure 4.24

Re-visualizing

This activity pertains only to visual forms of analysis. It involves changing the visual representation in some fundamental way, such as switching from one type of graph to another. Being able to do this quickly and easily is essential. Bertin expressed the need well when he wrote: "A graphic is no longer 'drawn' once and for all: it is 'constructed' and reconstructed (manipulated) until all the relationships which lie within it have been perceived...A graphic is never an end in itself: it is a moment in the process of decision making."[1] No single way of visualizing data can serve every analytical need. Different types of visualization have different strengths. If we don't have the ability to switch from one to another as fast as we recognize the need, our data analysis will be fragmented and slow, and we will probably end the process prematurely in frustration, missing the full range of possible insights standing in the wings.

1. *Information Visualization*, Robert Spence, Addison-Wesley, Essex England, 2001, p. 15.

Imagine that we're comparing actual expenses to the expense budget for a year's worth of data using a bar graph. Bars nicely support magnitude comparisons of individual values, such as actual expenses to budgeted expenses.

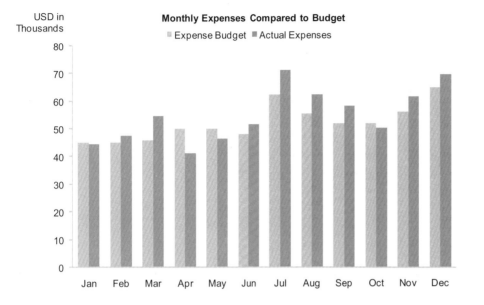

Figure 4.25

Before long, however, we want to see how the variation between actual and budgeted expenses changed through the year, which will be much easier if we switch from a bar to a line graph with a single line that expresses the difference between actual and budgeted expenses. We'll be grateful if we can switch the visualization from the one above to the one below with only a few keystrokes or movements of the mouse.

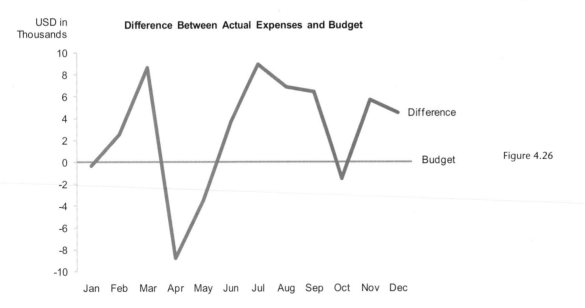

Figure 4.26

Information visualization software should support re-visualizing in the following ways:

- Provide a means to rapidly and easily switch from one type of graph to another.
- Provide a list of available graph types that is limited to only those that are appropriate for the data.
- Prevent or make more difficult the selection of a graph that would display the data inappropriately.

Zooming and Panning

When exploring and analyzing data visually, we sometimes want to take a closer look at a specific section of a graph. We can accomplish this by zooming in on the contents of a visualization, which enlarges the portion of the display that we wish to see more closely. The examples below illustrate this process. If we become particularly interested in what's happening during the specific period from February 14 through 20 while viewing the first graph below, we might want to zoom in on that portion, resulting in the bottom graph below.

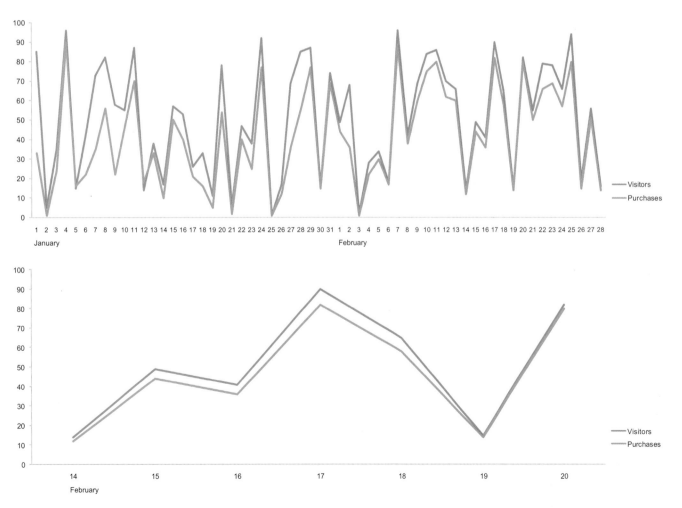

Figure 4.27

Zooming in on a graphical display can be accomplished in various ways: sometimes by using dedicated zoom controls and sometimes by simply narrowing a graph's quantitative scale (or both quantitative scales in a scatterplot) to include a subset of what's visible. Either way, the effect is much the same.

Usually, when we zoom in on a portion of the graph, it's as if we are using a magnifying glass to look at that specific section; that portion enlarges, and the other areas are no longer visible because they are outside the boundaries of the magnified view. We can always zoom back out to the graph's previous state to once again see the areas outside the magnified section, or we can change the view by panning, which involves moving up, down, right, or left in the larger display while maintaining the magnified (or "zoomed") scale. Panning brings into view areas of the graph that reside outside the boundaries of the current magnified portion. Panning is a familiar feature of many computer-based geographical displays, such as Google Maps. It is used in other graphical displays as well, such as panning from left to right in a line graph of time-series data to move the view to reveal different spans of time.

Information visualization software should support zooming and panning in the following ways:

- Provide the means to directly select an area of a graph and then zoom into it with a single click of the mouse.
- Provide the means to zoom back out just as easily.
- Provide the means, whenever a portion of what's in a graph is out of view, to pan in any direction directly with the mouse.

Re-scaling

This operation applies to quantitative graphs in particular. All graphs have at least one quantitative scale along an axis. Ordinarily, the quantitative scale places equal space between equal intervals of value. This common type of scale is sometimes called a *linear scale*. The following graph has a linear scale that ranges from $0 to $100,000 along equal intervals of $10,000 each. The distances between the tick marks are equal, reflecting that each jump in value is of equal size.

Figure 4.28

Another type of quantitative scale, which behaves differently, is a *logarithmic (log) scale*. Log scales occasionally come in handy. You might have avoided them until now because they were unfamiliar and perhaps a little intimidating, but they're really not that complicated. The little time it will take to get to know them will be worth the effort.

Along a log scale, each value is equal to the value of the previous interval multiplied by a base value. An example will clarify what I mean. Here's a log scale that has a base value of 10.

Figure 4.29

Notice that the second log value of 1 is equal to the actual value 10; that is, it is equal to the first actual value on the scale, 1, multiplied by the base value of 10 ($10 \times 1 = 10$). The third log value of 2 is computed by taking the second actual value, 10, and multiplying it by the base value, 10, which gives us 100. What's the fifth actual value along this scale? The answer is 10,000, which is the result of multiplying the actual value of 1 by the base value of 10 four times (that is, $1 \times 10 \times 10 \times 10 \times 10 = 10,000$).

So why bother with this seemingly unnatural scale? The primary reason, for our purposes at least, is because, by using a log scale to display time-series data, we can easily compare rates of change. We'll look at this use of log scales in *Chapter 7: Time-Series Analysis*, but here's a simple example to illustrate for now why they're handy. The graph below displays two sets of sales values: one for hardware sales and one for software sales. Which is increasing at a faster rate: hardware or software sales?

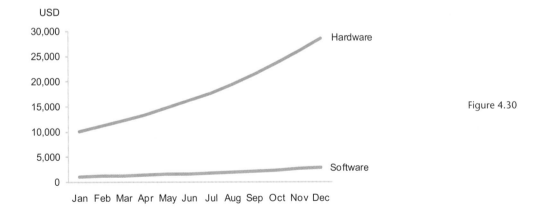

Figure 4.30

When I ask this question during classes, most people are quick to respond "hardware." The truth, however, is that both are increasing at the same 10% rate of change. The reason that hardware sales seem to increase at a faster rate is that a 10% increase in large dollar values produces a greater dollar increase than a 10% increase in low dollar values (software values are much smaller in this graph) even though the rate of change is the same. So the line for hardware has a steeper curve, but the rate of change, when normalized for the differences in the magnitude of the sales prices, is the same. When we wish to compare rates of change and avoid this optical suggestion that rate of change for higher-priced items is greater than for lower-priced items, log scales are a convenient solution. Look at what happens when I do nothing to the graph above but change it from a linear to a log scale.

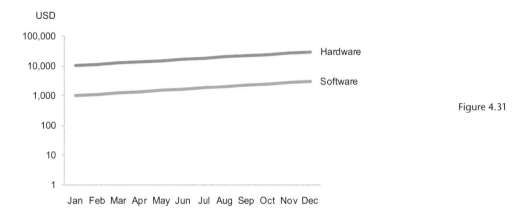

Figure 4.31

The slopes of the two lines are now identical. When using a log scale to display time-series values, identical slopes indicate identical rates of change. There are other scales besides the log scale that are sometimes useful for specific types of analytical problems, especially in science and engineering, but they are too specialized to include in this book.

Information visualization software should support re-scaling in the following ways:

- Provide a means to easily change the quantitative scale from linear to logarithmic and back.
- Provide the means to set a log scale's base. Although a base of 10 is typically used, others are sometimes useful. All bases display equal rates of change as equal slopes in lines, but the base value affects how many values appear on the scale. If, for example, a base 10 log scale results in too few values along the scale (for example, 1, 10, 100, and 1,000 only), switching to a lower base, such as base 2, will solve the problem.
- Provide a means to set the starting and ending values for the scale whether it's linear or logarithmic.
- Prevent or make inconvenient the use of a log scale with bar graphs and box plots. The height or length of a bar or a box encodes its value, but with a log scale we cannot rely on the bars or boxes as a means of comparing the actual values that they represent. Instead of regular values that are familiar, the heights or lengths of bars would encode log values, and most of us would find it difficult to meaningfully compare the magnitudes represented. For instance, in a log scale with a base of 10, a bar with a value of 100 would appear to have half the magnitude of a bar with a value of 10,000, even though it represented only 1/100th the value.

Accessing Details on Demand

Most of the time when we're exploring and examining data, we rely solely on visualizations, but from time to time we need details that either aren't included in a visualization or can't be discerned precisely enough. We want to call these details up instantly when we need them but keep them out of the way until then and put them out of the way once again after we've read them. A pop-up box (sometimes called a tool tip) containing details is the perfect solution. As shown in the example below, the box appears as a pop-up when we hover with the mouse over a particular item in a graph, such as a bar or point along a line. It disappears again when we move the mouse. In the field of information visualization, this is an example of what we call "details-on-demand."

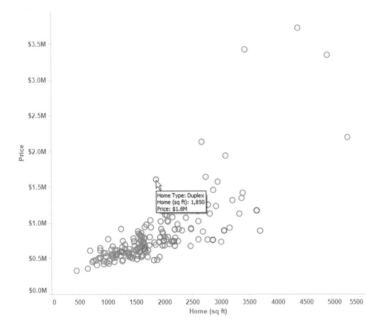

Figure 4.32. Created using Tableau Software

Information visualization software should support accessing details on demand in the following ways:

- Provide an easy means to view details related to an item in a visualization when needed, in the form of text.
- Provide an easy means to make details disappear from view when they are no longer needed.

Annotating

When we think about things, it often helps to make notes. Notes help us clarify our thinking and build an external repository of our thoughts (both questions and insights), documenting them for ourselves and allowing us to pass them on to others. When our thinking is about visualizations that we are studying, it is most effective to annotate the visualizations themselves rather than keeping notes in a separate, less accessible location. In the following example, I've annotated particular points in time to help me remember why traffic to my website exhibited particular behaviors.

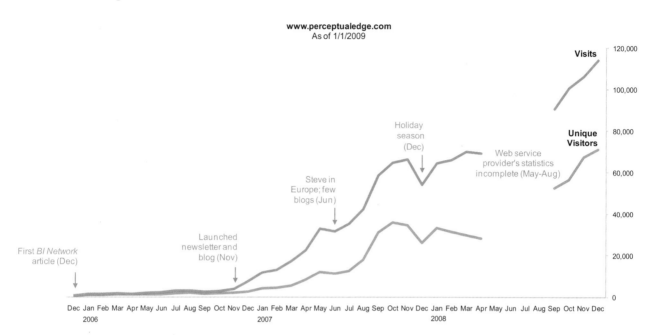

Figure 4.33

Unfortunately, because I can only annotate in Excel using text boxes that are independent of the graph, I'm forced to reposition the annotations every month when I update the graph with new statistics. Good visual analysis software supports richer annotation capabilities than this. In the two examples on the following page, I was able to attach the annotation to a specific data point in the scatterplot (left-hand example) so the annotation remained automatically tied to the point even when I filtered out some of the data, causing the annotated point to move (right-hand example). With annotation functionality such as this, we're encouraged to record our thoughts freely.

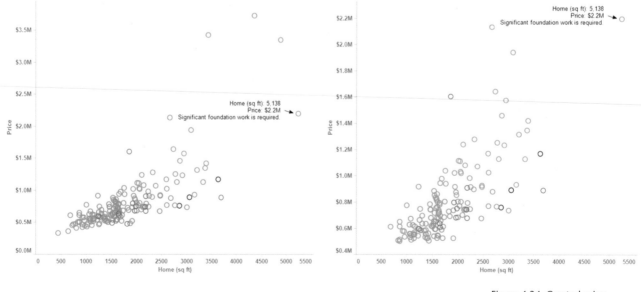

Figure 4.34. Created using Tableau Software

Information visualization software should support annotation in the following ways:

- Provide an easy means to add notes to a visualization so that they are associated with the visualization as a whole, a particular region, or one or more particular values.
- When notes are associated with particular items in a visualization and those items change position, the notes should automatically reposition to maintain the association.

Bookmarking

The analytical process does not follow a strict linear path; it meanders, bouncing back and forth. When we make an interesting discovery, it is often helpful to save that particular view, including its filters, sorts, and other features, so we can easily return to it later. This is similar to marking a page in a book or bookmarking a Web page for later access. Analytical software should allow us an easy, efficient way to save a particular view of the data so we can return to it whenever we wish. Sometimes this is accomplished by allowing us to save what we've created as a separate named worksheet or tabbed folder. How it's accomplished isn't important as long as it's easy to get back to it again with ease.

Sometimes we want to return to a previous view of the data that we didn't think to save at the time. This can only be accomplished if the software keeps a history of each view and allows us to navigate back through that history to get to particular prior states. It isn't as easy for software to maintain a history of the analytical process as it is to maintain a history of Web pages that we've visited during a single browsing session. What exactly constitutes a particular analytical state? We make so many changes during the analytical process, some big, such as changing from one type of graph to another, and some small such as turning on the grid lines or increasing font size. So it's hard to know where to draw the lines. Simply stepping backwards through a few individual changes, even small ones, is easy with a "back" or "undo" command, but what if the state that we wish to return to existed long ago? This requires some way to view the path we've followed in a manner that groups logically related changes together and perhaps branches off into separate paths when especially significant changes are made. This type of history tracking and navigation is more sophisticated than anything I've seen so far in a commercial visual analysis product, but some promising research has been done recently that is begging to be implemented.

The best work that I've seen so far for tracking and navigating analytical history was done by Jeffrey Heer, Jock D. Mackinlay, Chris Stolte, and Maneesh Agrawala and published in a paper titled "Graphical Histories for Visualization: Supporting Analysis, Communication, and Evaluation," published in *IEEE Transactions on Visualization and Computer Graphics*, Volume 14, Number 6, November/December 2008.

Information visualization software should support bookmarking in the following ways:

- Provide an easy means to save the current state of an analysis (visualizations, filters, sorts, data, etc.) for later access without interrupting the flow of analysis.
- Maintain a history of the steps and states during the analytical process so that it's easy to return to a particular former step or state as needed.
- Provide a means to review the history of steps and views in the analytical process so that it's easy to find a particular previous state.

The analytical interactions that I've identified and described become fluid, integrated, and seamless: a natural extension of our thoughts. They cease to function effectively if too much work is required to move from one to another; this interrupts the free flow and evolution of thought that is required for effective analysis.

Analytical Navigation

The visual analysis process involves many steps and potential paths to get us from where we begin—in the dark—to where we wish to be—in the light (enlightened). Some methods of navigating through data are more effective than others. Tukey once wrote:

> *Data analysis, like experimentation, must be considered as an open-minded, highly interactive, iterative process, whose actual steps are selected segments of a stubbily branching, tree-like pattern of possible actions.*[2]

2. "Proceedings of the Symposium on Information Processing in Sight Sensory Systems," John W. Tukey and M. B. Wilk, California Institute of Technology, Pasadena CA, 1965, pp. 5 and 6.

There is no one correct way to navigate through information analytically, but some navigational strategies are helpful general guidelines within which we can learn to improvise as our expertise grows.

Directed vs. Exploratory Navigation

At a fundamental level, analytical navigation can be divided into two approaches: directed or exploratory. Directed analysis begins with a specific question that we hope to answer, searches for an answer to that question (perhaps a particular pattern), and then produces an answer. With exploratory analysis, however, we begin by simply looking at data without predetermining what we might find; then, when we notice something that seems interesting and ask a question about it, we proceed in a directed fashion to find an answer to that question.

Directed

Figure 4.35

Exploratory

Both approaches are vital. Data analysis sometimes requires us to begin with a blank slate and let the information itself direct us to features worth examining. I agree with Howard Wainer, who wrote, "A graphic display has many purposes, but it achieves its highest value when it forces us to see what we were not expecting."[3] William Cleveland expresses this opinion as well:

> *Contained within the data of any investigation is information that can yield conclusions to questions not even originally asked. That is, there can be surprises in the data…To regularly miss surprises by failing to probe thoroughly with visualization tools is terribly inefficient because the cost of intensive data analysis is typically very small compared with the cost of data collection.[4]*

Information visualization is ideal for exploratory data analysis. Our eyes are naturally drawn to trends, patterns, and exceptions that would be difficult or impossible to find using more traditional approaches, such as tables of text, including pivot tables. When exploring data, even the best statisticians often set their calculations aside for a while and let their eyes take the lead.

Shneiderman's Mantra

When new recruits are trained in spy craft by intelligence organizations such as the Central Intelligence Agency (CIA), they are taught a method of observation that begins by getting an overview of the scene around them while simultaneously using a well-honed awareness of things that appear abnormal or not quite right. When an abnormality is spotted, they rapidly shift from broad awareness to close observation and analysis. A similar approach is often the best approach for visual data analysis as well. This was simply and elegantly expressed by Ben

3. *Graphic Discovery: A Trout in the Milk and Other Visual Adventures*, Howard Wainer, Princeton University Press, Princeton NJ, 2005, p. 59.

4. *The Elements of Graphing Data*, William S. Cleveland, Hobart Press, Summit NJ, 1994, pp. 8 and 9.

Shneiderman of the University of Maryland, and is known by people in the information visualization research community as *Shneiderman's Mantra*:

> *Overview first, zoom and filter, then details-on-demand.*[5]

In the book *Readings in Information Visualization*, Shneiderman and his co-authors elaborated on this navigational approach:

> *Having an overview is very important. It reduces search, allows the detection of overall patterns, and aids the user in choosing the next move. A general heuristic of visualization design, therefore, is to start with an overview. But it is also necessary for the user to access details rapidly. One solution is overview + detail: to provide multiple views, an overview for orientation, and a detailed view for further work.*[6]

> *Users often try to make a "good" choice by deciding first what they do not want, i.e. they first try to reduce the data set to a smaller, more manageable size. After some iterations, it is easier to make the final selection(s) from the reduced data set. This iterative refinement or progressive querying of data sets is sometimes known as hierarchical decision-making.*[7]

Shneiderman's technique begins with an overview of the data, looking at the big picture. We let our eyes search for overall patterns and detectable points of interest. Let your eyes roam over the graph below, which displays daily unit sales of five clothing products during three months.

5. *Readings in Information Visualization: Using Vision to Think*, Stuart K. Card, Jock D. Mackinlay, and Ben Shneiderman, Academic Press, San Diego CA, 1999, p. 625.

6. *Ibid.*, p. 285.

7. *Ibid.*, p. 295.

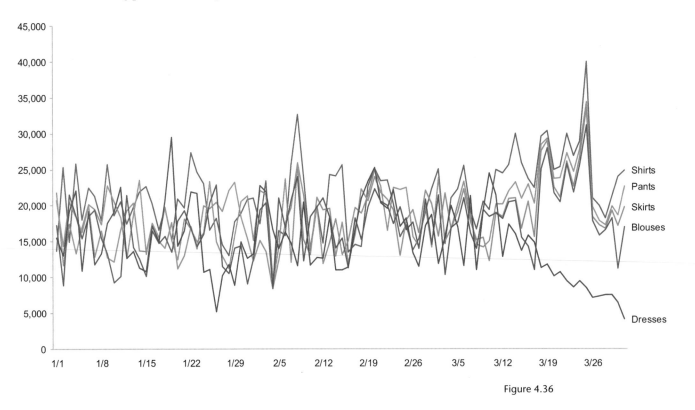

Figure 4.36

When we spot a particular point of interest, we can zoom in on it.

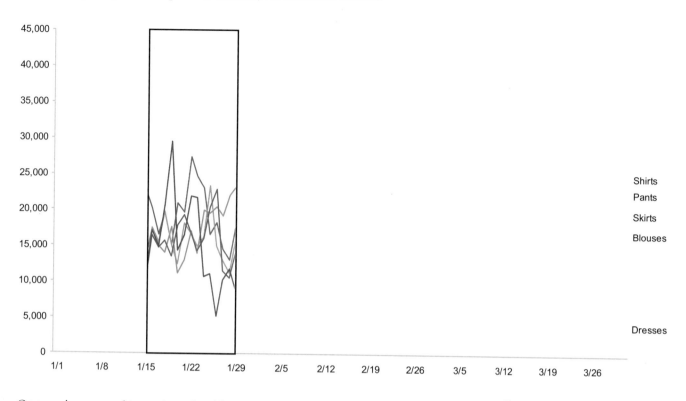

Figure 4.37

Once we've zoomed in on it, we're able to examine it more closely and in greater detail.

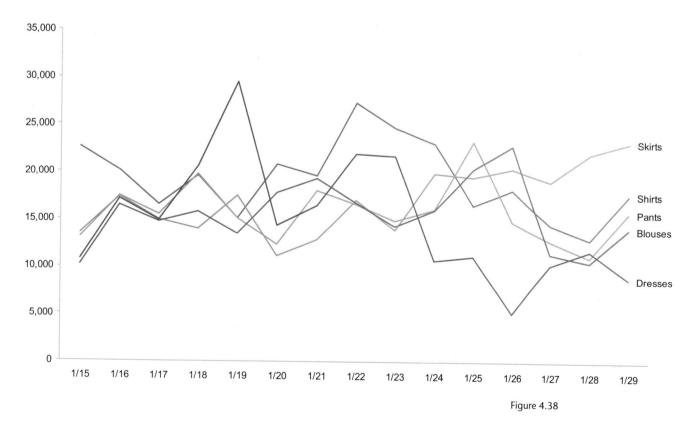

Figure 4.38

Often, to better focus on the relevant data, we must remove what's extraneous to our investigation.

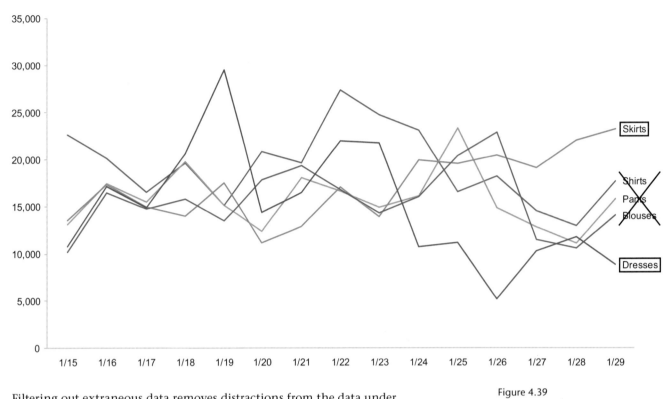

Figure 4.39

Filtering out extraneous data removes distractions from the data under investigation.

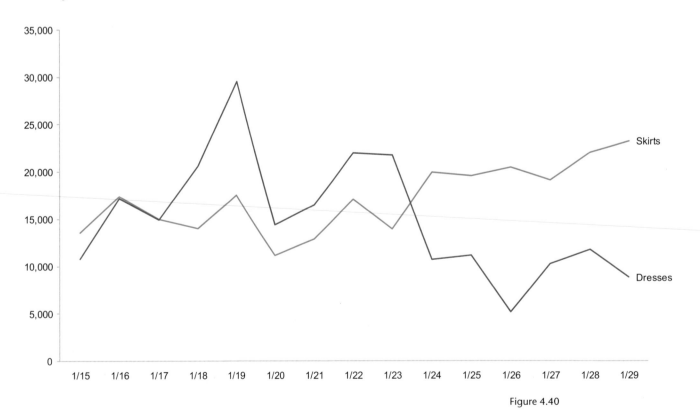

Figure 4.40

We rely mostly on the visual representations of information to reveal meanings that are embedded within data, but there are times when we need to see precise details that can't be discerned in the visualization. Here's another example of using a pop-up box in which information appears when we scroll over a specific area of an on-screen graph and disappears when we navigate away from the point.

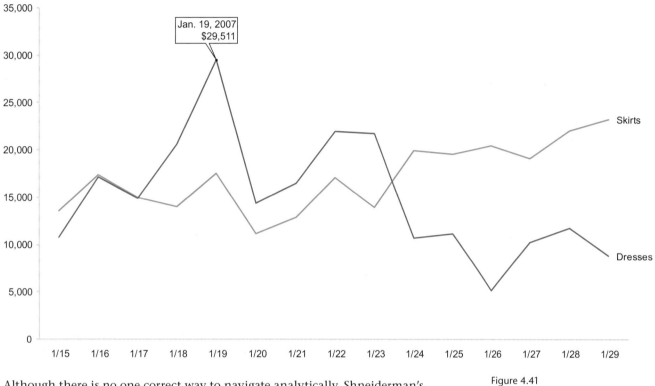

Figure 4.41

Although there is no one correct way to navigate analytically, Shneiderman's mantra describes the approach that often works best.

Hierarchical Navigation

It's frequently useful to navigate through information from a high-level view into progressively lower levels along a defined hierarchical structure and back up again. This is what I described earlier as drilling. A typical example involves sales analysis by region along a defined geographical hierarchy, such as continents at the highest level, then countries, followed by states or provinces, and perhaps down to cities at the lowest level. On the following page, the node-link diagram (also known as a tree diagram) illustrates a familiar way to display hierarchies.

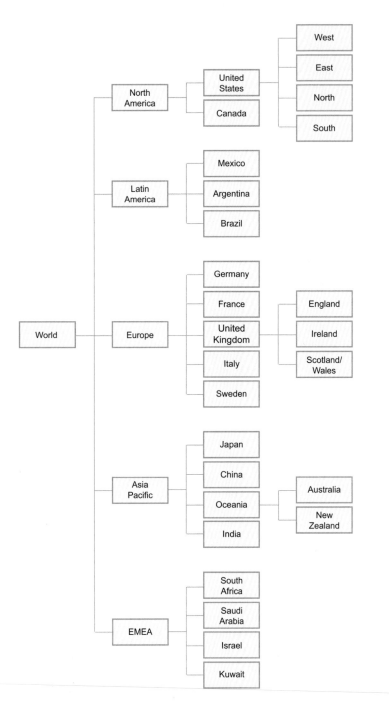

Figure 4.42

Node-link visualizations can be used to display quantitative values arranged hierarchically if variations in value are encoded using varying visual attributes such as the size or color intensity of each node. This approach quickly reaches the limits of what can be displayed on a single screen when we're dealing with large data sets. For this reason, Ben Shneiderman invented a visualization called a *treemap* (mentioned previously in *Chapter 3: Thinking with Our Eyes*), which he designed to display quantitative data arranged hierarchically in a manner that takes full advantage of limited screen space to include as much information as possible. Rather than representing hierarchical relationships by connecting nodes with lines and arranging them from top to bottom or left to right, treemaps use containment—the placement of child objects inside of parent objects—to display these relationships. Treemaps arrange rectangles within larger rectangles, which fit neatly within one another, so many items can be displayed on a single screen, as shown below.

Figure 4.43. Created using Panopticon Explorer

This example displays sales of Swedish beverages (can you guess where Panopticon, the vendor whose software I used to create this example, is located?), per country or region divided into several categories (Swedish Beer, Spirits, and so on). A fourth level, individual producers, also exists in the hierarchy but isn't currently visible.

Treemaps can display two quantitative variables simultaneously: one represented by each rectangle's size and the other represented by its color. In this example, size represents year-to-date sales, and color represents the percentage change in sales from last month (blue for increases and red for decreases, with greater color intensities for greater degrees of change).

Treemaps can display a great deal of information quite powerfully but for a limited set of purposes. That is, treemaps were not designed to support precise quantitative comparisons, which we can't make based on relative sizes and colors. Instead, treemaps allow us to simultaneously view two quantitative variables for a large number of hierarchically arranged entities. I don't know any other visualization that can display as many hierarchically structured items at once, but I do know visualizations, such as bar graphs, that can display the same two variables more effectively for smaller sets of data.

Another reason to reserve treemaps for large data sets is that rectangles within rectangles don't display hierarchical relationships as clearly as other types of displays, such as node-link visualizations, do. When used for large data sets, however, treemaps allow us to readily spot extremes and predominant patterns. For instance, our eyes are drawn to the darkest red rectangle located near the bottom right corner, with a country name that begins "Sout..." When I hover over the rectangle with my mouse, details about this county immediately appear, as shown below.

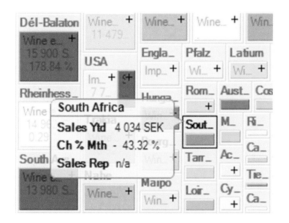

Figure 4.44. Created using Panopticon Explorer

We can also see a predominant pattern in this treemap: most of the countries with high sales (large rectangles) increased since the previous month (they're blue), with the notable exception of Spirits in Sweden, which decreased slightly.

Hierarchical navigation is easy with treemaps. If we want to take a closer look at sales of Spirits in Sweden to determine why they decreased, we can drill down into that category alone (by double-clicking it in this software program), causing it to fill the screen and automatically reveal the next level in the hierarchy (individual brands associated with each producer), shown on the following page.

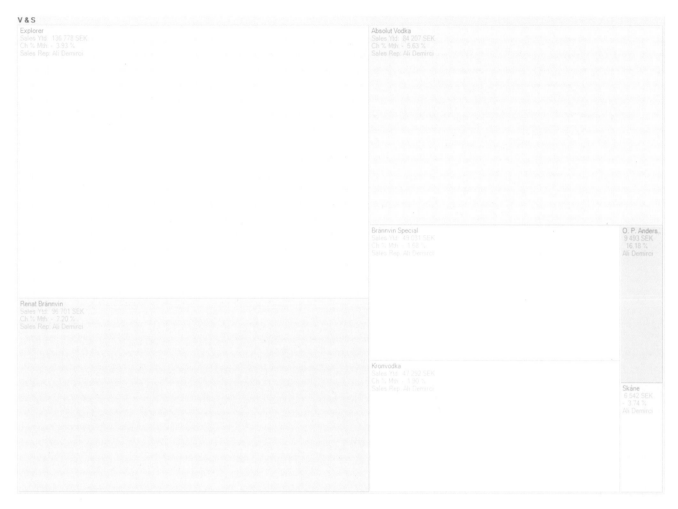

Figure 4.45. Created using
Panopticon Explorer

Now we can see that this decline cannot be attributed to any one product but
appears to be fairly evenly distributed across all brands except for one: O. P.
Anderson, the lone blue rectangle.

I've hardly done justice to treemaps in this short description. They merit
much more exploration, but my current purpose is only to illustrate how they
support hierarchical navigation especially when dealing with large quantities of
data.

Now that we've examined ways to interact with information and navigate
through the analytical process, it's time to move on to the techniques and best
practices that will keep our work on track and lead us to rich insights.

Let's now look at several general techniques and practices that can improve the effectiveness of visual analysis. These techniques and practices will also appear in later chapters to illustrate particular occasions when they're especially useful. But it's helpful to get to know them conceptually now before we focus on their practical use later.

Most of these techniques and practices were developed by the information visualization research community. We owe a lot to these folks, mostly university professors and doctoral students, who do the pioneering research and development that few commercial software vendors attempt.

We'll examine the following techniques and practices:

- Optimal quantitative scales
- Reference lines and regions
- Trellises and crosstabs
- Multiple concurrent views and brushing
- Focus and context together
- Details on demand
- Over-plotting reduction

A few of these terms were mentioned earlier in the book, but some might not mean a lot yet, and a few sound like they might be complicated. Rest assured, they'll all make sense when explained, and some might already be familiar. Let's look at each one in detail.

Optimal Quantitative Scales

I mentioned previously that it's sometimes useful to switch between linear and logarithmic scales. What I'm referring to now as optimal quantitative scales is different. This has to do with how we set a scale's range from beginning (the lowest value) to end (the highest value). The scale that's optimal depends on the nature of the information, the kind of graph we're using to view it, and what we're trying to discover and understand.

The basic rules of thumb are simple:

- When using a bar graph, begin the scale at zero, and end the scale a little above the highest value.
- With every type of graph other than a bar graph, begin the scale a little below the lowest value and end it a little above the highest value.
- Begin and end the scale at round numbers, and make the intervals round numbers as well.

I explained previously in *Chapter 4: Analytical Interaction and Navigation* why it's important in bar graphs to begin the scale at zero; otherwise, the relative heights or lengths of the bars won't accurately correspond to actual differences between the values. The following graph presents a visual lie because the heights of the bars cannot be compared to accurately determine differences in value.

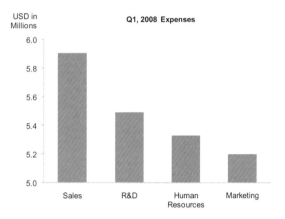

Figure 5.1

Expenses in the sales department are not 4 ½ times as great as expenses in the marketing department (5.9 is not 4 ½ times larger than 5.2), despite what the relative heights of the bars suggest. Now consider the next graph and notice that, because all of the values fall within a fairly narrow range, it is more difficult to discern small differences in the bars' heights. This is because, with such long bars, differences between the values represent small percentage differences in their heights.

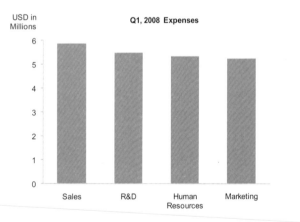

Figure 5.2

Keep in mind that our eyes perceive differences, not absolute values, and we perceive differences proportionally (that is, as percentage differences). Two long bars that are both roughly five inches tall but vary by 1/16th of an inch (a small percentage) would appear about the same height, yet two short bars—one 1/8th of an inch and the other 1/16th of an inch—would appear quite different in length because the percentage difference is great, even though they vary by the same 1/16th of an inch. When comparing values and patterns, it's helpful if their differences stand out so they're easy to see and compare. In a graph that uses the positions of objects to encode values, this means that we want to spread those differences in position across a fair amount of space rather than crowding them together in a small space. This is accomplished by narrowing the quantitative scale so that it begins a little below the lowest value in the data set and ends a little above the highest value. Because it isn't appropriate to narrow the scale in a bar graph so that the bars no longer begin at zero, we can replace the bars with data points and narrow the scale. Notice how much more easily you can compare the values and patterns that are represented in the graph above when they're displayed in the dot plot below with the values on the Y-axis narrowed to the range between 5 and 6 in contrast to the scale of 0 to 6.

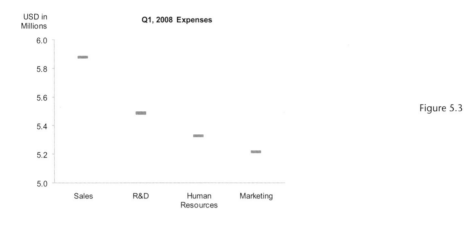

Figure 5.3

Unfortunately, few products support dot plots today, but sometimes we can work around this limitation. For instance, with Excel, we can produce a dot plot by starting with a line graph that uses dots to mark values along the line, and then we can remove the line, leaving only the dots. The example above was produced in Excel using this approach.

Scales can be narrowed in this way not only in dot plots but also in line graphs, scatterplots, and box plots. Here's an example of each:

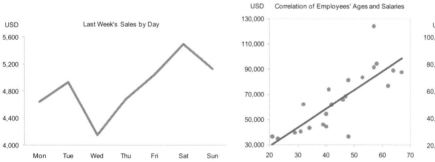
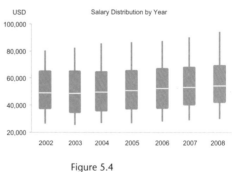

Figure 5.4

Notice that the scatterplot in the center has two quantitative scales, both of which have been narrowed, resulting in a plot area that is fully utilized.

The rules of thumb that I recommended above are designed for us, the analysts. If we go on to report our findings to others, however, we might, depending on who our audience is, choose to ignore the rule about beginning and ending the scale to closely fit the values and instead begin the scale at zero even when using line graphs, dot plots, and box plots. The larger distance between the objects that encode the values (for example, the dots above), which results from narrowing a quantitative scale, can sometimes mislead people into assuming that the large distances represent large differences in values, which isn't necessarily the case.

Information visualization software should support optimal quantitative scales in the following ways:

- Make it difficult or impossible to remove zero from the quantitative scale of a bar graph.
- Automatically set the quantitative scale for dot plots, line graphs, scatterplots, and box plots to begin a little below the lowest value in the data set and end a little above the highest value, based on round numbers.
- Provide a means to easily adjust the quantitative scale as needed.

Reference Lines and Regions

As I explained previously, comparisons are intimately interwoven into the analytical process. Therefore, anything that makes comparisons easier, such as including reference lines and reference regions, is worth doing. Imagine that we want to see how well our manufacturing process has been going relative to standards that have been established for an acceptable number of defects. Let's say that it's unacceptable when defects exceed 1% of the products manufactured on any given day. We could look at manufacturing quality for the current month using the following graph:

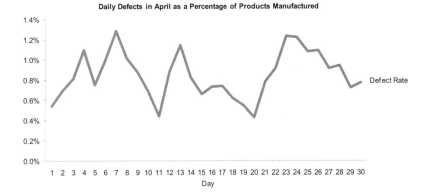

Figure 5.5

We could accomplish our task with the graph above, but notice how much easier and faster we could do this using the next graph, which has a reference line indicating the threshold for an acceptable percentage of defects:

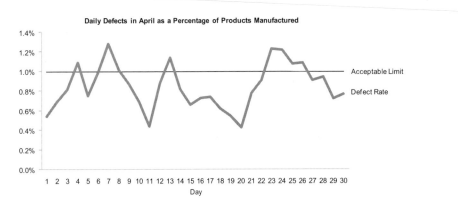

Figure 5.6

With the addition of the reference line, the days when the number of defects ventured into the unacceptable range pop out, and it's much easier to see the degree to which we exceeded the limits on those occasions. All we've done to create this clarity is mark the threshold with a reference line.

Information visualization software should support reference lines and regions in the following ways:

- Provide a means to include reference lines in graphs based on setting a specific value (for example, $10,000), an ad hoc calculation (for example, 1% of the number of manufactured products), or a statistical calculation.
- Provide automated calculations for the following statistical calculations: mean, median, standard deviation, specified percentiles, minimum, and maximum.
- Provide a means to base calculated reference lines either on the values that appear in the graph only or on a larger set of values. (I'll explain this with an example in a moment.)
- Provide a means to label reference lines to clearly indicate what the lines represent.
- Provide a means to format reference lines as needed, including a choice of hue, color intensity, line weight, and line style (solid, dashed, etc.).

When reference lines are automatically calculated, such as when the reference line is based on an average, we sometimes want that calculation to be based only on the values that appear in a given graph and sometimes on a larger set of values. In the following series of graphs, the reference line that appears in each graph represents the mean sales of products in that particular region only.

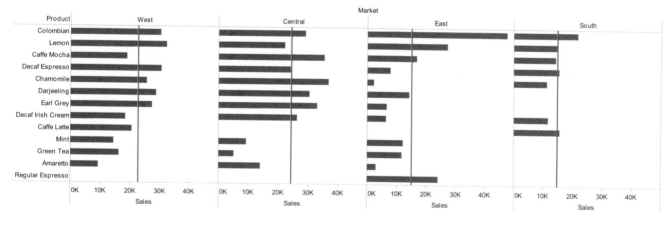

Figure 5.7. Created using Tableau Software

However, in this next example, the value marked by the reference lines is the same in each graph; it represents average sales revenues for products in all regions, not just the region represented in the particular graph.

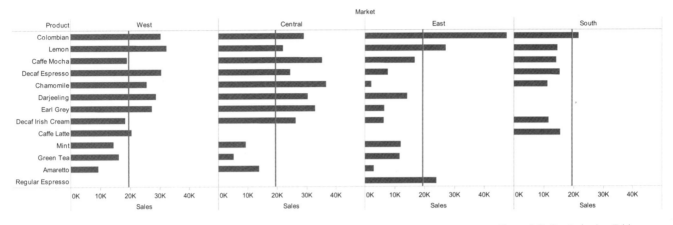

Figure 5.8. Created using Tableau Software

Both views are useful, so the ability to calculate reference lines in both ways is handy.

Trellises and Crosstabs

Figures 5.7 and 5.8 in the previous section preview the practice that I'll describe now. It is often helpful to divide the data set we wish to examine into multiple graphs, either because we can't display everything in a single graph without resorting to a 3-D display, which would be difficult to decipher, or because placing all the information in a single graph would make it too cluttered to read. By splitting the data into multiple graphs that appear on the screen at the same time in close proximity to one another, we can examine the data in any one graph more easily, and we can compare values and patterns among graphs with relative ease. Edward Tufte described displays of this type as *small multiples* in his 1983 book *The Visual Display of Quantitative Information*. Others refer to them as *trellis displays*, a term coined by William Cleveland and Rickard Becker in the early 1990s, which is how I'll refer to them in this book.

Trellis displays should exhibit the following characteristics:

- Individual graphs only differ in terms of the data that they display. Each graph displays a subset of a single larger set of data, divided according to some categorical variable, such as by region or department.
- Every graph is the same type, shape, and size, and shares the same categorical and quantitative scales. Quantitative scales in each graph begin and end with the same values (otherwise values in different graphs cannot be accurately compared).
- Graphs can be arranged horizontally (side by side), vertically (one above another), or both (as a matrix of columns and rows).
- Graphs are sequenced in a meaningful order, usually based on the values that are featured in the graphs (for example, sales revenues).

How we arrange the graphs—horizontally, vertically, or as a matrix—depends on the number of graphs that we're trying to squeeze into the space available on the screen as well as the types of comparisons that we're making among the graphs. In the following example, notice that it's easy to track a specific region, such as the east, through all the graphs because the bars that represent that region are aligned with one another across the page.

We can easily isolate the east region as we take in the full set of graphs. But if we want to accurately compare the magnitudes of the four bars that encode the east region's sales values, we could do that more easily using graphs arranged as illustrated below where quantitative scales are aligned with one another down the page:

Figure 5.9. Created using Tableau Software

Figure 5.10. Created using Tableau Software

When we can't display all the graphs in either a horizontal or vertical arrangement, we can shift to a matrix. Here are 15 graphs, one per department, that we can use to compare departmental expenses:

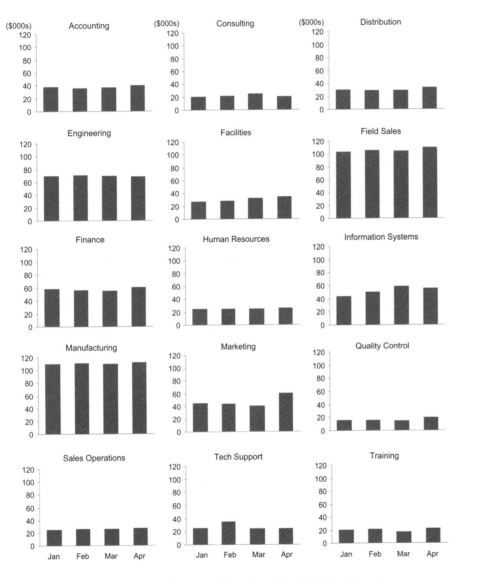

Figure 5.11

Trellis displays lose much of their value when the individual graphs are arranged in an arbitrary order—that is, an order that ignores the magnitudes of the values—such as in the alphabetical arrangement above. In the next example, the same 15 graphs have been arranged according to the magnitude of expenses for the four-month period in each, from the highest in the top left-hand corner, with expenses lowering as we move to the right across that row and continuing in the same manner on subsequent rows until the department with the lowest expenses appears in the bottom right-hand corner. Notice how much easier it is to use this trellis display than the previous one where the departments were arranged alphabetically.

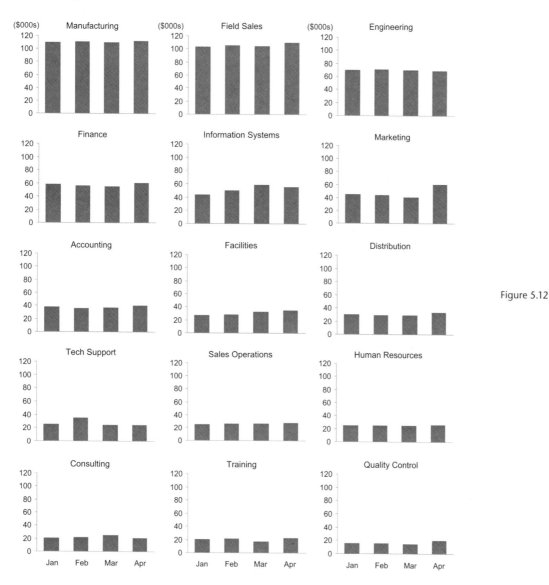

Figure 5.12

In a trellis display, the graphs differ according to a single variable, such as "department" in this example. Sometimes it's useful to arrange a series of graphs that differ according to more than one variable. This can be done using a *visual crosstab* display. In the next example, we have individual graphs for each intersection of region (columns) and product type (rows). This is similar to a crosstab that we might create in a spreadsheet product such as Excel, but the values are displayed visually rather than as text.

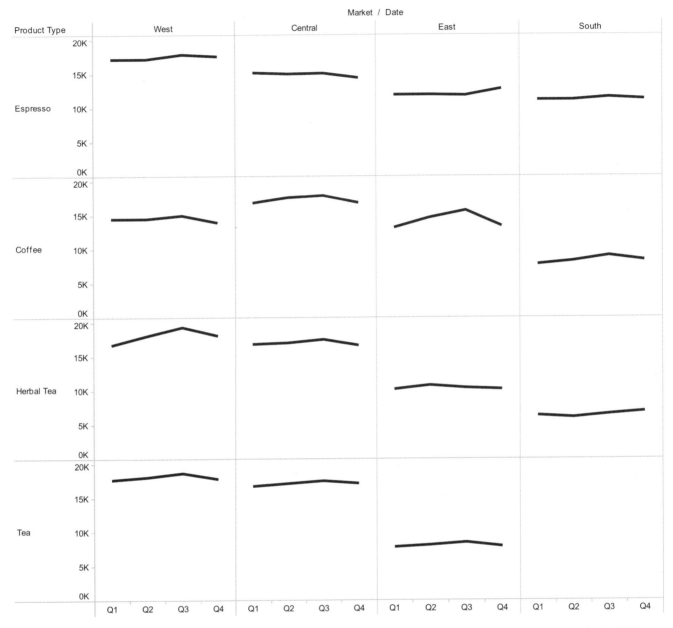

Figure 5.13. Created using Tableau
Software

Visual crosstabs are a powerful means to examine and compare data across several dimensions at once.

Another variation of the visual crosstab allows us to not only view a single quantitative variable across multiple categorical dimensions at once but to extend the analytical view to multiple quantitative variables as well. In the following example, we can now examine sales revenues, expenses, and profits together, divided into regions, product types, and products:

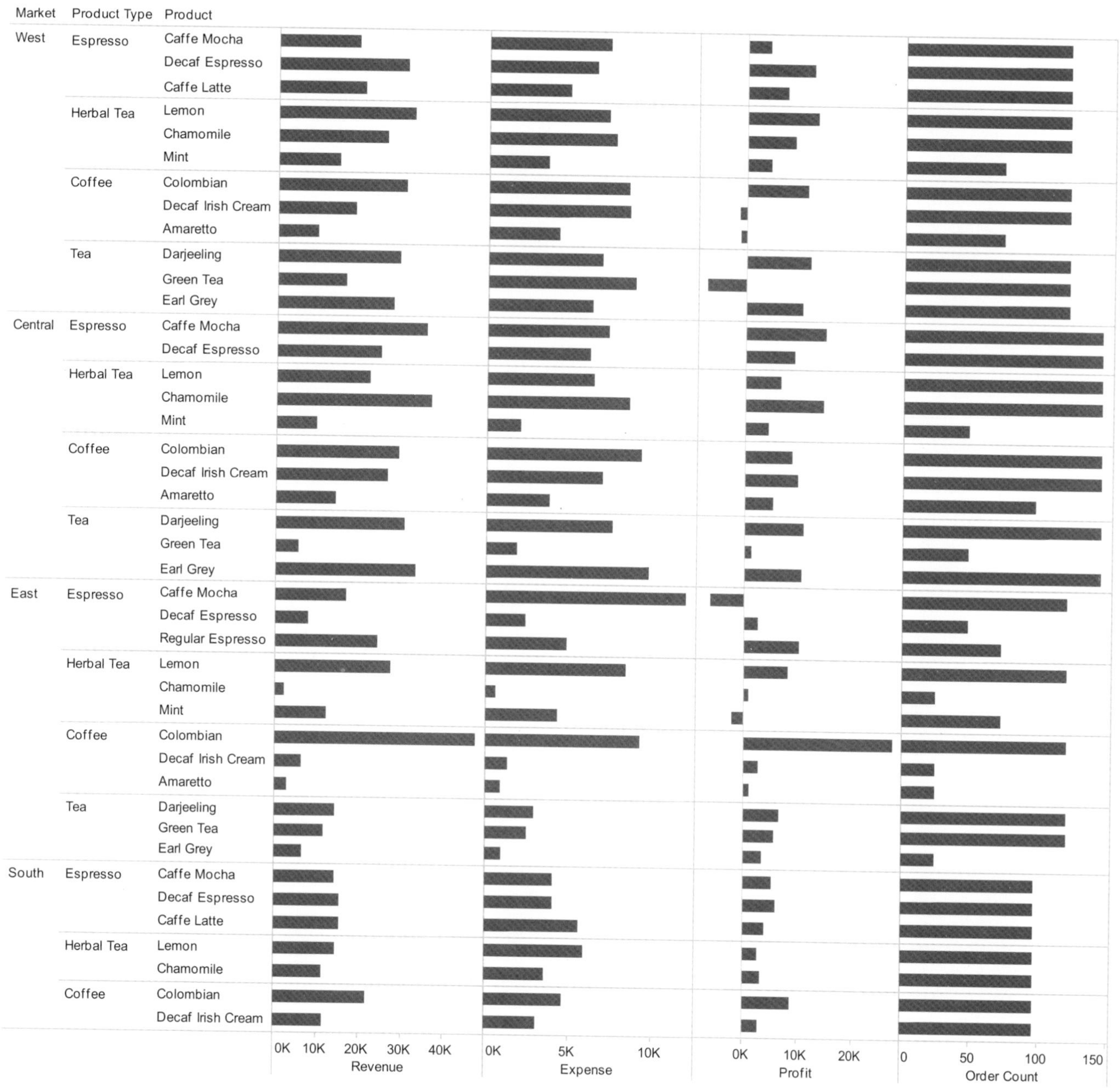

Figure 5.14. Created using Tableau Software

Notice that when multiple quantitative variables are included, their scales need not be the same. Quantitative scales must only be consistent among a series of graphs when it's appropriate and useful to compare the magnitudes of values between them. In fact, variables could be expressed as different units of measure entirely, such as dollars (revenue, expense, and profit above) versus number of items (order count), which would make it extremely impractical to use the same scales for all variables.

Information visualization software should support trellis and visual crosstab displays in the following ways:

- Provide a means to automatically arrange data as a trellis display simply by indicating the categorical variable on which the individual graphs should be based, the arrangement of the graphs (horizontally, vertically, or as a matrix), and the sorted order of the graphs (for example, by sales amounts in descending order).
- Automatically set the quantitative scales that appear in all graphs in a trellis display to be consistent with one another.
- Provide a means to automatically arrange data as a visual crosstab display by indicating one or more categorical variables on which columns of graphs should be based, one or more categorical variables on which rows of graphs should be based, and one or more quantitative variables that should be displayed in the graphs.
- Provide a means to display more than one quantitative variable in separate columns or rows of a visual crosstab display.
- Automatically set the quantitative scales that appear in all graphs in a visual crosstab display to be consistent with one another except when multiple quantitative variables are included in separate columns or rows of graphs, in which case each quantitative variable should be scaled independently.

Multiple Concurrent Views and Brushing

Not only is it useful to divide a data set into multiple instances of the same graph using trellis or visual crosstab displays, it is also useful to view a single data set from different perspectives concurrently using multiple graphs. An old folktale helps to explain the value of this kind of display. It is about three blind men who encounter an elephant for the first time and attempt to learn about it by touch alone. One touches the elephant's two front legs, another the tail, and the other the trunk. When they later discussed what they'd experienced, the first blind man proclaimed, "This queer animal resembles two big trees without any branches." The second said, "No, this queer animal is like our straw fans swinging back and forth to give us a breeze. However, it's not so big or well made. The main portion is rather wispy." The third in utter dismay said, "You're both wrong. This queer animal is similar to a snake; it's long and round, and very strong." The experience of each man was unique because each experienced different part of the elephant and that part alone.

Traditional data analysis tools make it unnecessarily difficult to explore data from multiple perspectives, so analysts tend to pursue only a limited set of predetermined questions. This is like the blind men perceiving the elephant from only a few limited interactions with it. It's simply too time consuming to explore the data thoroughly, allowing fresh discoveries to lead to comprehensive and free-flowing exploration. When we can't examine data from multiple perspectives simultaneously, many of the meaningful relationships that exist in our data will remain hidden.

Here's a display that combines several different views of the same data set on a single screen.

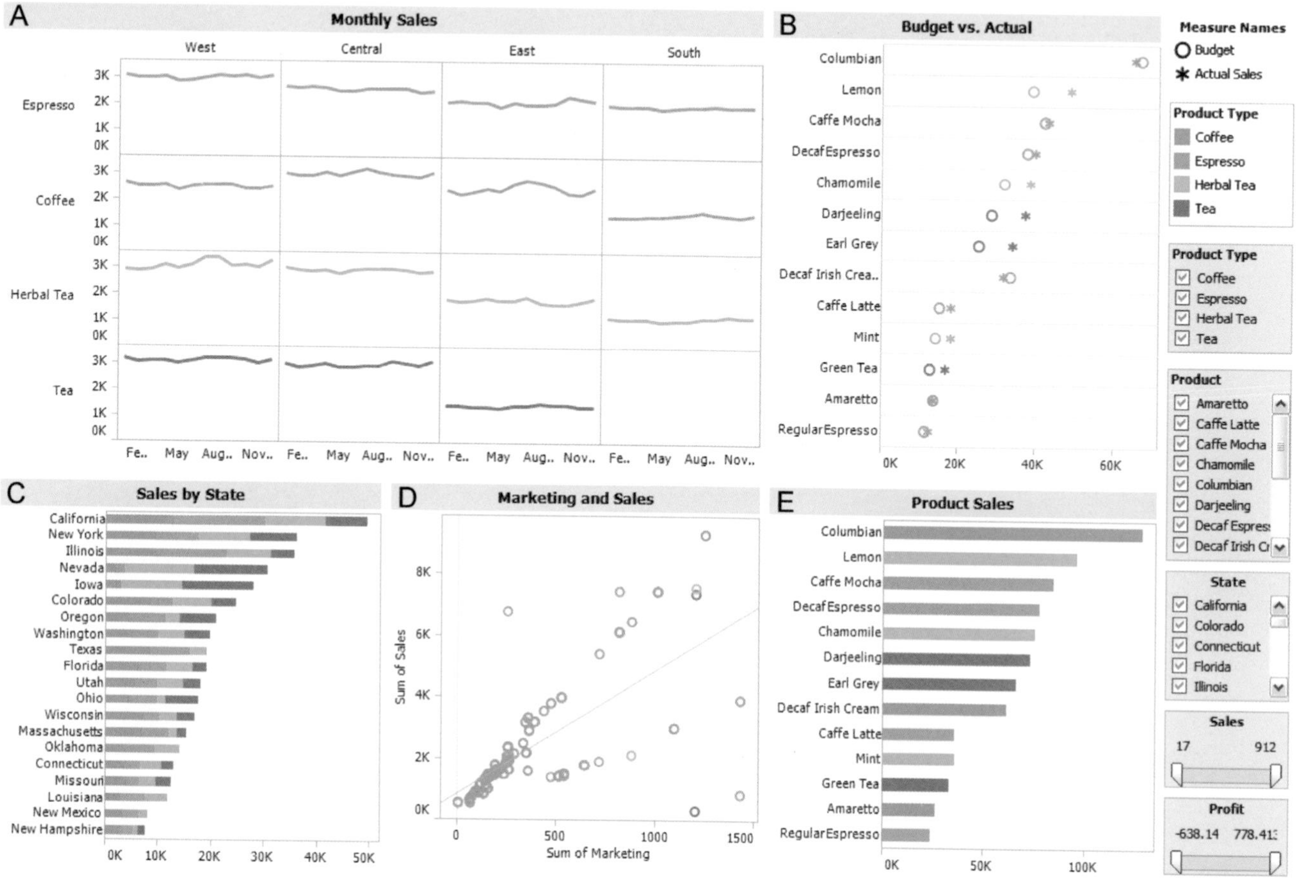

Each chart focuses on a different aspect of the data.

- In section A, we see a visual crosstab of line graphs that displays monthly sales by product type (the rows) and region (the columns).
- In section B, we see a comparison of actual sales (the asterisks) to the sales budget (the circles) by product, with color coding to associate individual products with product types.
- In section C, we see sales by state, further divided into product types by color.
- In section D, we see a scatterplot that examines the correlation between marketing expenses and sales, grouped by product type (using color), with a separate data point for each combination of state and product type.
- In section E, we see sales by product, once again grouped into product types by color.
- Finally, in the panel at the far right, two legends appear at the top, and below them appear five filter controls for product type, product, state, sales, and profit.

Figure 5.15. Created using Tableau Software; I've added the letter labels (A, B, C...) to make it easy to refer to particular sections of the display without confusion.

What we have here is a display that will allow us to explore a year's worth of sales data from several perspectives with little effort and no delay as we move rapidly from chart to chart, filtering the data as needed to examine particular subsets without distraction.

We can discern several facts about sales using this single display, including the following:

- Espresso sales were best overall, which I can see because the Monthly Sales graphs in section A are sorted by product type in descending order.

- Despite the fact that Espresso is the leading product type, the leading product is Colombian Coffee, followed by Lemon Tea in the number two position. Espresso sales take the overall lead, however, because the third and fourth products both fall into the Espresso category.

- Despite the fact that Colombian Coffee is the best sales performer overall, it is one of only two products that failed to meet the sales budget (see section B). The other is Decaf Irish Cream. Both are coffee products (the blue items). Perhaps the person in charge of budgeting coffee sales doesn't handle budgeting as well as the managers of the other product types. Of course, there are other possible explanations, so the truth requires digging deeper. I suppose it's possible that the high sales performance of tea products (the red items) compared to budget might also be due to poor budgeting skills.

- Sales are highest in the west region, probably because sales in the state of California lead the nation (see section C). Although the central region does not perform as well as the west overall, it outperforms the west in coffee sales. Coffee sales increase in the central and east regions in the month of July, and then a month later in the south. A similar summer peak, however, does not occur in the west for coffee, but it does for herbal tea.

- In general, there is a positive correlation between marketing expenses and sales (see section D), and no single product type stands out as being better or worse than the others in this respect. The scatterplot reveals a few outliers in the data—data points that seem far removed from the norm— and there appear to be two separate groups of data points that form what are called positive linear correlations, revealed by the one linear series of points that appears above the trend line and the other that appears below it. This is worth further investigation. (We'll take a closer look at correlations in *Chapter 11: Correlation Analysis*.) The two outliers in the bottom right of the scatterplot represent Green Tea in Nevada and Caffe Mocha in New York. I was able to determine this by hovering over these points with the mouse, which caused the details to appear as text in a pop-up window.

- Multi-perspective displays like this really come alive when we begin to filter the data. Filtering data in a display like this usually works best when filters affect all the charts.

Displays that combine multiple views of a common data set on a single screen are called by different names. When they're used to make sense of the data, that is, for analysis, I call them *faceted analytical displays*. I don't call them *dashboards* because dashboards are used to *monitor* what's going on, not to *analyze* what's going on, and are therefore designed and function differently.

Not only do the individual charts display the same data set, they are also intimately linked together so that all interactions with the data affect all views, automatically and immediately. Whenever multiple tables and graphs are linked in this manner, they are, in information visualization nomenclature, *tightly coupled*. I've already mentioned how this applies to filtering, but it can apply to other interactions as well.

Filtering the same data from all the views simultaneously brings the data to life. In the following version of the faceted analytical display that appears above, I have filtered out the state of California.

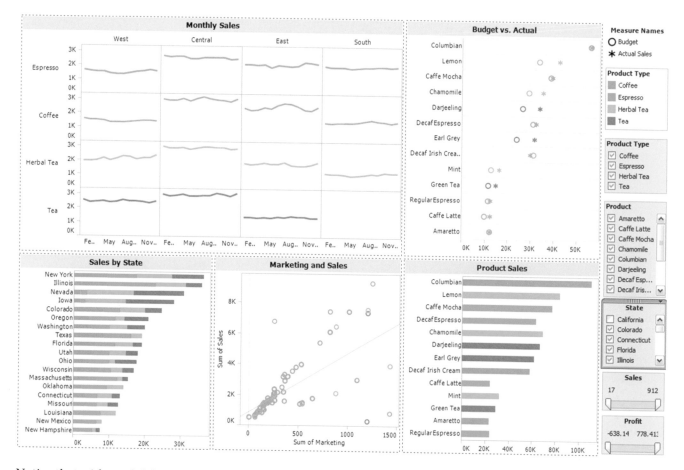

Notice that without California the order of the products in the Budget vs. Actual graph product sales has been rearranged. I intentionally set this graph to automatically re-sort if filtering affects the relative order of product sales, but the Product Sales graph is not set to automatically re-sort. This allows me to look at the Product Sales graph to easily spot when bars are no longer in order by size. Short bars that appear above longer bars represent products that have decreased

Figure 5.16. Created using Tableau Software

in sales relative to those that had lower sales before California was removed from the display. For instance, notice that the Decaf Espresso and Caffe Latte bars are both smaller than those immediately below them. Now, by looking up at the Budget vs. Actual graph, we can see that Decaf Espresso has fallen from the 4th position to 6th and that Caffe Latte has fallen from 9th to 12th. These products obviously sold better in California than they did overall. We can also tell by glancing at the Budget vs. Actual graph that the poor budget performance of Colombian Coffee has been corrected by removing the state of California, so California must have been primarily responsible for this performance issue.

Now let's see if we can learn something about profits, first by filtering out all but negative profits (that is, losses). Here's the result:

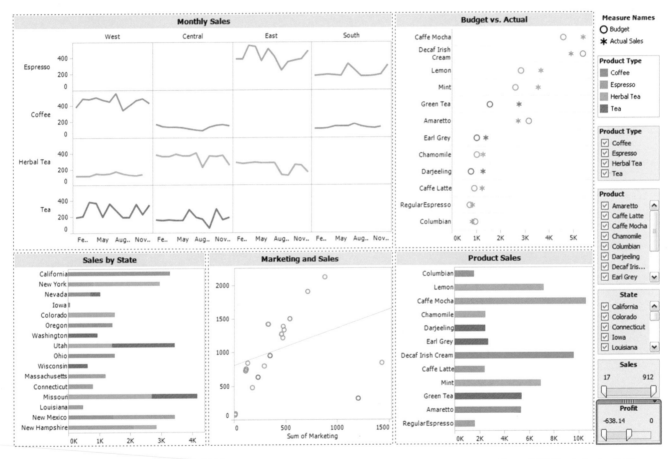

Figure 5.17. Created using Tableau Software

Filtering out all but the losses has affected the overall sales picture dramatically. Notice how many differences now catch your eye. Looking at the Sales by State graph, you can easily see that the states of Missouri, Utah, and New Mexico now show higher sales than all of the other states, including the three overall top-ranking states of California, New York, and Nevada. Move your attention to the Marketing vs. Sales scatterplot, and you will probably be surprised to find that, with the exception of two outliers in the bottom right corner, most sales seem to exhibit a fairly linear positive correlation between marketing expenses and sales, so we probably can't blame the losses on marketing expenses. Now look at the Product Sales graph and you can see that Caffe Mocha and Decaf Irish Cream appear to have a disproportionate influence on losses, which you can further confirm by glancing up at the Budget vs. Actual graph where these products are now ranked first and second. Before moving on, notice also how little Colombian Coffee contributed to the losses, which appears dead last in rank, even though it was previously ranked #1. Finally, notice how jagged the lines are in the Monthly Sales graphs. With the exception of Herbal Tea in the west region and Coffee in the central and south regions, low profits appear to be related to volatile sales with lots of dramatic ups and downs throughout the year.

Let's look at one more example, this time the reverse of what we just examined. Here's the picture that results from filtering out all sales except those with high profits ranging from $362 to the maximum amount of $778 per customer:

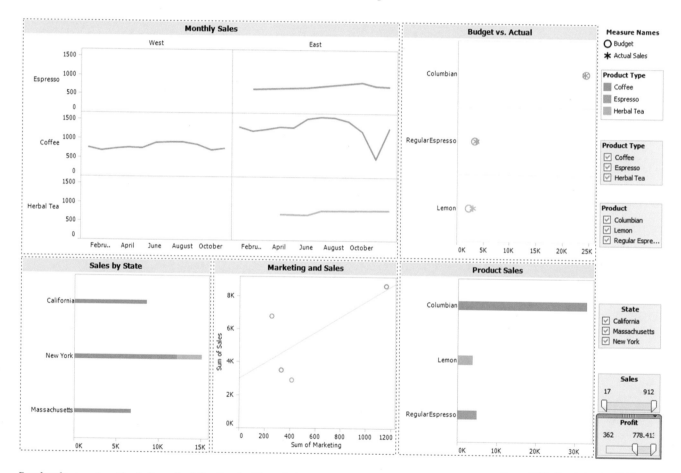

Figure 5.18. Created using Tableau Software

By slowly moving the left end of the Profit filter slider control (the one in the bottom right corner) to the right, gradually removing low profits and all but higher and higher profits, I noticed that as soon as I passed the threshold of $361 in profit, the number of products dropped from seven to the three that now remain, eliminating the Tea product type altogether. I also noticed the number of states drops from 16 to 3, eliminating the central and south regions. Looking at the Monthly Sales graphs, we can see that high profits are associated with sales of Coffee, specifically Colombian Coffee, throughout the year, except in November, primarily in the east.

In addition to filtering, another analytical interaction called *brushing* brings data to life. Brushing is the act of selecting a subset of the items that appear in one table or graph to highlight them, which automatically results in those same items being highlighted where they appear in each tightly-coupled view. To illustrate brushing, let's look at another example of a faceted analytical display.

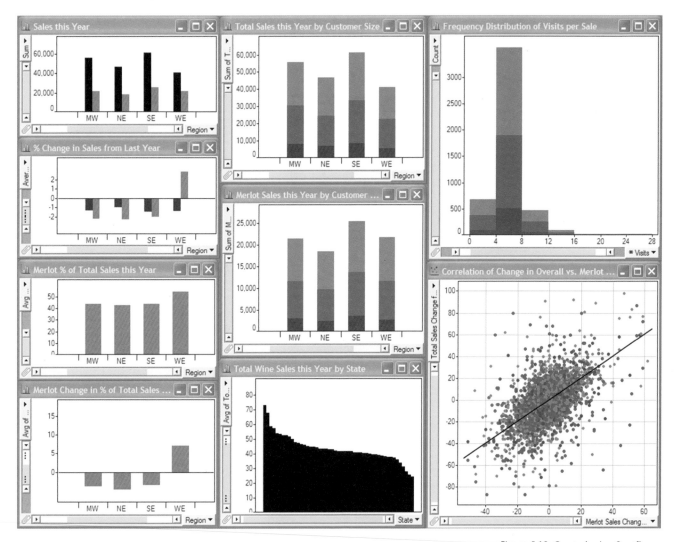

Figure 5.19. Created using Spotfire

Let's say that, while looking at one of the graphs in the example above, we become interested in a particular subset of the data, such as customers whose purchases of Merlot have decreased since last year even though their overall wine purchases increased, as shown in the upper left quadrant of the scatterplot. Now imagine that we have a brush that we can use to paint a rectangle around these particular data points in the scatterplot to highlight them, resulting in the following:

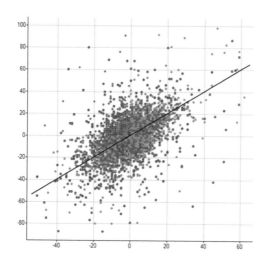

Figure 5.20. Created using Spotfire

Now all customers whose overall wine purchases increased (above zero on the Y-axis) but whose Merlot sales decreased (left of zero on the X-axis) are highlighted in red. Simply making them stand out in the scatterplot, however, is not the point of this exercise. What we really want to see is how these particular customers look from all perspectives displayed in this group of graphs. That's exactly what brushing does for us automatically. Let's take a look at the full screen to see if brushing leads us to any interesting insights.

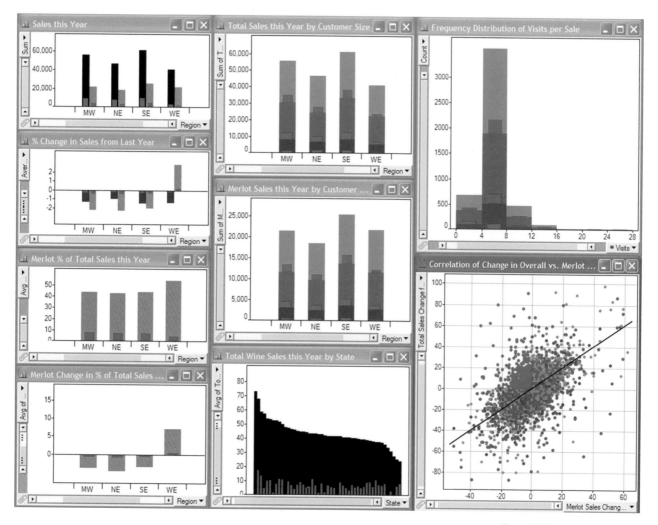

Figure 5.21. Created using Spotfire

One thing we can see is that decreases in Merlot sales that are out of sync with corresponding increases in overall wine sales occurred less often in the west (especially evident in the upper graph in the left column and the middle graph in the center column). Relative to customer size, this pattern also seems to be disproportionately strong in the southeast (see the top and middle graphs in the center column).

Now let's say that we want to see if sales in the west fall disproportionately in any particular area of the scatterplot. To see this, we can brush the west region in any of the graphs in the left or center columns and see the results highlighted in every graph, including the scatterplot shown below.

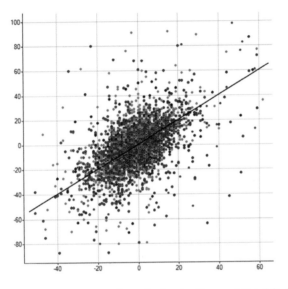

Figure 5.22. Created using Spotfire

Notice that a disproportionate number of sales in the west (highlighted in red) appear below the trend line and in the right half (increases in Merlot sales) of the graph. This reaffirms our previous observation that the west has contributed more than other regions to increases in Merlot sales, especially when overall wine sales changed less than the average.

The ability to see data from multiple perspectives simultaneously brings a great deal of information together, reducing our need to rely on limited working memory. When these different views of the data are tightly coupled, the potential of faceted analytical displays can be expanded dramatically, especially through filtering and brushing.

Information visualization software should support multiple concurrent views and brushing in the following ways:

- Provide a means to easily create, co-locate, and tightly couple multiple tables and graphs based on a shared set of data on a single screen.
- Provide a means to easily place particular tables and graphs anywhere and to size them as necessary.
- Provide a means to easily filter all tightly-coupled tables and graphs together by a single action.
- Provide a means to directly brush (that is, select) any subset of data in a single view (table or graph) to highlight it and have that same subset of data automatically highlighted in all the other tables and graphs that are tightly coupled to that view.
- When a subset of data is brushed in a particular table or graph, and that subset is associated with a bar or box in a graph, highlight only that portion of the bar of box that is made up of that subset.

Focus and Context Together

Losing sight of the forest when all we can see is the grove of trees that surrounds us is a common metaphor and it applies especially to data analysis. When we are focusing on details, it is easy to forget the big picture, the larger context that shapes the meaning of the details. We need to somehow be able to duck into the corners of the data, to feel our way down dark halls of meaning, without the risk of losing our way. In other words, we need a way to focus on details without losing a clear view of the larger context that frames them.

This need to hold onto the big picture while analyzing data has received a great deal of attention from the information research community. The solutions that have been proposed are generically called *focus+context*. When we're focusing on details, the whole doesn't need to be visible in high resolution, but we need to see where the details that we are focusing on reside within the bigger picture and how they relate to it. How this is achieved varies depending on the nature of the data and the visualization. For our concern with quantitative visualization in the form of graphs, we want a way to zoom into a selected portion of the data in a graph so that we can closely view that portion while a picture of the whole remains available to us, with an indication of the location and extent of the selected data within that whole.

The next few examples feature an application called *TimeSearcher 2*, developed by the University of Maryland's Human-Computer Interaction Lab (HCIL) under the direction of Ben Shneiderman. This application provides a way to focus on a period of time that is a part of a larger time-series display without losing sight of the whole display. In the first example on the next page, we see the daily closing prices of 1,430 stocks (each line is a single stock) across 52 weeks.

TimeSearcher 2 is not a commercial software product. It was developed as a research project and is freely available at the website of the Human-Computer Interaction Lab (HCIL) at the University of Maryland to those who wish to use it for academic or other non-commercial purposes (www.cs.umd.edu/hcil/).

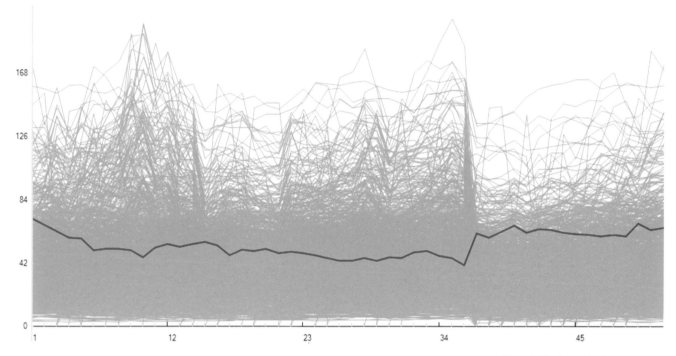

The blue line highlights a single stock. Imagine that we have noticed some interesting activity around weeks 9 through 12. TimeSearcher 2 would allow us to narrow the dates that appear in the graph to this range by sliding the ends of the orange selection box that appears in the small graph of the entire data set at the bottom of the example below.

Figure 5.23. Created using TimeSearcher 2, developed at the University of Maryland's Human-Computer Interaction Lab (HCIL)

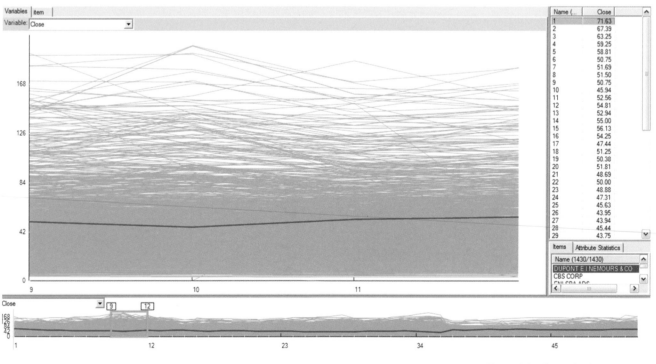

Figure 5.24. Created using TimeSearcher 2

This arrangement enables us to focus on what's happening during weeks 9 through 12 in greater detail while still remaining aware of where we are in the larger context of 52 weeks of stock prices. We could choose to focus with less distraction on those stocks that closed high during the 10th week by drawing a rectangle (what TimeSearcher 2 calls a *timebox*) around those stocks, resulting in the following picture:

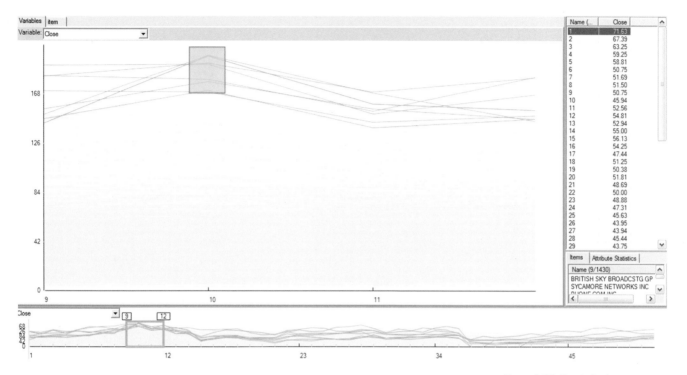

Figure 5.25. Created using TimeSearcher 2

Not only are the stocks with high closing prices shown in the details above, but they're also highlighted in the picture of the larger context below in the orange rectangle, which makes it possible to understand their behavior beyond the immediate point of focus. We could do a great deal more with this tool, but the only point that I'm trying to illustrate right now is how useful it can be to focus in on details without losing sight of the whole.

Information visualization software should support concurrent focus and context views in the following ways:

- Provide a means, while viewing a subset of a larger set of data, to simultaneously see a visual representation of the whole that indicates the subset of data as part of the whole.
- Provide a way for the larger context view to be removed to free up screen space when it isn't needed.

Details on Demand

Information visualization gives us the means to explore and make sense of data visually. Most of the time, visual representation is exactly what we need because we're looking for meaningful trends, patterns, and exceptions that we can most easily identify in graphical form. From time to time, however, we need precise details that we cannot see by looking at a picture of the data. We could switch from the graphical representation to a table of text for a precise representation of the values, but in doing so we risk breaking the flow of analysis and losing sight of meaningful patterns. What we need is a way to access the details without departing from the rich visual environment. This is called *details on demand* (mentioned previously in *Chapter 4: Analytical Interaction and Navigation*), a feature that allows the details to become visible when we need them and to disappear when we don't, so that they don't clutter the screen and distract us when they are not needed. In the following example, a pop-up box appeared when I hovered over a particular point on the brown line. After I read it to get the details I wanted, I simply moved the mouse away from that point and the pop-up box disappeared. Once it was out of the way, I could continue exploring the data without distraction.

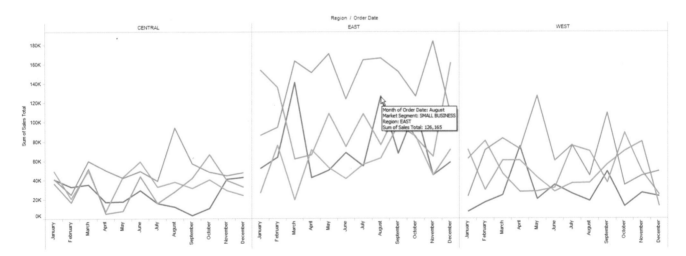

Figure 5.26. Created using Tableau Software

There are other ways besides hover or pop-up boxes to provide details on demand. For instance, in the following example, I wanted details about a collection of points, rather than only one. I used the mouse to highlight those points (the points in red in the left-hand graph below), then right-clicked to access a pop-up command menu and chose "Show Underlying Data." A window then appeared that displayed the underlying records that were associated with the points that I selected, which, in this case, were all of the individual sales orders during the months of May and June in the central region for all types of products.

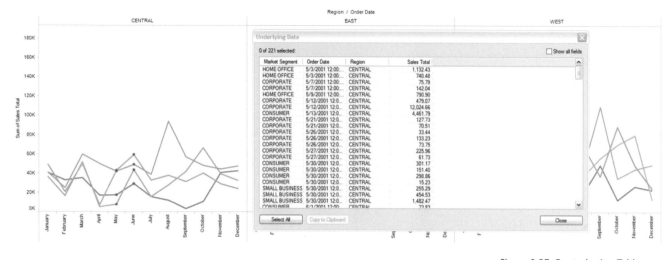

Figure 5.27. Created using Tableau Software

Information visualization software should support access to details on demand in the following ways:

- Provide a means to directly and easily select one or more data points in a graph and then request details on demand simply by hovering or by a single mouse click or keystroke.
- Cause the details-on-demand display to disappear with a movement of the mouse or single mouse click.
- Provide a means to define the information that will be included in a details-on-demand display. This should include both the actual data fields included and the level at which they're displayed (for example, the level that's displayed in the graph or some finer level of detail).

Over-Plotting Reduction

In some graphs, especially those that use data points or lines to encode data, multiple objects can end up sharing the same space, positioned on top of one another. This makes it difficult or impossible to see the individual values, which in turn makes analysis of the data difficult. This problem is called *over-plotting*. When it gets in the way, we need some way to eliminate or at least reduce the problem. The information visualization research community has worked hard to come up with methods to do this. We'll take a look at the following seven methods:

- Reducing the size of data objects
- Removing fill color from data objects
- Changing the shape of data objects
- Jittering data objects
- Making data objects transparent
- Encoding the density of values
- Reducing the number of values

Reducing the Size of Data Objects

Consider the following scatterplot filled with data. Notice that, in some areas, multiple data points fight for the same location and as a result sit on top of one another.

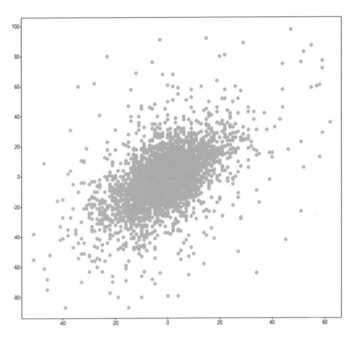

Figure 5.28. Created using Spotfire

Sometimes the problem can be adequately resolved simply by reducing the size of the objects that encode the data, in this case the dots. Here is the same data set with the size of the dots reduced:

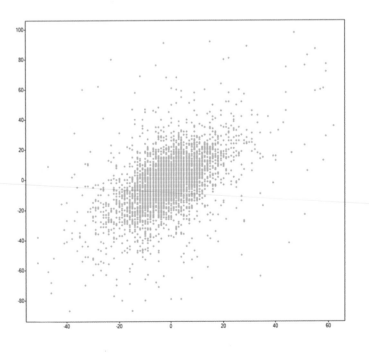

Figure 5.29. Created using Spotfire

When the problem of over-plotting is relatively minor, reducing the size of data objects can often do the job, but in this case it doesn't overcome the problem altogether, though it enables us to see more than we could before.

Removing Fill Color from Data Objects

Another simple method to reduce over-plotting involves removing the fill color from the objects that encode the data, which allows us to see better how the objects overlap. In this next example, the dots are slightly enlarged and the fill color is removed. The color is also changed so that it that stands out more clearly against the white background even when the amount of color in each dot has been reduced.

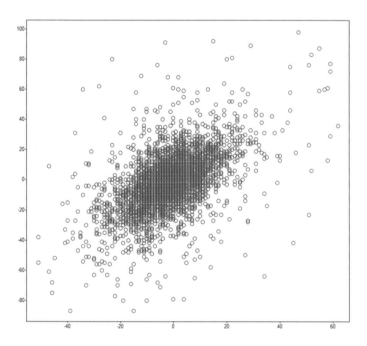

Figure 5.30. Created using Spotfire

Once again, even though this method is often quite useful, it hasn't done the job for this particular graph.

Changing the Shape of Data Objects

Another simple way to address over-plotting is to change the shape of the data objects. We can change shapes from the circles above, which function like containers with an interior and require a fair amount of space, to shapes that are not container-like, such as plus signs or X's.

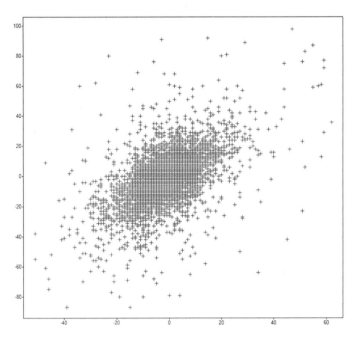

Figure 5.31. Created using Spotfire

This method often does the trick but does not reduce over-plotting when multiple objects encode the same exact value as they will continue to occupy the exact same space as one another.

Jittering Data Objects

One of the best ways to reduce over-plotting when multiple data objects have the same exact values is to change something about the data rather than changing the appearance of the object. *Jittering* slightly alters the actual values so they are no longer precisely the same, moving them to slightly different positions. In the scatterplot below, we can now see more detail than we could in the previous versions above. For instance, we can see that there are more values in the center of the cluster, which was not apparent in the previous example.

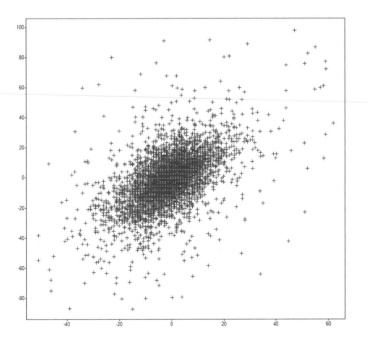

Figure 5.32. Created using Spotfire

We've made significant progress in reducing over-plotting in the above graph; it is much easier to see the differences in the density of data in contrast to the mass of undifferentiated clutter that was in the original scatterplot. Jittering wouldn't be practical if we had to change the values manually. Fortunately, many good visual analysis products support jittering as a function that can be turned on and off as needed and can be adjusted by degrees, from slightly jittered to greatly jittered. If you are fortunate enough to use one of these products, don't get carried away because if you jitter data too much, you will produce patterns that don't actually reflect the data values.

Making Data Objects Transparent

A newer method, which in many cases works even better than jittering and does not entail altering the data values or changing the shape of the data objects, makes the objects partially transparent. The proper degree of transparency allows us to see through the objects to perceive differences in the amount of over-plotting as variations in color intensity. The following scatterplot allows us to easily detect differences between the dense center of the cluster, which is intensely blue, and surrounding areas of progressively less concentration (less intensely blue). Using a slider control to vary the degree of transparency, we can quickly and easily adjust a display that suffers from over-plotting to reveal nuance in the midst of clutter.

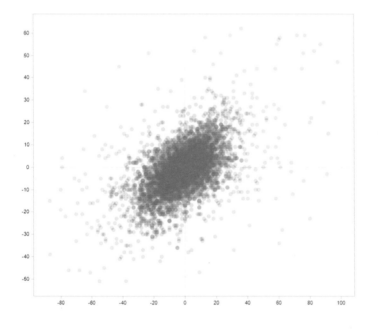

Figure 5.33. Created using Tableau Software

Encoding the Density of Values

Another approach encodes the density of the overlapping data points located in each region of the graph. Consider the scatterplot on the next page, which suffers from a great deal of over-plotting, prior to any attempt to reduce it.

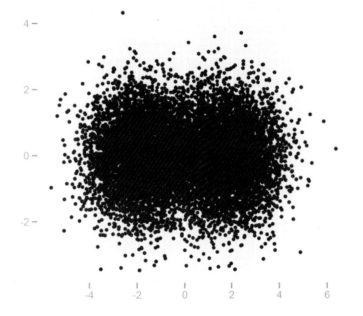

Figure 5.34. The scatterplot was created by Wayne Folta using the statistical analysis software "R."

One density-encoding method uses yellow contour lines to outline areas that contain varying densities of data points. This approach makes it possible for us to still see the individual data points where no over-plotting occurs, while at the same time it helps us to differentiate dense areas of over-plotting (the innermost contours) from those that are less dense.

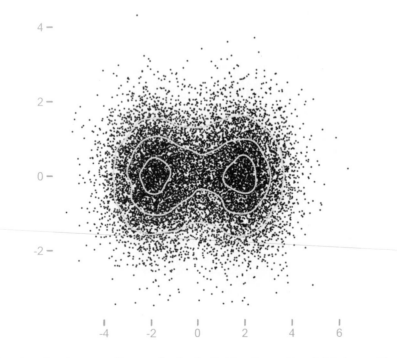

Figure 5.35. The scatterplot was provided by Wayne Folta to illustrate how contours can be used to differentiate varying degrees of data density, which he created with the statistical analysis software "R."

Another density-encoding method sub-divides the scatterplot into small regions (usually square in shape) and displays the number of data points in each region as colors of varying intensities. Here's the same data as before, but this time the color key on the right provides the means to differentiate four different levels of data density: 0 to 20, 21 to 40, 41 to 60, and 61 to 80 data points.

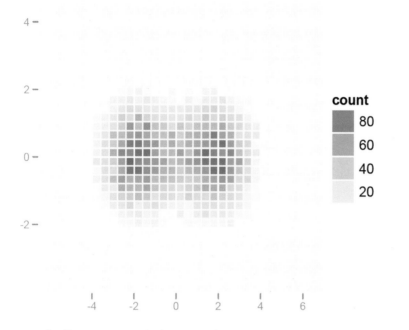

Figure 5.36. The scatterplot was provided by Wayne Folta to illustrate how colors can be used to differentiate varying degrees of data density, which he created with the statistical analysis software "R."

This approach allows us to easily focus on the varying levels of data density, but in a way that has removed the individual data points entirely. When the details that have been lost aren't necessary, this approach works quite well.

Reducing the Number of Values

The remaining methods for reducing over-plotting don't involve changes to the objects that encode the data or to the values; they involve reductions in the number of values that are displayed. The four most useful methods of this type are:

- *Aggregating the data.* This can be done when we really don't need to view the data at its current level of detail and can accomplish our analytical objectives by viewing the data at a more general or summarized level.
- *Filtering the data.* This is a simple solution that can be used to remove unnecessary values in the graph if there are any.
- *Breaking the data up into a series of separate graphs.* When we cannot aggregate or filter the data any further without losing important information, we can sometimes reduce over-plotting by breaking the data into individual graphs in a trellis or visual crosstab display.
- *Statistically sampling the data.* This technique involves reducing the total data set using statistical sampling techniques to produce a subset that represents the whole. This is a promising method for the reduction of over-plotting, but it is relatively new and still under development. If it is successfully refined, it could become a useful standard feature of visual analysis software in the near future.

Trellis and visual crosstab displays can often solve over-plotting problems quite easily. Here's the same information that we've been looking at in previous graphs, this time broken into four graphs, one per region.

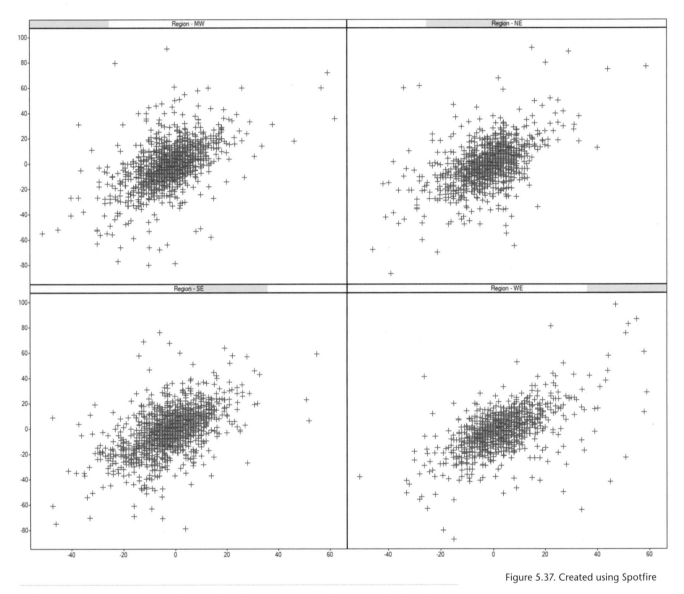

Figure 5.37. Created using Spotfire

Information visualization software should support over-plotting reduction in the following ways:

- Provide a means to easily change the size of data objects, such as by using a slider control.
- Provide a means to remove fill color from data objects that have interiors, such as circles (dots), squares, triangles, and diamonds.
- Provide a means to select from an assortment of simple shapes for encoding data points.
- Provide a means to jitter data objects, and offer a simple way to vary the degree of jittering.

- Provide a means to make data objects transparent.
- Provide a means to aggregate and filter data.
- Provide a means to break data up into a series of graphs in the form of a trellis or visual crosstab display.
- Provide a means to reduce the quantity of data through statistical sampling.

Now that we've examined general practices that enhance visual analysis, we'll turn to the actual steps that we must take to analyze data and see how they allow us to navigate an enlightening path through a landscape full of potential surprises.

6 ANALYTICAL PATTERNS

Quantitative analysis involves examining relationships among values. In this book, I've categorized data analysis based on the nature of the relationship that's being examined. Analyzing these relationships requires us to search for particular patterns in data and to use particular analytical techniques. Part II, which begins with the next chapter, explains how to analyze each of these types of relationships, one per chapter:

- Time-series
- Ranking and Part-to-Whole
- Deviation
- Distribution
- Correlation
- Multivariate

This chapter gives an overview of different ways that we can represent data visually before we begin to examine the relationships above in depth in the next few chapters.

When any of the relationships above are represented properly in visual form, we can see particular patterns and analyze them to make sense of the data. To prime our eyes for pattern perception before diving into specific types of analysis, we'll take some time now to think about patterns that are meaningful in several types of analysis.

Remember that in *Chapter 3: Visual Perception and Information Visualization*, I explained that our visual sense receptors are highly tuned to respond to particular low-level characteristics of objects called pre-attentive attributes. These basic attributes of form, color, position, and motion can be used to display abstract data in ways that are rapidly perceptible and easily graspable. When we look at a properly designed graph, we can spot patterns that reveal what the information means. Although graphs inform us differently than spoken or written words, both involve language: one is visual and the other verbal. Similar to verbal language, visual displays involve semantics (meanings) and syntax (rules of structure). Letters of the alphabet are the basic units of verbal language, which we combine to form words and sentences according to rules of syntax that enable us to effectively communicate the meanings we intend. In the same way, simple objects such as points, lines, bars, and boxes are basic units of visual language, which are combined in particular ways according to rules of perception to reveal quantitative meaning.

Guidelines for Representing Quantitative Data

Particular visual objects are best suited to communicating particular quantitative relationships for particular purposes. It helps to know the strengths and weaknesses of each type of visual object so that we can choose the type of graph that will best help us find what we're looking for, examine it in the way will most likely to lead to understanding, and, when necessary, communicate the information to others.

Bars

When you look at two objects like the two dark rectangles below, what do you notice and what meanings come to mind?

Figure 6.1

What likely stands out most prominently to most of us is the difference in their heights. This difference invites us to notice that one bar is taller than the other. This is what bars are especially good at: displaying differences in magnitude and making it easy for us to compare those differences. Also, because bars have such great visual weight and independence from one another, like great columns rising into the sky, they emphasize the individuality of each value.

The following graph makes it quite easy to see planned versus actual sales in each region as distinct and to compare magnitudes with accuracy and little effort. It is especially easy to compare planned versus actual sales because they are next to one another. In other words, this graph, by the way it has been designed, guides us to make that particular comparison, just as the choice and arrangement of words in a spoken or written sentence points us toward certain meanings and interpretations and away from others. This is what I meant previously when I said that we must understand and honor a visual equivalent of vocabulary and syntax—the rules of perception—when we use graphs.

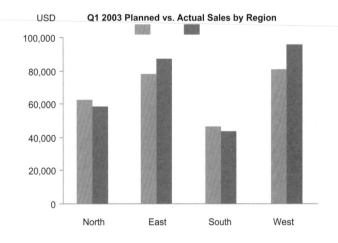

Figure 6.2

We'll usually choose bar graphs when we want to emphasize the individuality of values and compare their magnitudes.

Boxes

When you look at objects like the two subdivided rectangles below, what are you inclined to notice and what meanings come to mind?

Figure 6.3

Although these rectangles are similar to bars, they don't share a common baseline, so we tend to notice the differences between the positions of their tops and their bottoms, the difference between the horizontal lines that divide them, and the difference between their total lengths. This is precisely what these rectangles are designed to help us do. They are called boxes, and the graphs in which they are used are called box plots. Each box represents the distribution of an entire set of values: the bottom represents the lowest value, the top represents the highest value, and the length represents the full spread of the values from lowest to highest. The mark that divides the box into two sections, in this case a light line, indicates the center of the distribution, usually the median or mean value. A central measure (also called an average) gives us a single number that we can use to summarize an entire set of values. Notice how your eyes are encouraged to observe and compare the different positions of the centers of these boxes, and how the difference in the position of the center lines conveys that, on average, the values represented by the box on the right are higher than those on the left. The graph below illustrates the usefulness of box plots. In this case, the graph can be used to compare the distributions of salaries for five years and to see how they changed from year to year.

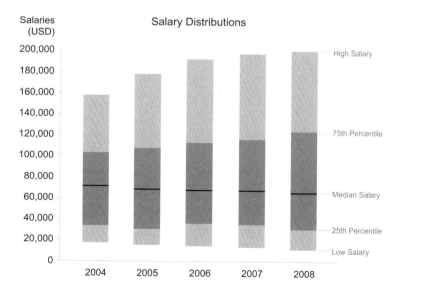

Figure 6.4

The box plot on the previous page tells the story of how employees are compensated in an organization, based on five values that summarize each year's distribution: the highest, lowest, and middle values as well as the point at and above which the top 25% of salaries fall (the 75th percentile), and the point at and below which the bottom 25% of salaries fall (the 25th percentile). The example below displays the same exact salary distributions in a way that is more typical of how box plots are usually drawn.

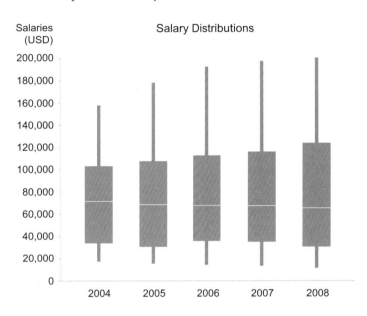

Figure 6.5

We'll take the time to learn more about box plots in *Chapter 10: Distribution Analysis*. If you haven't used them before, you'll find that they'll become familiar in no time.

Lines

When you see an object like the line below, what does it suggest?

Figure 6.6

This particular line, which angles upwards from left to right, suggests an increase, something moving upward. Lines do a great job of showing the shape of change from one value to the next, especially change through time.

The strength of lines is their ability to emphasize the overall trend and specific patterns of change in a set of values. The following graph tells a vivid story of how sales changed throughout the year.

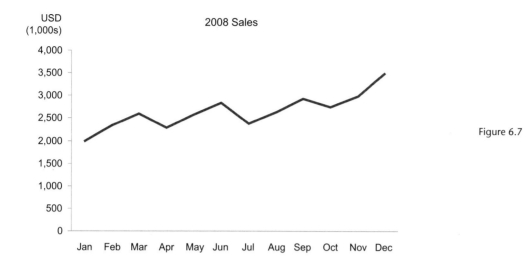

Figure 6.7

Points

When you see points scattered about, as illustrated below, what features attract your attention?

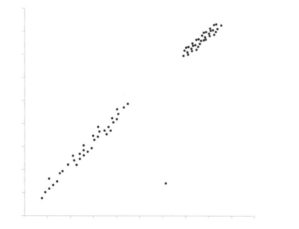

Figure 6.8

Points, such as those in a scatterplot, encourage us to notice patterns such as clusters, linear or curved arrangements, gaps, and points that appear isolated from the majority. These are precisely the patterns that are meaningful in correlation relationships, which is what scatterplots were designed to display.

Perhaps the greatest strength of points is the ability of each to encode two quantitative values: one based on its horizontal position and one based on its vertical position. Looking at the scatterplot on the following page, which displays a potential correlation between advertisements and resulting sales orders (two quantitative variables), it is hard to imagine any object other than a point that could do the job as well. Bars certainly wouldn't work when the X – axis and Y-axis both host quantitative scales, and if we connected the points with a line, the result would be a meaningless string of spaghetti.

Number of
Orders

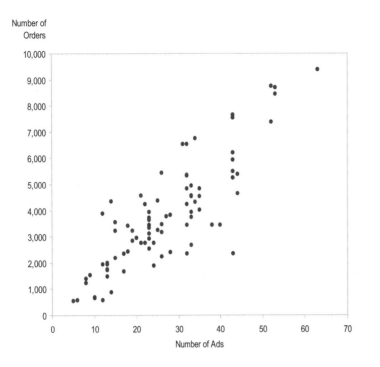

Figure 6.9

Points can also be used as a substitute for bars when there is an advantage to narrowing the quantitative scale so that zero is no longer included. Remember that, when bars are used, the quantitative scale must include zero as the baseline for the bars because otherwise the lengths of the bars will not accurately encode their values. (See the section on comparing and contrasting in *Chapter 4: Analytical Interaction and Navigation* for a more detailed explanation of this issue). In the bar graph below, all of the values fall between 62% and 83%. Most of each bar's length doesn't tell us much because we are mostly concerned with the differences between the values, and they all fall within a relatively narrow range at the right.

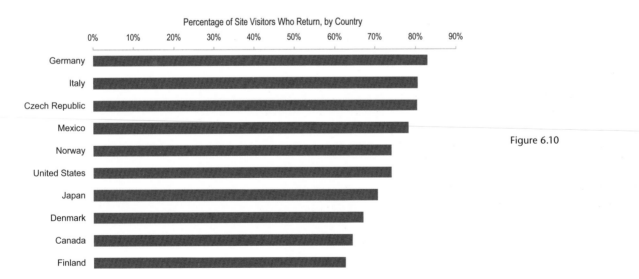

Figure 6.10

If we want to examine these differences more clearly, we can't just narrow the scale to begin around 60% because then the bars' lengths would no longer accurately encode the values. We could narrow the scale, however, if we replace the bars with points to create a dot plot, as shown below.

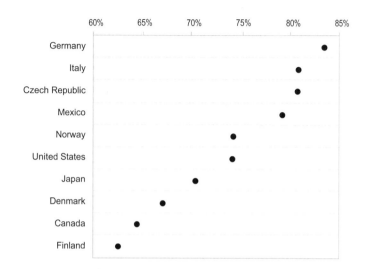

Figure 6.11

These points encode values based on their horizontal position in relation to the quantitative scale along the top. We are no longer comparing the lengths of objects, so the elimination of zero from the scale does not create the same perceptual problem that would have been created with bars.

Points and lines can be used together in a line graph to clearly mark the actual positions of values along the line. This is especially helpful when a graph displays more than one line, and we need to compare the magnitudes of values on different lines. For example, in the example below, if we want to compare domestic and international sales in the month of June, the points make it easier for our eyes to focus on the exact position on the line where the comparison should be made. When we primarily want to see the shape of change through time but secondarily also want to make magnitude comparisons between the lines, a line graph with data points works well.

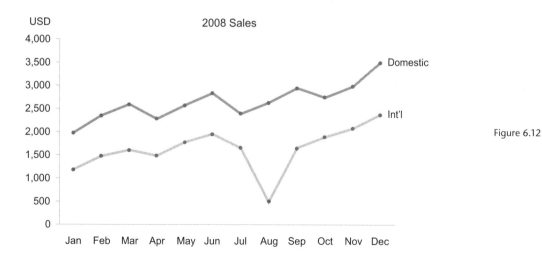

Figure 6.12

In the Smooth and in the Rough

Borrowing terms from statisticians, we can speak of data as falling into two categories: *in the smooth* and *in the rough*. Values that are relatively typical of the set as a whole reside in the smooth. Technically, *smooth* is just another term for "fit," that is a line or curve that fits the shape of the data (also known as a trend line), which we use to describe the overall pattern in the data. Atypical values, those that fall outside the normal range and therefore cannot be described by the smooth, are said to reside in the rough. The total set of data therefore equals the smooth plus the rough.

> *The smooth is the underlying, simplified structure of a set of observations. It may be represented by a straight line describing the relationship between two variables or by a curve describing the distribution of a single variable, but in either case the smooth is an important feature of the data. It is the general shape of a distribution or the general shape of a relationship. It is the regularity or pattern in the data...What is left behind is the rough, the deviations from the smooth.*[1]

1. *Exploratory Data Analysis*, Frederick Hartwig with Brian E. Dearing, Sage Publications, Inc., Thousand Oaks CA, 1979, pp. 10 and 11.

I'll usually use the term *exceptions* to refer to abnormal values in a set of data. Exceptions are sometimes called *outliers*. Technically, the terms exception and outlier differ slightly in meaning. Both, however, are worth examining. A value is an exception whenever it falls outside defined standards, expectations, or any other definition of normal. Outlier, by contrast, is a statistical term that refers to values that fall outside the norm based on a statistical calculation, such as anything beyond three standard deviations from the mean.

> *An outlier is a value which lies outside the normal range of the data, i.e., lies well above or well below most, or even all, of the other values... It is difficult to say at just what point a value becomes an outlier since much depends upon its relationship to the rest of the data and the use for which the data is intended. One may want to identify and set aside outlying cases in order to concentrate on the bulk of the data, but, on the other hand, it may be the outliers themselves on which the analysis should be concentrated. For example, communities with abnormally low crime rates may be the most instructive ones.*[2]

2. *Ibid.*, pp. 27 and 28.

> *Outliers can...be described as data elements that deviate from other observations by so much that they arouse suspicion of being produced by a mechanism different than that which generated the other observations.*[3]

3. "Summarization Techniques for Visualization of Large Multidimensional Datasets," Sarat M. Kocherlakota, Christopher G. Healey, Technical Report TR-2005-35, North Carolina State University, 2005, p. 4.

Whether we use a strict statistical method to identify true outliers or some other approach to identify exceptions, we must first define what is normal in a way that excludes only those values that are extraordinary. Every abnormal value, whether an exception or an outlier, can and ought to be explained. Something has caused these unusual values. There are always reasons and it's up to us to find them.

Values can fall outside the norm for three possible reasons:

- Errors
- Extraordinary events
- Extraordinary entities

Exceptions are often errors caused by inaccurate data entry, inaccurate measurements, or other mistakes. Some exceptions are not errors but are the result of extraordinary events: something happened, such as a storm, the loss of a key employee, or an exceptionally successful promotional campaign, that caused atypical behavior or results. And, finally, exceptions sometimes result from the behavior of a person, organization, or some other entity that itself falls outside of the norm, such as an order from a country that rarely makes purchases or a person with highly unusual tastes.

When examining information, we want spotting exceptions to be as easy as possible. Because memory is fallible, and working memory is in limited supply, we shouldn't rely on memory to know the boundaries of normal. One of the great benefits of information visualization is the opportunity to offload cognitive workload to our eyes. Let's not waste our brains on activities that our eyes can do faster and with much less effort. So in this example, it's a good idea to display explicitly the boundaries that define the range of normal. The upper and lower boundaries of what we define as normal can be easily shown on a graph as reference lines or as reference areas of fill color that either define the range or define areas outside of the range. Standards that define what is acceptable can be displayed similarly.

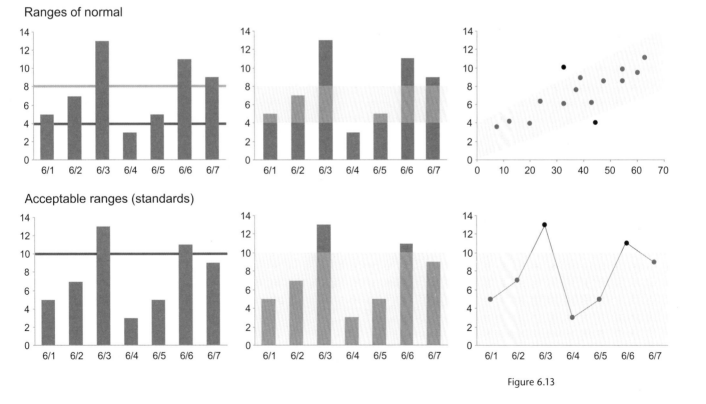

Figure 6.13

Pattern Examples

The number of unique visual patterns that exist in the world is virtually infinite. The number of patterns that represent meaningful quantitative information in 2-D graphs, however, is not. If we learn to recognize the patterns that are most meaningful in our data, we'll be able to spot them faster and more often, which will save us time and effort.

The example below no doubt appears overwhelmingly complex to most of us. But to someone who has been trained and developed expertise in reading this type of display, it isn't overwhelming at all.

Colin Ware states:

> *People can learn pattern-detection skills, although the ease of gaining these skills will depend on the specific nature of the patterns involved. Experts do indeed have special expertise. The radiologist interpreting an X-ray, the meteorologist interpreting radar, and the statistician interpreting a scatter plot will each bring a differently tuned visual system to bear on his or her particular problem. People who work with visualizations must learn the skill of seeing patterns in data.[4]*

Figure 6.14. Example of a *horizon graph*, created using Panopticon Explorer

4. *Information Visualization: Perception for Design*, Second Edition, Colin Ware, Morgan Kaufmann Publishers, San Francisco CA, 2004, p. 209

To an expert, much of what appears in the display isn't important; it's visual noise from which the meanings that matter can be easily and rapidly extracted. As visual data analysts, we must learn to separate the signal from the noise.

A number of basic patterns are almost always meaningful when they appear in graphs. They're not always relevant to the task at hand, so we won't always attend to them, but it's useful to hone our skills to easily spot them.

While looking at the blank graph below, try to imagine some of the meaningful patterns that might be formed in it by points, lines, bars, and boxes. Think about your own work, the data that you analyze, and call to mind patterns that catch your attention (or ought to) when present. Take a minute to list or draw examples of a few right now.

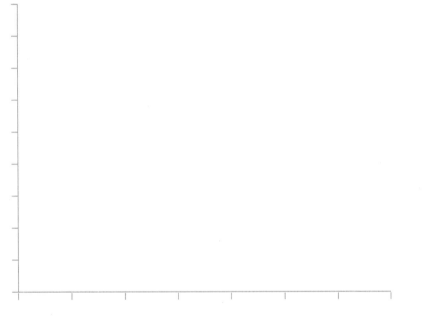

Figure 6.15

It helps to bring patterns to mind and understand what they mean when we spot them in various contexts. Doing this primes our perceptual faculties, sensitizing them to particular patterns, which helps us spot them more readily.

On the next page are examples of several patterns that are worth noticing when they show up in our data. Others might come to mind that are specific to your work and the kinds of data you encounter but I'm focusing here on patterns that are commonly found in data from lots of different types of businesses and other sources. This is by no means an exhaustive list, but we're likely to run across these patterns often. Part II presents more information on patterns as each chapter lists the specific patterns that apply to the type of analysis discussed in that chapter.

Pattern	Example	Pattern	Example
High, low, and in between		Non-intersecting and intersecting	
Going up, going down, and remaining flat		Symmetrical and skewed	
Steep and gradual		Wide and narrow	
Steady and fluctuating		Clusters and gaps	
Random and repeating		Tightly and loosely distributed	
Straight and curved		Normal and abnormal	

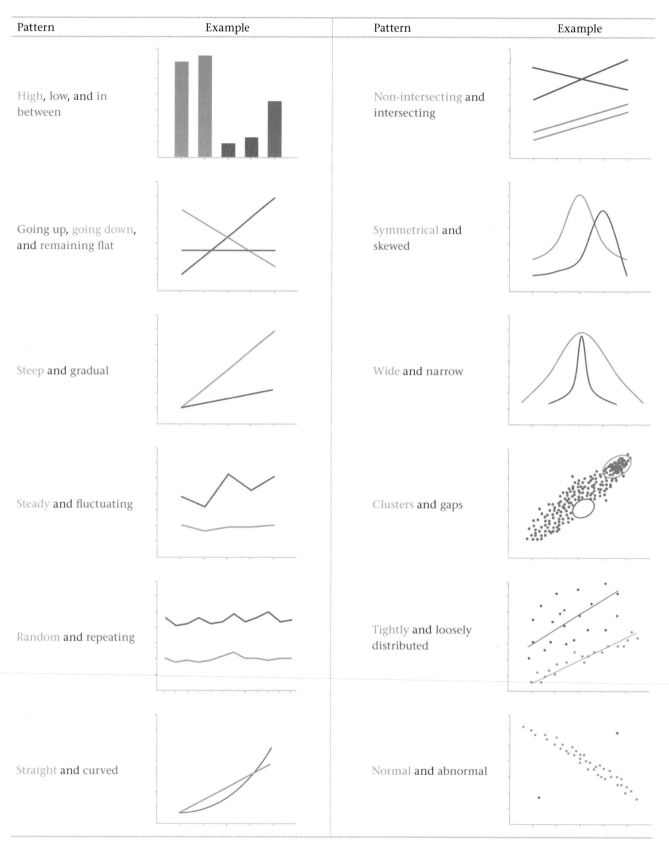

Beware of Patterns that Aren't Actually There

Humans' pattern recognition skills are amazing and the source of great insights, but sometimes they're too good. We are so adept at finding patterns that we sometimes detect ones that aren't really there. Even when a pattern is real, we often err by ceasing our exploration once we've spotted a single pattern, especially one that we were primed to find, so we miss others that are unfamiliar and unexpected. We should never become so good at spotting patterns that we lose sight of the information that composes them.

It is important, at times, to disregard familiar patterns and view data with fresh eyes. Take the time to look at the pieces—the details—for sometimes that is where truth lives. New patterns and meanings emerge that are unexpected if we let ourselves look without preconceptions and drill down to the specifics as well as scanning the big picture. Only when we empty our minds of the expected can we make room for something new. Zen Buddhism speaks of this approach as having a *beginner's mind*. In his marvelous book *Presentation Zen*, Garr Reynolds describes this state of mind:

> *Like a child, one who approaches life with a beginner's mind is fresh, enthusiastic, and open to the vast possibilities of ideas and solutions before them. A child does not know what is not possible and so is open to exploration, discovery, and experimentation. If you approach creative tasks with a beginner's mind, you can see things more clearly as they are, unburdened by your fixed view, habits, or what conventional wisdom say it is (or should be).*[5]

5. *Presentation Zen*, Garr Reynolds, New Riders, Berkeley CA, 2008, p. 33

Never let yourself become such an expert, so adept at spotting patterns, that you can no longer be surprised by the unexpected. Set the easy, obvious answers aside long enough to examine the details and see what might be there that you can't anticipate. Let yourself get to know the trees before mapping the forest.

PART II HONING SKILLS FOR DIVERSE TYPES OF VISUAL ANALYSIS

SPECIFIC PATTERNS, DISPLAYS, AND TECHNIQUES

Near the beginning of this book, I said that the meanings we seek to find and understand in quantitative information come to light when we examine the parts of that information and how they relate to one another. We strive to understand quantitative data by focusing on particular relationships between individual values and groups of values. Each chapter in Part II covers one of these relationships and describes the visualizations and techniques that enable us to discover and make sense of its meanings. We'll learn how to analyze each of the following quantitative relationships:

Chapter 7—Time-Series Analysis

Chapter 8—Ranking and Part-to-Whole Analysis

Chapter 9—Deviation Analysis

Chapter 10—Distribution Analysis

Chapter 11—Correlation Analysis

Chapter 12—Multivariate Analysis

We'll consider the following aspects of each:

- Visual patterns that are particularly meaningful
- Graphs that display meaningful patterns most effectively
- Analytical techniques that are useful and best practices we should follow

7   TIME-SERIES ANALYSIS

Introduction

No quantitative relationship receives more attention than values changing through time. "A random sample of 4,000 graphics from 15 of the world's newspapers published from 1974 to 1989 found that more than 75% of them featured time series."[1] Business analysts hope to see profits increase over time. Government and non-governmental organization (NGO) analysts expect to see changes in relation to influential events, such as natural disasters or tax increases. More than any other variable, time gives us a context for understanding data. The present can only be understood and the future can only be predicted in light of the past.

1. "An Augmented Visual Query Mechanism for Finding Patterns in Time Series Data," Eamonn Keogh, Harry Hochheiser, and Ben Shneiderman. *Proc. Fifth International Conference on Flexible Query Answering Systems*, Copenhagen Denmark, Oct 2002.

Time-Series Patterns

Six basic patterns are especially meaningful when we analyze change through time:

- Trend
- Variability
- Rate of change
- Co-variation
- Cycles
- Exceptions

Trend

A trend is the overall tendency of a series of values to increase, decrease, or remain relatively stable during a particular period of time. For example, it is common to refer to sales during a 12-month period as trending upward, downward, or remaining flat (also known as "no trend"). Any period of time can be the basis for determining a trend. We select a starting point and an ending point in time and then look to see whether the values during that period tended to move in a particular direction.

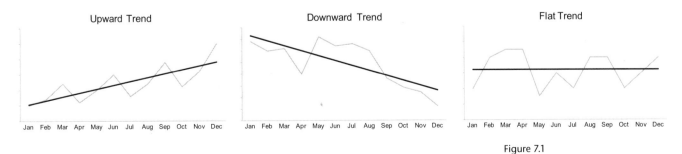

Figure 7.1

Line graphs work particularly well for visualizing trends. Trends are often obvious from the general slope of a line, but when the line moves both up and down throughout the period, the overall trend might be difficult to determine based on the appearance of the line alone (see the top graph below). At such times, most software can display a trend line to show the overall slope of change, but we must rely on trend lines with caution as I will explain later in this chapter, in the *Time-Series Analysis and Best Practices* section, where I propose an alternative to trend lines.

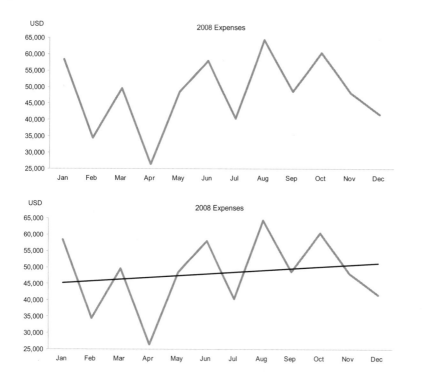

Figure 7.2

Variability

Variability is the average degree of change from one point in time to the next throughout a particular span of time. If sales revenues changed dramatically from month to month during a particular year, we can describe them as highly variable.

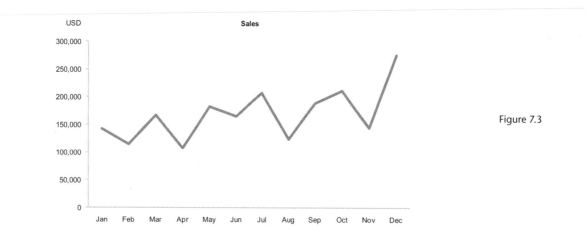

Figure 7.3

If sales decreased significantly from November to December, but remained fairly steady from month to month during the rest of the year, overall variability would not be considered high.

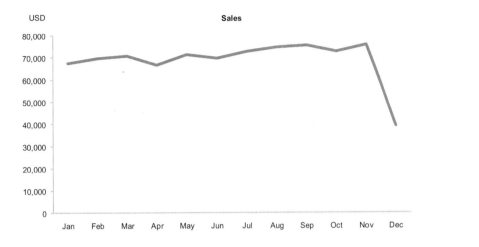

Figure 7.4

Line graphs do a good job of displaying variability. A jagged line indicates a greater degree of variability than another line in the same graph that is relatively smooth. Beware, however, of assuming a high degree of variability when viewing a graph that contains only a single jagged line. The appearance of jaggedness could be the result of a narrow quantitative scale. For example, in the graph below, revenues vary by less than 1% per month, but the pattern looks highly variable because its scale is so narrow.

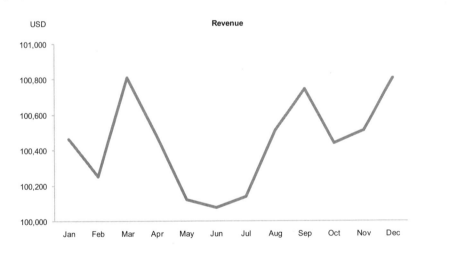

Figure 7.5

When interpreting variability based on the jaggedness or smoothness of a line, our judgments will be more reliable if we begin the quantitative scale at zero or, if examining a graph with multiple lines, restrict ourselves to relative assessments of more or less variability among the lines. In the following example, we can conclude with certainty that the monthly revenues in the east division experienced greater variability than those in the west division. We must be careful when judging the overall degree of variability in the east, however, because the narrow scale exaggerates its appearance.

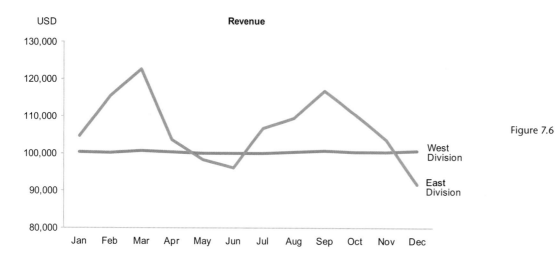

Figure 7.6

Rate of Change

The rate of change from one value to the next can be directly expressed as the percentage difference between the two. It is often enlightening to view change in this manner, especially when comparing multiple series of values, such as sales per region. For example, consider a comparison of domestic and foreign sales per month expressed in dollars, as illustrated below.

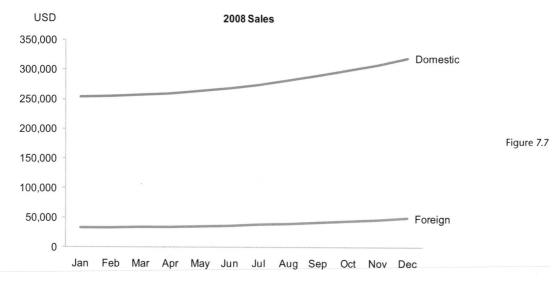

Figure 7.7

The amount of increase from month to month, measured in terms of U.S. dollars, is much greater for domestic sales than for foreign sales ($1,000 versus $250). However, this isn't a good way to compare rates of change between these two regions because even though foreign sales are increasing by smaller dollar amounts, they might in fact be increasing at a faster rate. In the next example, we see the same sales data, this time expressed as the rate of change from one month to the next.

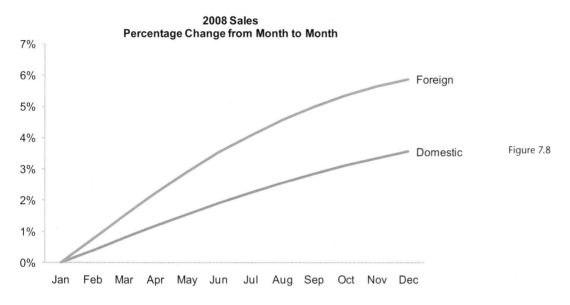

2008 Sales
Percentage Change from Month to Month

Figure 7.8

This graph tells a much different story than the previous one. Foreign sales are, in fact, increasing at a faster rate and thus might represent a better potential market. We'll look at various ways to examine rates of change later in the *Time-Series Analysis Techniques and Best Practices* section of this chapter.

Co-variation

When two time series relate to one another so that changes in one are reflected as changes in the other, either immediately or later, this is called co-variation. The pattern can qualify as co-variation even if changes in one time series move in a different direction (up or down) from corresponding changes in the other. For example, expenses could co-vary with profits such that decreases in expenses are reflected as increases in profits. When related changes don't occur simultaneously, but, instead, changes in one time series always occur before or after related changes in another, we have what are called *leading indicators* or *lagging indicators*. A leading indicator is a change that occurs in one time series that relates to a change that takes place in another at a later time. A lagging indicator is the reverse. The line graphs on the following page illustrate co-variation between newspaper ads (leading indicator) and orders (lagging indicator), which occur four days later.

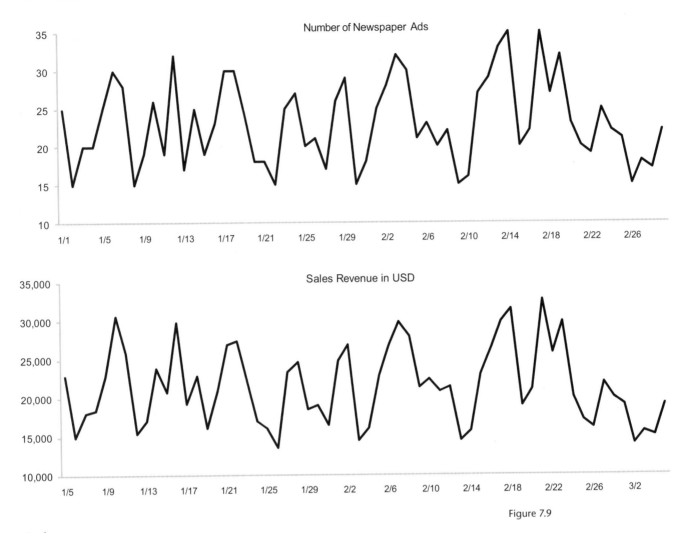

Figure 7.9

Cycles

All the patterns that we've covered so far are usually examined in a linear fashion, by viewing a period of time from beginning to end. For example, the question "At what time during the last five years did expenses hit their peak?" would be investigated using a linear view. Cycles, by contrast, are patterns that repeat at regular intervals, such as daily, weekly, monthly, quarterly, yearly, or seasonally (winter, spring, summer and fall). Cyclical patterns are often easier to examine using visualizations that don't display time linearly from beginning to end but instead display the interval at which the cycles occur (for example, days of the week, months of the year) positioned close to one another where they can be easily compared. The question "Did expenses consistently hit their peak during a particular month of the year during each of the last five years?" could be pursued using a cyclical view. The following line graph allows us to examine cyclical sales behavior by month in a manner that features quarterly patterns.

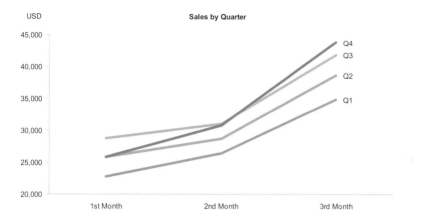

Figure 7.10

This particular sales pattern, which exhibits a peak in the last month of each quarter, is sometimes called the *hockey stick* pattern because it's shaped like a hockey stick with an upward bend near the end. If you've ever seen this pattern in your own company's sales data, you probably know that it is not the result of customer buying preferences but rather a result of the sales compensation plan, which awards bonuses to salespeople for reaching quarterly quotas. As the end of each quarter approaches, sales people get serious about closing as many deals as possible to reach or exceed their quota before the deadline. Once the end of the quarter is past, they relax for a while, sometimes on the golf course (sales-people do this, right?), until the next deadline looms.

Exceptions

We care about exceptions—values that fall outside the norm—in every type of analysis. How exceptions reveal themselves in graphs differs depending on the nature of the relationships that we're analyzing (time-series, distribution, correlation, and so on). In time series, they appear as values that are well above or below the norm, regardless of how we define the norm. In the following example, the number of employees hired during the month of November is a very visible exception, falling far below the number in other months.

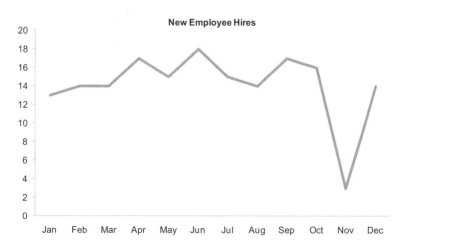

Figure 7.11

Every industry, work function, or group in an organization has particular and sometimes unique time-series patterns that are of special interest. Think about the data that you analyze and some of the patterns of change through time that are particularly interesting to your organization. Take a few minutes to list a few (or for "extra credit," you might even draw a few) of the patterns that are of interest in your work. Calling these patterns to mind when they are not in front of you helps to build them into memory in a way that makes them easier to spot.

Time-Series Displays

It's hard to beat a line graph for displaying change through time. Most time-series analysis can and should be accomplished using line graphs. Sometimes, however, other graphs do a better job. Five types of graphs are useful, some more than others, for examining quantitative change through time:

- Line graphs
- Bar graphs
- Dot plots
- Radar graphs
- Heatmaps

Each of these is the best solution for examining a particular type of time-series data or to help uncover a particular aspect of the data. Two more graphs are also useful for analyzing data when change through time is secondary in importance to another quantitative relationship:

- Box plots (and similarly constructed high-low plots), to analyze how distributions of values have changed
- Scatterplots, using animation to analyze correlation changes

Let's take a look at the design, uses, and benefits of each.

Line Graphs for Analyzing Patterns and Exceptions

If your objective is to see how quantitative values have changed during a continuous period of time, nothing works better than a line graph. Lines work better than any other means to make visible the sequential flow of values as they have changed with the passage of time. By its very nature, a line clearly traces the connection from one value to the next and through its slope displays the extent and direction of change. In the next example, the overall trend of sales throughout the year and the ups and downs from month to month are both easy to see in the line.

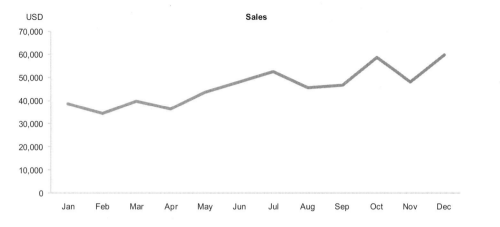

Figure 7.12

When we want to compare individual values at specific points in time, such as actual and budgeted expenses in a given month, bar graphs do this better. As I mentioned previously, if we wish primarily to see the shape of change through time, but to also compare the magnitudes of values at a particular point in time, we can include points along the lines to mark the precise location of each value, which makes it easier to compare values on separate lines at precisely the right location.

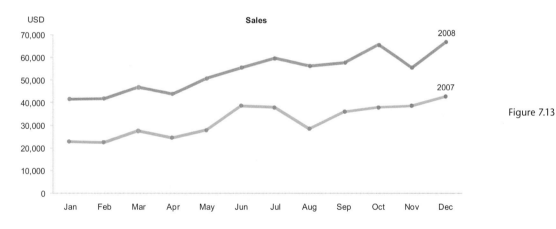

Figure 7.13

Bar Graphs for Emphasizing and Comparing Individual Values

As mentioned previously, the lengths of bars encode values in a way that allows us to simply and accurately compare individual values to one another. The visual weight of bars and their clear separation from one another encourages our eyes to focus on individual values rather than the patterns they form as a whole. Consequently, if you are trying to compare individual values, such as actual to budgeted expenses in particular months as illustrated on the next page, bars graphs do the job nicely.

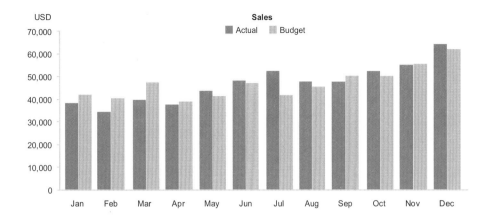

Figure 7.14

Dot Plots for Analyzing Irregular Intervals

Usually when we're analyzing time-series data, each interval along the timeline for each series of data contains a value. Sometimes, however, the values that we're examining are not distributed at regular intervals throughout the period but instead were recorded sporadically. For example, imagine that you're an inspector who measures contaminant levels at a particular location in a river, but not at regular intervals. If you used a line graph to display these values, it might look something like this:

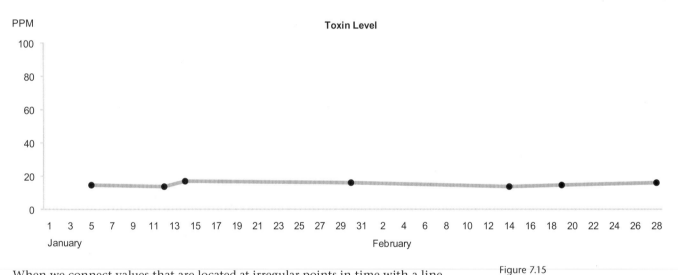

Figure 7.15

When we connect values that are located at irregular points in time with a line as I've done above, the resulting shape suggests a smooth linear change from one value to the next. This is a problem, however, because these smooth transitions might not at all correspond to what actually happened. If the toxin levels had been measured every day, the picture of change might look quite different, such as shown in the following graph.

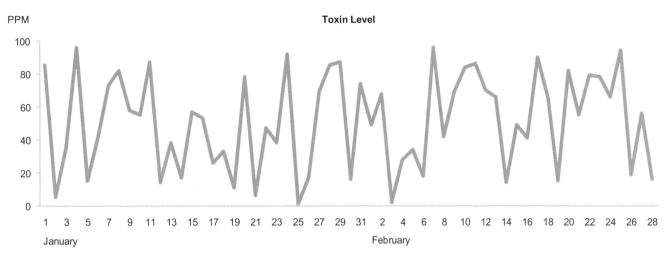

Figure 7.16

Therefore, when analyzing values that are spaced at irregular intervals of time, don't connect them with a line. Instead, use a data point, such as a dot, to mark each value separately. This type of graph is called a *dot plot*, illustrated below.

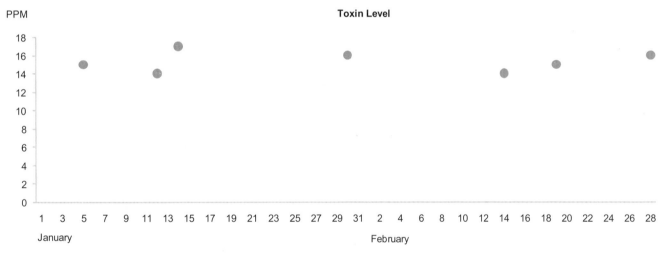

Figure 7.17

Dot plots discourage the misleading assumption that there was a direct transition from one value to the next. Few software products provide dot plots, but you can use many products to produce them, including Excel, by using a line graph with data points to mark the values and then eliminating the line.

Radar Graphs for Comparing Cycles

I'm not a big fan of *radar graphs* (also known as *spider graphs*) because their usefulness is limited to rare situations. Sometimes, however, they can be useful for time-series analysis. The circular shape of a radar graph can be used to represent the cyclical nature of time. For example, similar to the way hours are sequentially arranged in a circle on a clock, the axes of a radar graph can be used to mark the hours of the day, as shown in the example on the following page.

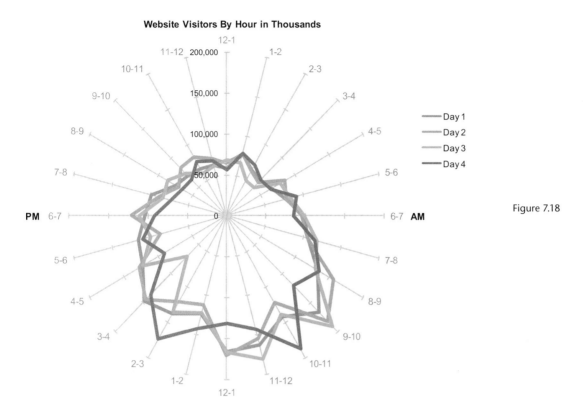

Figure 7.18

The same data can also be displayed using a line graph, as shown below, which I believe works just as well for analytical purposes. But if you prefer the way radar graphs represent the cyclical nature of time—the minutes of the hour, hours of the day, or even days of the week or month, months of the year, and so on— you'll find them useful.

Figure 7.19

Both line and radar graphs can become cluttered when we use them to analyze cyclical patterns. The following example displays 30 days' worth of data, one line per day, resulting in a great deal of over-plotting, which makes it impossible to compare individual days to one another or to closely examine anything that appears in one of the cluttered areas.

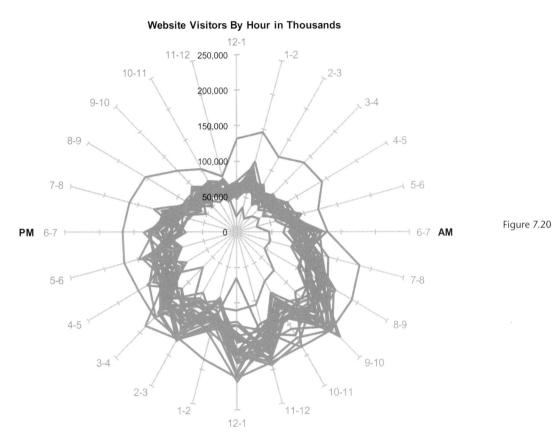

Figure 7.20

Despite the over-plotting, it is still possible to spot exceptions to the norm, such as the line that circles far outside the others or the one that is close to the center. It is also possible to discern predominant patterns, such as the high number of website visits that almost always occurs during the noon hour or the low number during the midnight hour. This is a useful overview of what's going on, which is a good place to begin. To dive down into the details using this display, we would need to reduce the over-plotting, such as by selectively filtering out days that aren't relevant to the question we're trying to answer.

Heatmaps for Analyzing High-Volume Cyclical Patterns and Exceptions

We can visualize large quantities of cyclical data that would likely produce over-plotting in a line or radar graph by using a *heatmap*. The term heatmap refers to any display that uses color to encode quantitative values. Weather maps are a familiar example of heatmaps. Typically, weather maps use variations in color on a geographical map to display temperatures or levels of rainfall. Another form of heatmap uses a matrix (rows and columns) of cells, each color coded to display a value. The following example, created using a product called

Trixie Tracker, is used by parents to track and attempt to understand the daily sleeping patterns of a young child over a period of one month.

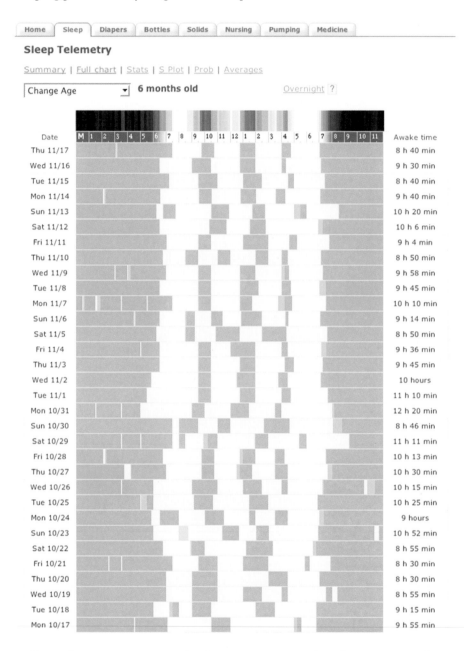

Figure 7.21. This chart was produced using a product called Trixie Tracker, which can be found at www.trixietracker.com.

Notice how easy it is to see the dominant patterns of awake time versus sleep time, especially using the summary in the row of grayscale colors at the top. This particular heatmap tracks and summarizes daily binary values (either on or off) of awake versus asleep, but heatmaps are not restricted to binary displays. The next example displays Web traffic, measured as the number of visits to a site during each hour of the day for 30 days. The number of visits in each hour has been encoded as varying intensities of red, with the highest values represented by the most intense color.

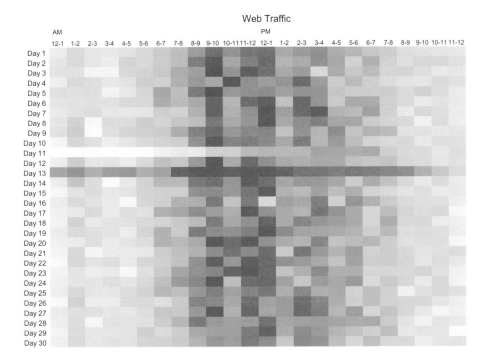

Figure 7.22

A heatmap matrix can be constructed in Excel using the *conditional formatting* feature. Other products handle heatmaps with more sophistication. Don't ever use a heatmap for time-series analysis just because it's novel or colorful. Use it only when it can display cyclical data that could not be as clearly displayed using a line or radar graph because of over-plotting.

Box Plots for Analyzing Distribution Changes

Box plots work superbly for analyzing how values are distributed across a range and how that distribution changes through time. For example, imagine that you're an analyst working in the Human Resources department of a large company; you've been asked to examine how salaries are distributed across the full range from the lowest to highest and how that distribution has changed during the past five years. A box plot such as the one below could be used for this task.

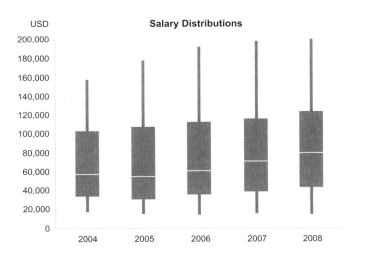

Figure 7.23

If you're not already familiar with box plots (most people aren't), don't worry. We'll spend quite a bit of time on them in *Chapter 10: Distribution Analysis*, and you'll become comfortable with them in no time at all. For now, here's an abbreviated version of the story that's told by the previous example. The typical salary paid in 2005 of about $56,000 (the light horizontal line that divides the box near the middle, which represents the median salary) was slightly lower than it was in 2004 (about $58,000), as was the lowest salary (the bottom of the vertical line). The highest salary (the top of the vertical line), however, increased significantly from around $158,000 to $179,000.The bottom half of salaries were crowded into a fairly narrow $41,000 range, compared to the top half, which were more liberally spread across a $123,000 range. In 2006, the typical salary switched directions and increased a fair amount, as did the highest salary, which happened again in 2007. In the final year, 2008, although 50% of the employees made less than $80,000 (far lower than the midpoint between the highest and lowest salaries near $100,000), salaries were more evenly distributed across the range than they ever were previously during this five-year period.

This next example is the same as the previous, except that the median values have been connected from one point in time to the next with a line to make it a little easier to see how the salaries have changed through time. This version of a box plot is not available in most products, but I find it quite useful for displaying how distributions have changed through time.

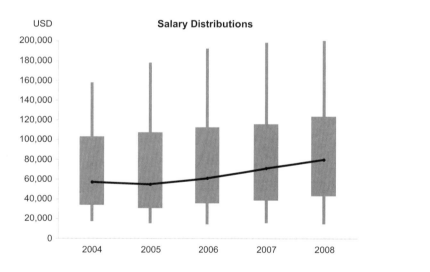

Figure 7.24

Animated Scatterplots for Analyzing Correlation Changes

Scatterplots are a wonderful way to compare two quantitative variables to determine whether, how, and to what extent they are correlated. We'll talk a lot about scatterplots in *Chapter 11: Correlation Analysis*; for now, I only want to describe how data points can be animated (given motion) to display how the relationship between two sets of quantitative values changed through time. This is accomplished by moving the data points around in the scatterplot to show

how values changed from one point in time to the next. This technique was pioneered and has been popularized by Hans Rosling of GapMinder (www.GapMinder.org), a Swedish professor and social scientist who uses it to tell important statistical stories. Here's an example that Rosling created, which shows this relationship between fertility rates and child mortality by country, grouped into continents by color, as it existed in 1962.

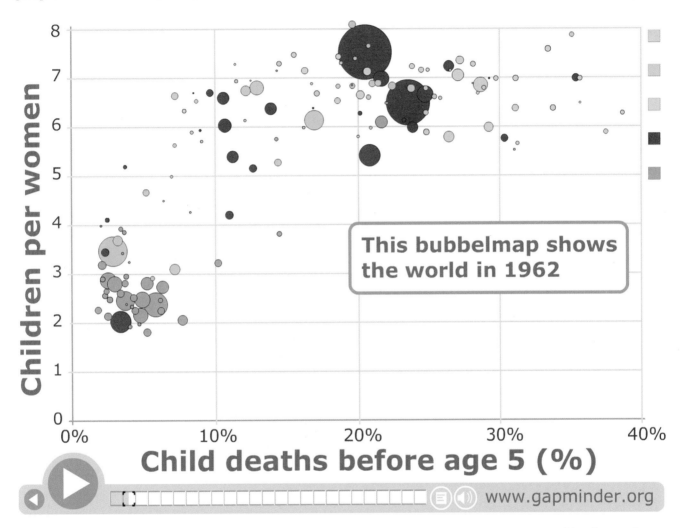

When Rosling appeared for the first time at the Technology, Entertainment, and Design (TED) conference in Monterey, California in 2006, he had 20 minutes to tell the story of world fertility rates (number of births per woman) related to life expectancy (years). He stood in front of a huge projection of a chart while bubbles (one per country) moved around the screen to show how these values of fertility and life expectancy have changed from 1962 to 2003. People sat in awe as he ran around pointing to bubbles and speaking until he was winded, mesmerized by the story and his highly animated presentation style. Perhaps never before in history did a crowd of people find a bubble chart

Figure 7.25. This and many other wonderful examples can be viewed in animated form at www.GapMinder.org. The software that was originally developed by Gapminder, called *Trendalyzer*, was purchased by Google, and a new version called *Motion Charts* is now freely available.

so fascinating. Why? I believe both because the story itself was compelling and important and because the animated bubble chart brought the story to life in a way that made it easy to understand.

Figure 7.26. Hans Rosling during his presentation at the TED conference in 2006.

Animations can be used in powerful ways to tell the story of change through time. Of this I have no doubt, but, for our purposes, the question is: "Can animations of change through time be used for analysis?" Several researchers recently tackled this question, conducting a series of experiments with enlightening findings. Animation works very effectively for telling a story because a narrator tells us where to focus our attention as facts unfold across the screen. It does not demonstrate the same benefits when used for analysis. If we're trying to watch all the little bubbles as they move around, we can only take in a fraction of what's going on. To make sense of it, we end up rerunning the animation over and over, attending to a different bubble or two each time, which is not only time consuming, it also makes it impossible to stitch the pieces together into a big picture of what went on because, as you recall, our working memory is limited.

For analytical purposes, times-series animations must be supplemented by other displays that allow us to follow what happened, discern the pattern of change, and make comparisons. The study of animation for data analysis confirmed the effectiveness of two approaches that allow us to perform these tasks:

- Trails to show the complete pattern of change through time from start to finish
- Small multiples, such as trellis displays, to compare the patterns of change among multiple items

"Effectiveness of Animation in Trend Visualization," George Robertson, Roland Fernandez, Danyel Fisher, Bongshin Lee, and John Stasko, *IEEE Transactions on Visualization and Computer Graphics*, Volume 14, Number 6, November/December 2008.

Rosling uses trails in the form of a separate bubble per interval of time (for example, for each year) to help people see and compare patterns for the entire span of time. This study of animation techniques improved the effectiveness of trails by connecting each bubble that represents a point in time with a line and using color intensity from light to dark to show the direction of change along the trail.

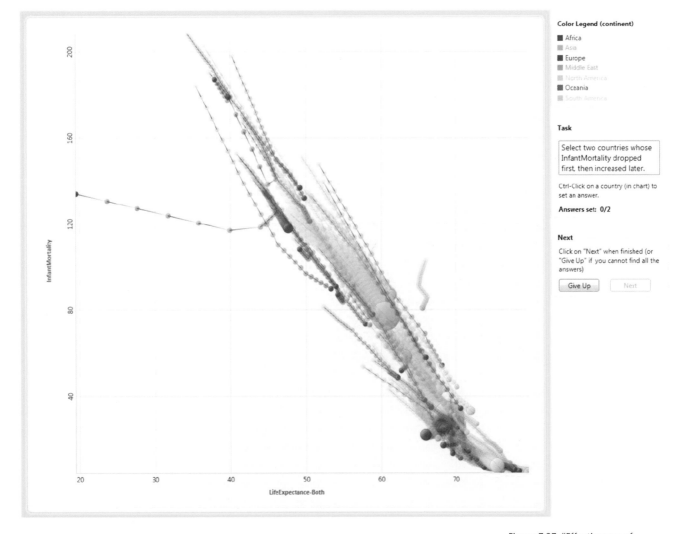

By looking at a display like this, we can discern predominant patterns and outliers, but we cannot easily compare specific patterns because of the visual clutter and over-plotting. Trellis displays solve this problem by separating each of the trails into its own graph, as you can see in the next example.

Figure 7.27. "Effectiveness of Animation in Trend Visualization," George Robertson, Roland Fernandez, Danyel Fisher, Bongshin Lee, and John Stasko, *IEEE Transactions on Visualization and Computer Graphics*, Volume 14, Number 6, November/December 2008, p. 1327.

Figure 7.28. "Effectiveness of Animation in Trend Visualization," George Robertson, Roland Fernandez, Danyel Fisher, Bongshin Lee, and John Stasko, *IEEE Transactions on Visualization and Computer Graphics*, Volume 14, Number 6, November/December 2008, p. 1328.

Thanks to the innovative efforts of Rosling and fine-tuning by several exceptional researchers, we now know the usefulness of time-series animations, their limitations for analysis, and alternative complementary displays that enable us to see and compare patterns of change.

Time-Series Analysis Techniques and Best Practices

Given how important time-series analysis is to most organizations, it is no surprise that several techniques have been developed to peek under the covers to observe time's mysteries. It should also come as no surprise that a few guidelines (best practices) should be followed to avoid mistakes in visualizing and analyzing time series.

We'll look at the following techniques and best practices:

- Aggregating to various time intervals
- Viewing time periods in context
- Grouping related time intervals
- Using running averages to enhance perception of high-level patterns
- Omitting missing values from a display
- Optimizing a graph's aspect ratio
- Using logarithmic scales to compare rates of change
- Overlapping time scales to compare cyclical patterns
- Using cycle plots to examine trends and cycles together
- Combining individual and cumulative values to compare actuals to a target
- Shifting time to compare leading and lagging indicators
- Stacking line graphs to compare multiple variables
- Expressing time as 0-100% to compare asynchronous processes

Aggregating to Various Time Intervals

Have you ever noticed that time-series data can look quite different if you change the level of aggregation? For example, if you're examining a year's worth of visits to your website per quarter, and then per month, and then per day, the patterns of change revealed at each level might look quite different.

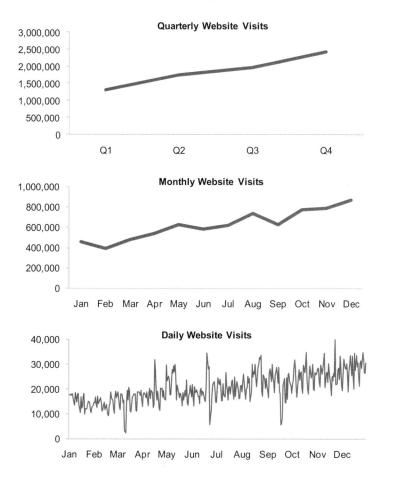

Figure 7.29

All three versions of the previous graph are useful and correct. The daily version reveals details that aren't visible when viewing the same data by month or quarter, such as the fact that Web traffic is higher on weekdays than on weekends. However, the overall trend is difficult to discern from the daily view. One view isn't better than the others in general, but one is definitely better than the others for specific analytical purposes. Don't restrict your view of time series to a single level of aggregation, especially when searching without preconceptions for anything that seems interesting. Switch the level from year to quarter, quarter to month, month to week, week to day, and so on (and back and forth) to tease out the insights that will only emerge when we look at the data from all perspectives.

To encourage this practice, software tools are needed that allow us to quickly and easily switch between various intervals of time while examining data. The ability to switch time intervals with a mouse click or two, or by using something as simple as an interval slider control, sets us free to explore.

Viewing Time Periods in Context

It is easy to read too much into a time-series pattern when viewing a brief span of time. This can easily happen if we restrict our analysis to a relatively short period and never view it in the context of a longer period. Consider the following example.

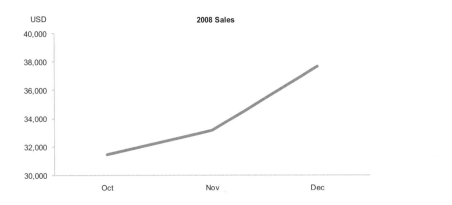

Figure 7.30

Based on this graph, we might conclude that sales are trending upward. Now look at the same three months of data, this time in the context of the entire year.

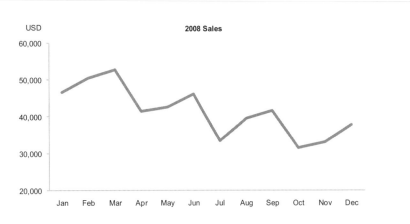

Figure 7.31

The lesson is clear, isn't it? When we examine short periods of time in isolation, we run the risk of assuming that observed patterns are more significant or more representative of what's happening overall than they in fact are. Is a year's worth of data enough? Five years? Ten years? There is no single right answer. Develop the habit of occasionally extending your view to longer stretches of time. Views of various time spans might each lead to insights that are not available if we stick to one time span.

Grouping Related Time Intervals

Sometimes it's useful to arrange time intervals into larger groups. For example, if we're examining three years' worth of monthly expenses, it would be useful to see the months grouped by year and perhaps also by quarter. As you can see in the second graph below, the addition of vertical lines to divide the quarters makes it easier to examine and understand quarterly patterns.

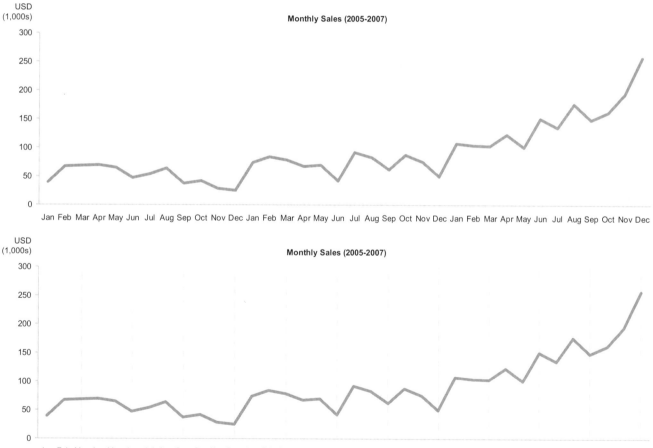

Figure 7.32

Another useful example is illustrated on the next page. When we are viewing three months' worth of daily website visits, it helps to clearly separate weekdays from weekends so we can, for example, differentiate expected drops in Web traffic on weekends from unexpected drops on weekdays, which ought to be investigated.

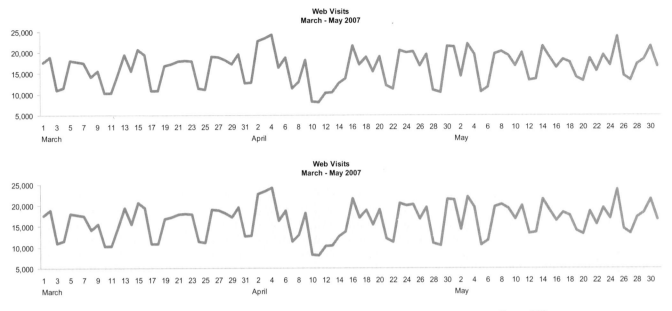

Figure 7.33

Unfortunately, few software products support the ability to group periods of time in this manner. If yours does not, let your vendor know how useful this would be.

Using Running Averages to Enhance Perception of High-Level Patterns

It is sometimes difficult to discern the overall trend of values during a span of time, especially when values are highly volatile. It's hard to picture how the general pattern might look if we could smooth out a jagged line of time-series values, taking all the increases and decreases into account, to discern what's happening overall. Trend lines are often used in attempts to solve this problem, but this approach can be misleading.

Bear in mind that whenever you take advantage of a software product's generous offer to draw a trend line for you, you are not only trusting it to do so accurately, you are also asking it to display a trend across a particular stretch of time that will fail to account for what has happened before or after. In the following example, I allowed Excel to display the overall trend of expenses for the current year to date (January through November).

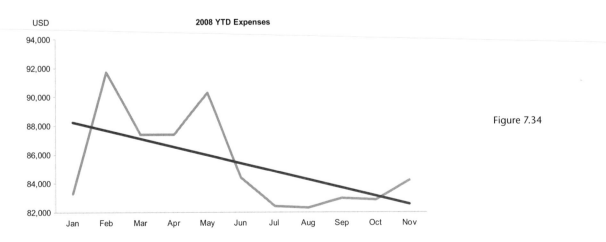

Figure 7.34

As you can see, the black trend line suggests that expenses are trending downward. Now look at how different the trend looks when I add a single month—December from the previous year—to include a full 12 months of expenses:

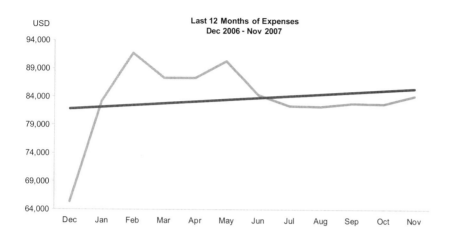

Figure 7.35

Quite a different trend, isn't it? Both graphs are accurate, based on the data they were asked to include when calculating the trend. If you associate a trend line with time-series data, be sure to examine values that fall outside the specified time period you're basing it on, to make sure you haven't isolated a section that would trend quite differently if the period were slightly altered.

A straight line of best fit, which is the type of trend line that appears in both examples above, is based on a calculation called a *linear regression*. It's determined by finding the straight line that passes through the full set of values from left to right such that the sum of the squares of the distance between each data point and the trend line is the least possible. Unless you understand this calculation and its proper use when applied to time series, it's easy to get into trouble. For this reason, I suggest a different approach to solving the problem: *running averages*.

Variability in time series can be smoothed out to some degree if, rather than displaying the actual value for each point in time (for example, for each month in the graph below), we display an average for each value and a few that precede it. For example, in the graph below we can see the pattern formed by taking the same values that appear in the two examples above and displaying each month's value as a five-month running average.

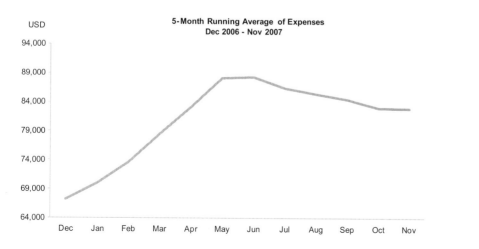

Figure 7.36

The graph on the previous page displays each month's value as the average (mean) of that particular month and the four preceding it. It is often appropriate to examine time series from a smoothed (high-level) and an actual (low-level) value perspective at the same time, as shown in the example below. Seeing both perspectives at once can help us avoid reading too much meaning into either one.

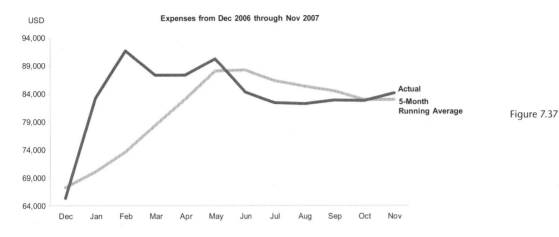

Figure 7.37

Omitting Missing Values from a Display

There's a difference between a value of zero and a value that's missing from the data. The following graph suggests that no employees worked for the company during the month of July.

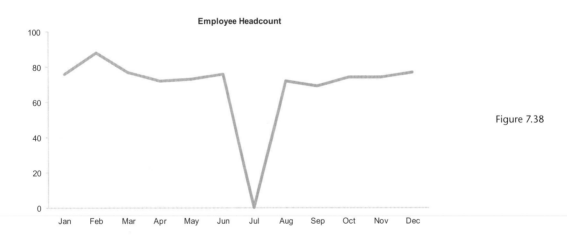

Figure 7.38

It is unlikely that everyone left the company in July and then staffing returned to its previous level in the month of August. Rather, July's employee count is missing from the data, and the graph displayed this omission as a value of zero. Bad graph! This choice produced a picture that doesn't reflect reality. The best way to handle missing values is to omit them from the graph. This makes the fact that values are missing noticeable, and the meaning obvious. Missing values can be visualized in either of the following two ways:

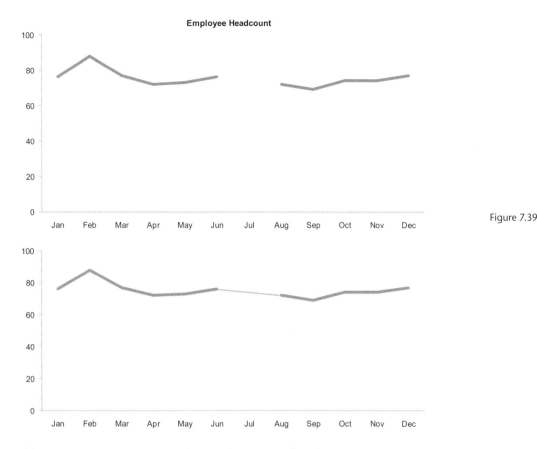

Figure 7.39

When we spot missing values during the course of analysis, we can estimate what's missing or take the time to track down the real values. In the headcount example above, no matter how it's displayed, the value for July is obviously missing because any other interpretation would be absurd, but when we're examining information that at times legitimately includes zeroes, we might not be able to discern the difference between a zero that's real and a value that's missing if both are represented as zero. For this reason, missing values should always be omitted from a graph. If you use software that automatically treats missing values in a graph as zeroes, let the vendor know that this is a bug.

Optimizing a Graph's Aspect Ratio

The aspect ratio of a graph is the ratio of the length of the X-axis to the length of the Y-axis. For example, if the plot area of a graph is exactly as tall as it is wide, it has an aspect ratio of 1 to 1 (sometimes written as 1:1). The aspect ratio of a time-series graph usually works best when it is wider than it is tall. In the example on the following page, the same values are displayed with a 1:1 aspect ratio above and a 2:1 aspect ratio below.

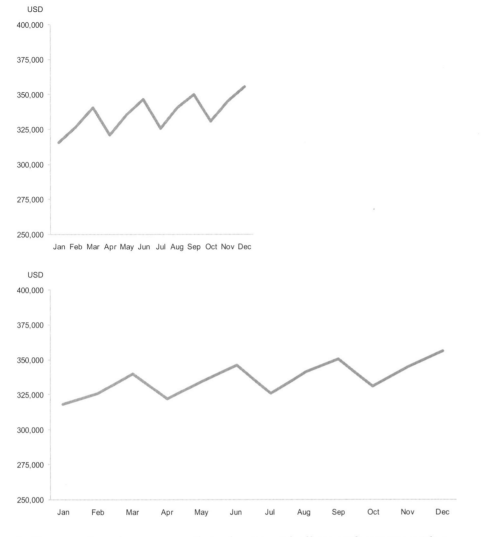

Figure 7.40

In the second graph, we can see that sales rise gradually in each quarter, with a steep decline in the first month of each new quarter. This pattern is much harder to discern in the upper graph, however, because of its aspect ratio.

Despite the usual advantage of making time-series graphs wider than they are tall, no single aspect ratio is always best. The choice of aspect ratio depends on what you're trying to see. It is sometimes worthwhile to experiment with the aspect ratio to see if something meaningful comes to light that wasn't noticeable before. William Cleveland took the time to test various aspect ratios and found that it is often helpful to set them so that the patterns we're focusing on have slopes that are approximately 45°. This is because a 45° slope is easier to see and interpret than one that is flatter or steeper. Cleveland explains the reasons:

> If the aspect ratio of a display gets too big, we can no longer discriminate two positive slopes or two negative slopes because the orientations get too close. A similar statement holds when the aspect ratio is too small...The orientations of two line segments with positive slopes are most accurately estimated when the average of the orientations is 45°, and the orientations of two line segments with negative slopes are most accurately estimated when the average of the orientations is −45°...The 45° principle applies to

the estimation of the slopes of two line segments. But we seldom have just two segments to judge on a display, and the aspect ratio that centers one pair of segments with positive slopes on 45° will not in general center some other pair of segments with positive slopes on 45°. Banking to 45° is a compromise method that centers the absolute values of the orientations of the entire collection of line segments on 45° to enhance overall estimation of the rate of change.[2]

As long as we're relying on our eyes to estimate the optimal aspect ratio, it isn't necessary to follow Cleveland's suggestion precisely. Tufte offers a practical solution for time-series displays: "Aspect ratios should be such that time-series graphics tend toward a lumpy profile rather than a spiky profile or a flat profile."[3] The middle graph below illustrates the lumpiness that Tufte advocates, in contrast to the examples of the flatness in the bottom graph and spikiness in the top graph.

2. *The Elements of Graphing Data*, William S. Cleveland, Hobart Press, 1994, pp. 252-254.

3. *Beautiful Evidence*, Edward R. Tufte, Graphics Press, Cheshire CT, 2006, p. 60.

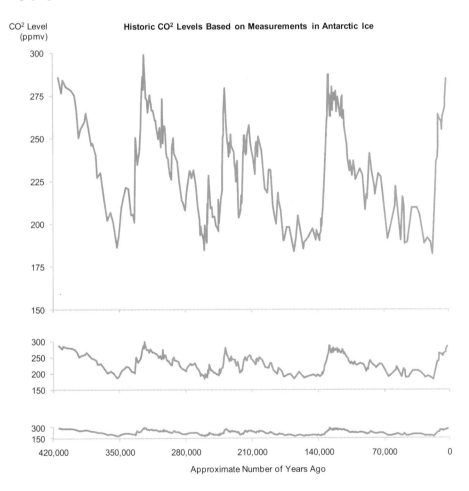

Figure 7.41. Data source: National Climatic Data Center website, based on measurements published by Petit et al., 1999.

Today, to achieve optimal slope, we must manually adjust a graph's aspect ratio, using our eyes alone to roughly determine what's most effective unless we happen to use one of the few products that includes automated banking to 45° algorithms, such as the "R" and "S" languages, which have supported this for many years. Recent work has been done by Jeffrey Heer and Maneesh Agrawala at the University of California, Berkeley to develop even better algorithms for banking to 45° that could be incorporated into software to improve this process. The option of simply turning on a "banking to 45°" feature in software and having it do the work for us, faster and more accurately than we could possibly do ourselves, is one that I'll welcome with enthusiasm.

Jeffrey Heer and Maneesh Agrawala, "Multi-Scale Banking to 45°," *IEEE Transactions on Visualization and Computer Graphics*, Vol. 12, No. 5, Sept/Oct, 2006.

Using Logarithmic Scales and Percentages to Compare Rates of Change

As we discussed in *Chapter 4: Analytical Interaction and Navigation*, it is natural, when looking at the time-series graph below, to assume that the blue line increased at a faster rate than the brown line.

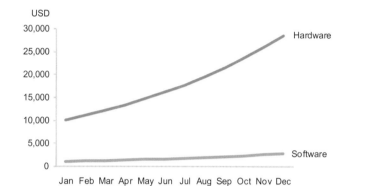

Figure 7.42

In fact, they both increased at precisely the same 10% rate. A 10% increase starting from $1,000 amounts to $100, while a 10% increase starting from $10,000 amounts to $1,000. In a graph with a standard linear scale, the slope of a line that increased by $100 is less steep than one that increased by $1,000. This does not hold true, however, for a graph with a logarithmic (log) scale. The graph below displays the same data, this time using a log scale. Now, equal rates of change appear as equal slopes, no matter how much the actual values are or how great the difference between them.

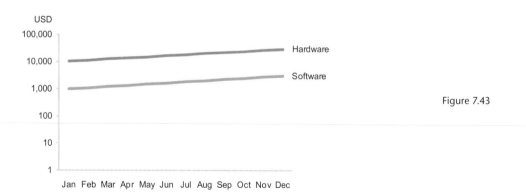

Figure 7.43

The next graph illustrates this from a different perspective. Using a standard linear scale, this graph contains two lines that exhibit precisely the same visual patterns and slopes, which makes it appear that their rates of change were the same.

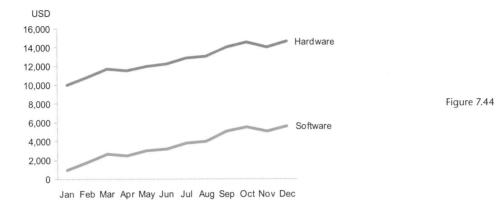

Figure 7.44

The graph below uses a log scale to display the same data, which reveals that the rates of change for hardware and software were, in fact, quite different.

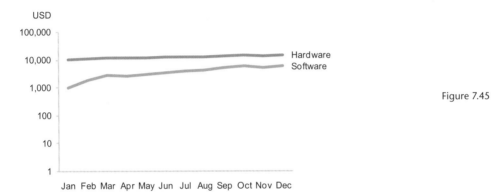

Figure 7.45

Another way to compare rates of change is to graph the rates directly, expressed as the percentage difference between each value and the next. To see how this works, let's begin with a regular graph that compares hardware and software sales throughout a single year.

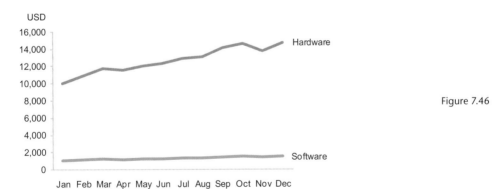

Figure 7.46

As we've learned, it's difficult to compare rates of change using a standard linear scale in this manner. Rather than switching to a log scale, this time let's graph the rates of change directly. The two graphs on the following page display hardware and software sales separately as the percentage change from each month to the next.

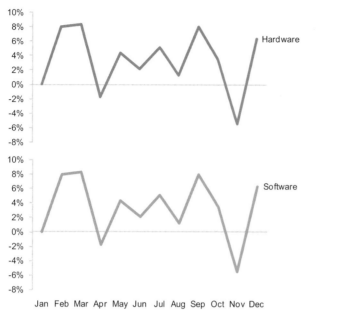

Figure 7.47

As you can see, hardware and software sales exhibited the exact same rates of change from month to month throughout the year. I displayed them in separate graphs only because, had I used a single graph, the two lines would have occupied the same exact space, causing one to be completely hidden by the other. In the next example, rather than graphing the percentage change from one month to the next, I display each month as the percentage difference from a single baseline month, in this case January, the first month of the year. Once again, we can see that the patterns and magnitudes were precisely the same.

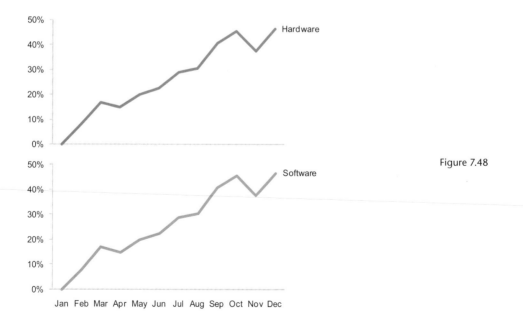

Figure 7.48

Overlapping Time Scales to Compare Cyclical Patterns

We can strengthen our ability to detect and compare cyclical patterns stretching across multiple cycles in a line graph by displaying each cycle as a separate line. As you can see in the following two graphs, the cycles that are difficult to compare in the top graph, are much easier to compare in the bottom graph.

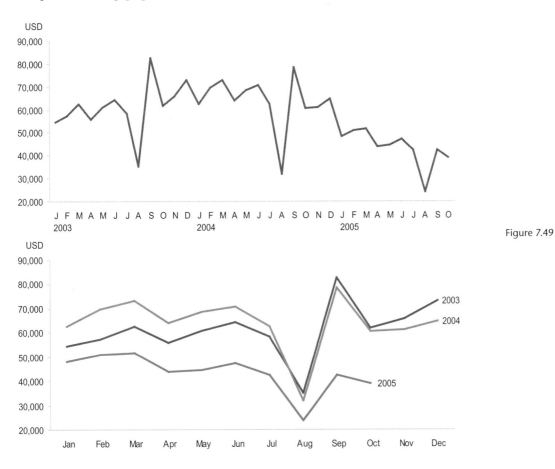

Figure 7.49

This type of graph is particularly easy to create when using Excel, simply by treating each year as a separate data set.

Using Cycle Plots to Examine Trends and Cycles Together

You might have noticed that the technique we just covered in the section above makes it easy to compare cycles to one another but does not allow us to see trends that extend across multiple cycles. A display that makes it possible to both compare cycles and see trends extending across multiple cycles would be useful. The line graph on the next page displays 56 days' worth of sales, which gives us a sense of weekly cycles, but to understand the cycles clearly, we need a different view.

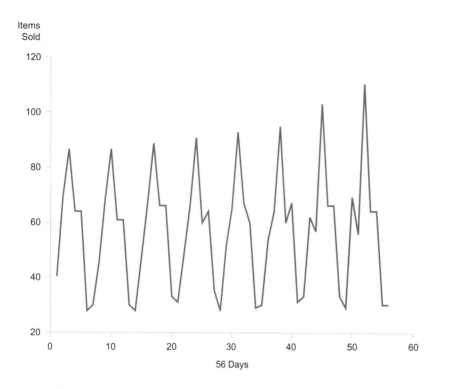

Figure 7.50

The graph below displays the average sales per day of the week for these same eight weeks.

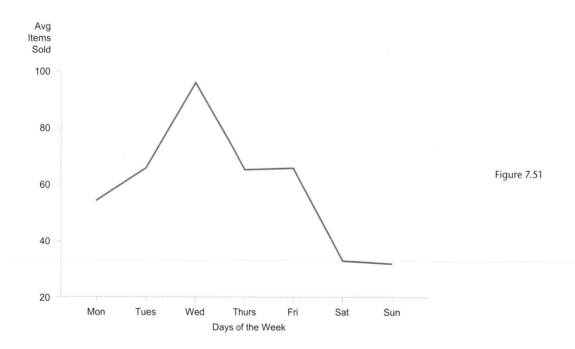

Figure 7.51

We can now see what the overall weekly pattern is for the eight-week period, but we've lost sight of the variation from week to week. In the 1970s, Cleveland, Dunn, and Terpenning developed the *cycle plot*, which can be used to solve this problem.

Cycle plots allow us to see two fundamental characteristics of time-series data in a single graph:

- The overall pattern across the entire cycle
- The trend for each point in the cycle across the entire range of time

Here are the same weekly values that were displayed in the previous graph, this time displayed in a cycle plot:

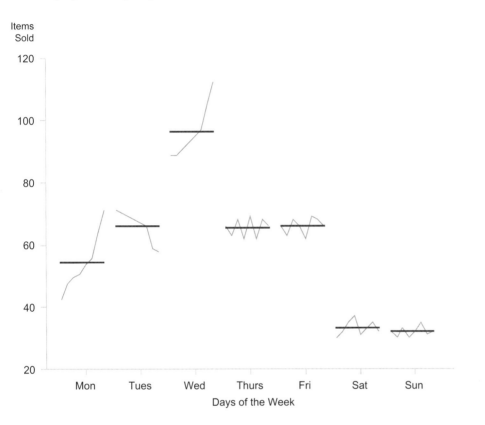

William Cleveland, Douglas Dunn, and Irma Terpenning, "The SABL Seasonal Analysis Package— Statistical and Graphical Procedures," Bell Laboratories, Murray Hill NJ: Computing Information Service, 1978. This paper was brought to my attention by Naomi B. Robbins in the article, "Introduction to Cycle Plots," *Visual Business Intelligence Newsletter*, Perceptual Edge, Berkeley CA, 2008. Most of the examples of cycle plots shown here were derived from examples that Robbins created for the article.

Figure 7.52

In this cycle plot, the typical weekly pattern is formed across the entire graph by the means (averages) for each day of the week, which are encoded as short, straight horizontal lines. The actual values for any given day of the week across the entire range of time are displayed by each of the small curvy lines. These begin with the value for that particular day of the week during the first week and continue with a value for each week until the last. By looking at the weekly values for Tuesday and comparing them to Monday, we can now see that values consistently increased on Mondays during this eight-week period and consistently decreased on Tuesdays. The two values that stand out as the lowest on Tuesdays occurred during the last two weeks of the period. We can also see that Wednesday also consistently increased, but the other days of the week went up and down without exhibiting a predominant trend.

The ability to summarize cycles and view longer trends without shifting from graph to graph can lead us to insights that we might not otherwise discover. It's useful to have the option of connecting the data points across the graph for any single cycle (such as any one day of the week in the example above) or across the mean values for all the cycles. In the example below, I've connected the mean values, which makes it easier to see the weekly trend based on the means of each day of the week for the entire 56-day period. Unfortunately, this option doesn't seem to be available in any software that I've seen.

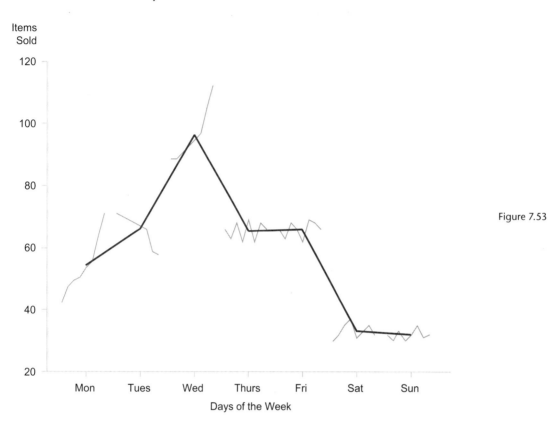

Figure 7.53

Some software products support cycle plots as a special form of line graph. The following example was produced using Tableau Software:

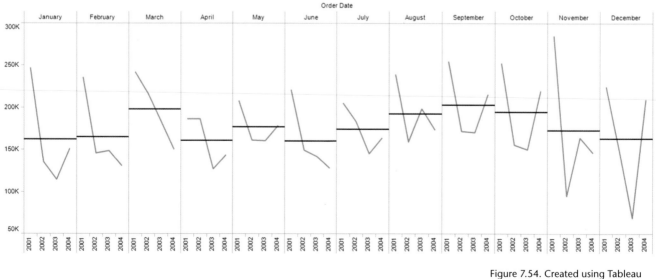

Figure 7.54. Created using Tableau Software

All I had to do to shift from a normal line graph to a cycle plot was to reverse the order of the "month" and "year" fields when I constructed the graph, placing month before year, which caused the years (2001-2004) to be grouped within the months. In other words, it took no longer to construct this cycle plot than it did to construct the normal line graph, and I could quickly and easily switch back and forth between the two simply by reversing the order of the years and months.

Even if you don't have a product like Tableau Software, you can produce cycle plots in Excel with some time and effort. The example below was produced by first creating a single graph for January values (one graph per year from 1993 through 2005), then copying and pasting that graph 11 times to create the others, and finally by selecting the appropriate source data for each month.

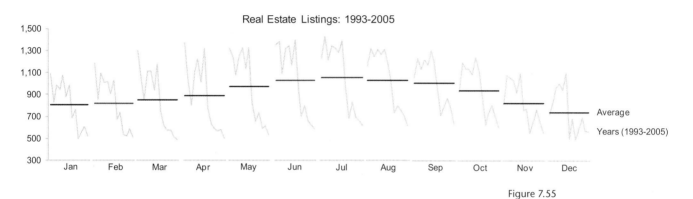

Figure 7.55

Combining Individual and Cumulative Values to Compare Actuals to a Target

Often when we monitor a time series, we assess how well things are going by comparing actual values to targets. If we're tracking expenses on a monthly basis, but the target that's used to judge performance is for the year as a whole, a graph that displays each month's expenses during the course of the year, such as the graph below, would make it hard to compare year-to-date performance to the target.

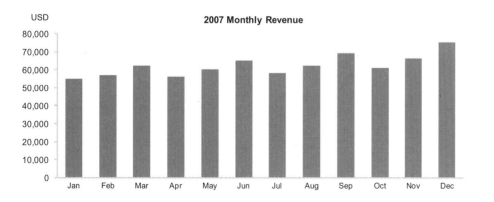

Figure 7.56

We could create a separate graph with just two values—the actual year-to-date expenses and the annual target—but what if we don't want to lose sight of monthly expenses? A simple solution involves a combination bar and line graph, with a bar for each month's expenses, a line to display cumulative year-to-date expenses per month, and a reference line to mark the target, as illustrated below.

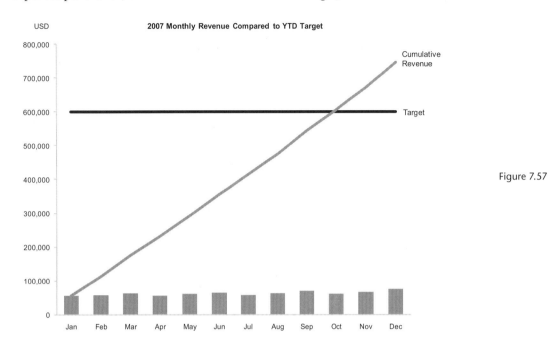

Figure 7.57

A graph of this type is difficult to use to precisely compare individual bars because, when we scale the graph to accommodate the cumulative values, the bars become too short in comparison. If we want to keep the bars longer to eliminate this problem, we can display the data in two graphs, arranged one above the other: a bar graph for monthly values and a line graph for year-to-date cumulative values compared to the target. As illustrated below, we can scale each graph independently, thereby getting the best of both worlds.

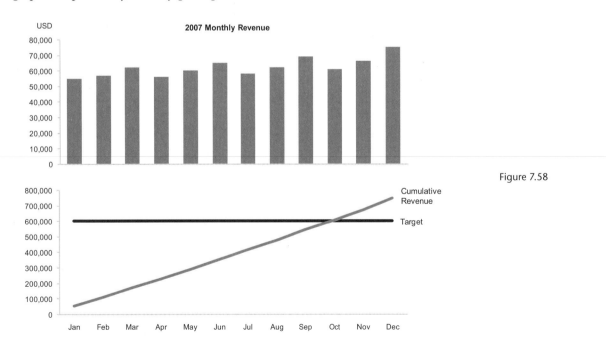

Figure 7.58

Shifting Time to Compare Leading and Lagging Indicators

It is sometimes useful to examine how one variable (the independent variable) affects another (the dependent variable). When we do this in the context of time, it's sometimes difficult to see how the dependent variable is affected by the independent variable if there is a lag in time between the cause and the effect. The following example illustrates this difficulty.

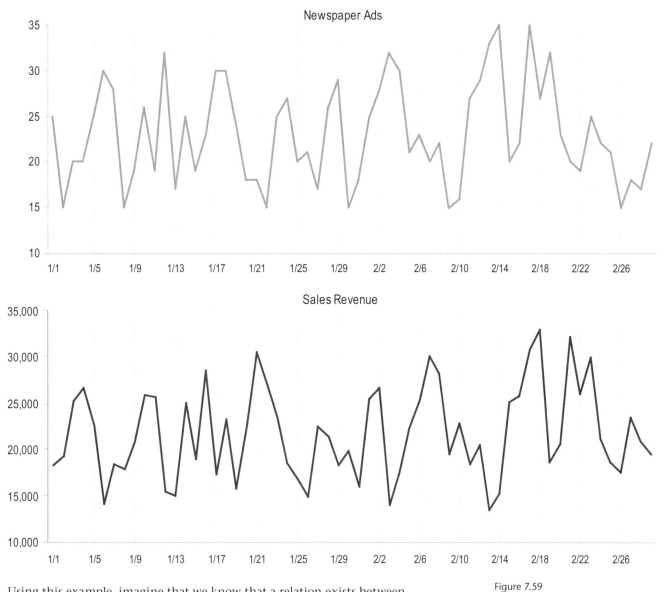

Figure 7.59

Using this example, imagine that we know that a relation exists between newspaper ads and resulting sales such that a greater number of ads results in increased sales four days later. In other words, newspaper ads are a leading indicator of sales revenues, and there is a lag of four days between them. Because of the lag, the up and down patterns formed by the number of newspaper ads don't line up with the related patterns formed by sales revenues. To examine their relationship more closely, we need to align the leading and lagging events.

This example was created using Excel. We can now reposition the sales revenue graph to the left by four days to align the related values, and also move it up a bit to get the two lines closer to one another.

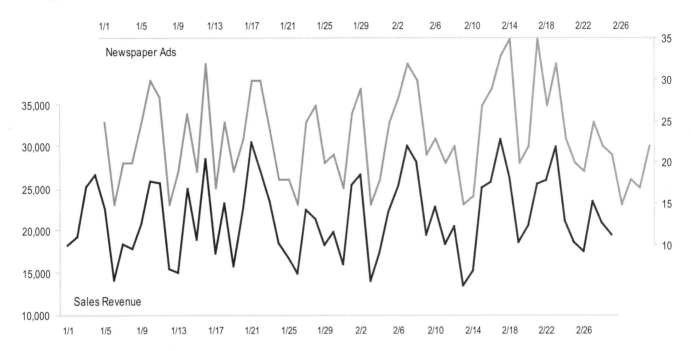

Figure 7.60

Now the leading and lagging values are aligned and can be compared with ease. Doing this in Excel doesn't require anything fancy. Because graphs can be positioned wherever you want them, Excel does a particularly good job of supporting this technique. To place graphs on top of one another so that you can see through the one on top to the one beneath, you simply need to set the chart's background fill color to "none" rather than "white."

A simple solution that I haven't seen so far in a product would involve a feature that allowed us to shift time in a graph to the left or right by any specified amount without affecting time in other graphs that are also on display. Perhaps this feature exists, and I just haven't seen it. If so, the innovative vendor deserves our thanks.

Stacking Line Graphs to Compare Multiple Variables

Often, time-series data sets that are useful to compare can't all reside in a single graph either because they are expressed using different units of measure, or there are huge differences in where they fall along the quantitative scale. For example, we can't compare a product's sales revenues in U.S. dollars to the number of units sold in the same graph without using two scales, which can lead to confusion. Also, it is difficult to compare a product's profits to its average selling price in a single graph when monthly profits range in the millions of dollars and the average price per product is $500. Scaling the graph to accommodate values in the millions of dollars would cause the average selling prices to barely register as a straight line hugging the bottom of the plot area with no discernable pattern. But it is useful to compare these things, so how can we do it?

This problem can be solved by using a series of graphs arranged above and below one another with the same points in time aligned. Here's an example that compares the number of units sold, revenues, profits, average selling price, and customer satisfaction.

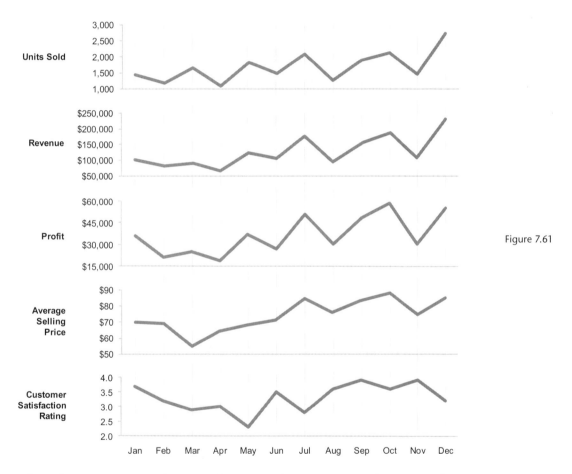

Figure 7.61

When the quantitative scales in graphs are not the same, you can't compare the magnitudes of values in one graph to those in another, but you can compare patterns of change. This technique can be executed in Excel simply by creating separate graphs with the same time scale along their X-axes, and arranging them so that the same points in time are aligned. Other, more powerful products are available for doing this that reduce labor by arranging the graphs automatically.

The following example illustrates how this is done using Tableau Software.

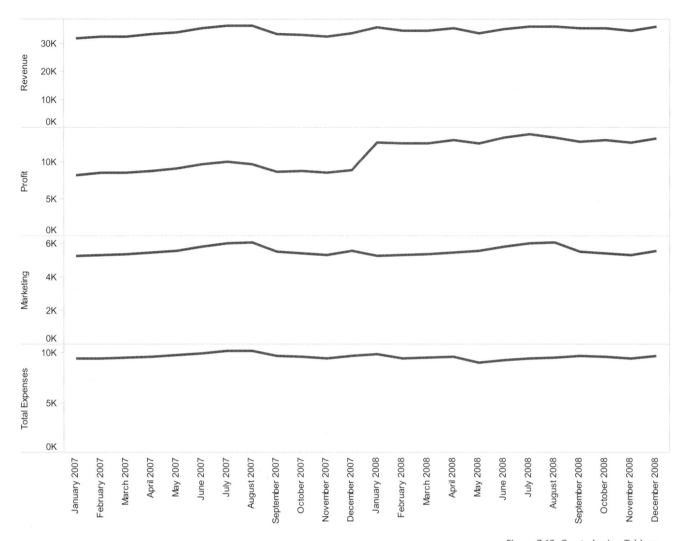

Figure 7.62. Created using Tableau Software

Expressing Time as 0-100% to Compare Asynchronous Processes

Imagine the following situation. You work in the Information Technology (IT) department of a company, and you want to compare costs in person hours associated with 50 projects that IT managed during the past five years. You're interested in finding out whether project costs exhibit particular time-based patterns, such as high costs during the start-up phase, increasing rates of costs near the end, or other patterns that you have yet to imagine. The problem that prevents you from analyzing these costs as you would any other time series is the fact that the 50 projects did not all start at the same time, nor did they all last the same length of time. In other words, they were asynchronous. What can you do?

One answer involves making starting time, ending time, and duration consistent for all projects. This can be done by expressing each project's duration as a percentage, beginning at 0% and ending at 100%, no matter when the project began, when it ended, or how long it lasted. This approach makes it possible to compare what's happening at the beginning of each process, at the end of each process, halfway through each process, 90% through each process, and so on, despite their asynchronous nature. I ran across this solution in a research project done by the Human-Computer Interaction Lab (HCIL) at the University of Maryland, which produced a software application called *TimeSearcher*.

The example below, prepared using TimeSearcher 2, compares the bid prices (top graph) and velocities (bottom graph) of 227 eBay auctions (one line per auction). Velocity is the rate at which bids were being made.

TimeSearcher 1 and *TimeSearcher 2* were developed at the University of Maryland (www.cs.umd.edu/hcil/ timesearcher). TimeSearcher 1 was developed under the direction of Ben Shneiderman by Harry Hochheiser. TimeSearcher 2 is described in the following research paper: Aleks Aris, Ben Shneiderman, Catherine Plaisant, Galit Shmueli, and Wolfgang Jank, "Representing Unevenly-Spaced Time Series Data for Visualization and Interactive Exploration." *Proceedings of the International Conference on Human-Computer Interaction*, 2005, pp. 835-846.

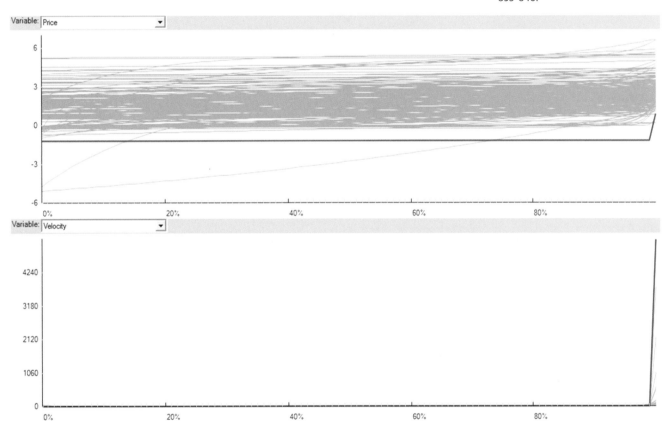

These auctions started on different days and lasted different numbers of days, yet their time-based patterns can be meaningfully compared in this manner. The lines that are highlighted in blue represent an auction that I found interesting because it exhibited the greatest surge of bid velocity of all, revealed by steep line at the right end of the bottom graph. As you can see, the bid price for this auction remained constant until the very end, when the surge in bidding activity produced a slight increase in the price.

Figure 7.63. Created using TimeSearcher 2

In the following example, I highlighted the 10 auctions with the highest final bid prices using the aqua colored rectangle, which TimerSearcher 2 calls a *timebox*, to see whether auctions with high final prices exhibit a particular velocity pattern.

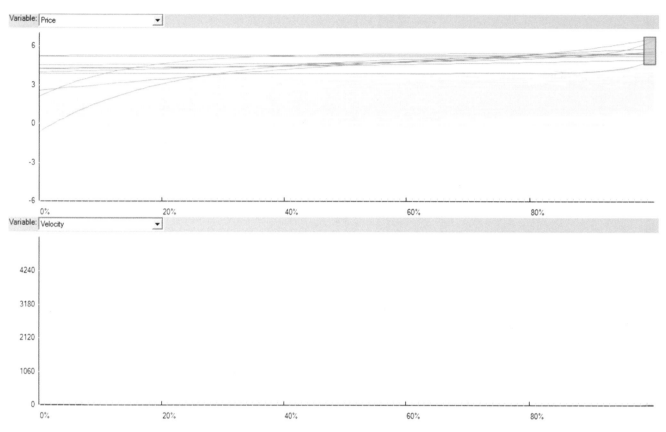

Of the 10 auctions that are highlighted in the price graph (the darker graph lines in the top graph), none is highlighted in the velocity graph, which tells us that none exhibited a significant velocity increase near the end of the auction.

So far, I haven't seen any software that automatically converts time to percentages in the manner described above. TimeSearcher requires that this conversion be done before the program accesses the data. For now, we can do this conversion ourselves. For example, with Excel, we can convert dates to a 100% scale by following a relatively simple procedure, described in *Appendix A: Expressing Time as a Percentage in Excel*. Once this is done for the dates associated with each process that we want to compare, we can use an Excel scatterplot—the version that connects values sequentially with a straight line—to display the data, which I did to produce the following example.

Figure 7.64. Created using TimeSearcher 2

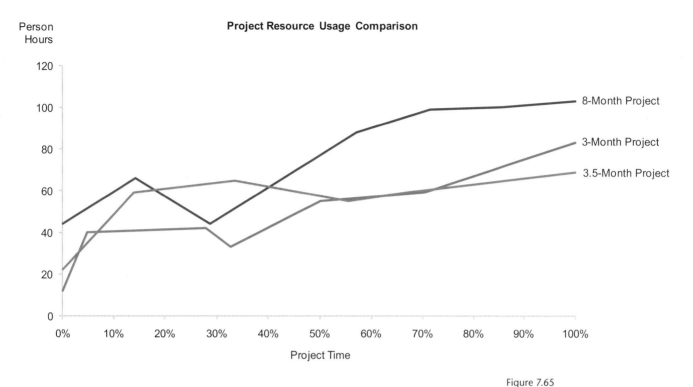

Figure 7.65

Searching for Specified Patterns of Change

The technique of searching for specific patterns was brought to my attention initially by the TimeSearcher applications mentioned above. Wouldn't it be great if you could draw a time-series pattern in the form of a line, such as and tell your software to find and display every line that exhibits a similar pattern within a specified range of variation? TimeSearcher doesn't do this exactly, but it does let you pick a section of a line in a graph and then instruct the software to find all other patterns throughout the data set that are similar in shape. The ability to draw a pattern and instruct the software to look for it was implemented by Martin Wattenberg in the research project that produced *QuerySketch*, but it has never, to my knowledge, been implemented in commercial software. Unlike most of the analysis techniques that I describe in this book, this one won't be practical until a software product supports it. I hope that by the time you read this, products will save us time by searching massive amounts of data to find specific patterns much faster than we could ever do with our eyes alone.

"Sketching a Graph to Query a Time-Series Database", Martin Wattenberg, Dow Jones / SmartMoney.com, New York NY, 2001; Wattenberg currently works for IBM Research and is responsible for some of the best information visualization research and development being done today.

Maintaining Consistency through Time

I've found that business analysts often ignore two important practices that are necessary to maintain consistency in time-series values, especially when those values extend across several years:

- Adjusting for inflation when examining currency
- Taking into account differences in how the information was collected or defined over time

When we wish to examine and compare monetary values across multiple years, inaccuracies will arise if we fail to account for the changing value of money that results from inflation. This failure can cause us to conclude that a product's sales performance is greater today than it was five years ago, even when its performance has in fact decreased. I believe that adjusting for inflation is seldom done primarily because people simply don't think about it or they assume that it's much harder than it actually is. Indexes that can be used to adjust for inflation are readily available for download from the Internet and can be plugged right into software such as Excel. Instructions for finding these indexes and using them in Excel can be found in *Appendix B: Adjusting for Inflation in Excel.*

In *Chapter 2: Prerequisites for Enlightening Analysis*, I mentioned how important it is to know the pedigree of your data. One reason is that sometimes a particular measure, even of something as common as sales bookings, could have been defined or calculated in the past differently than it is now. Differences like this are especially common if your organization switched between computer systems at some point in the past, and the old system calculated or defined some things differently than the current system does. Another common cause in business is the acquisition of another company whose systems defined measures differently than yours, and the merging of that company's data with yours. For example, if one system defined revenues such that sales taxes were included and the other treated sales taxes as separate from revenues, and information from them was merged five years ago without taking this difference into account, comparing six-year-old revenues to current revenues would be like comparing apples and oranges (or at least McIntosh and Granny Smith apples) unless you adjusted for this difference. If someone else, such as a data warehousing team, takes care of adjustments like these, you're lucky. If not, you ought to make these adjustments yourself.

8 PART-TO-WHOLE AND RANKING ANALYSIS

Introduction

Two of the most frequently performed and simplest types of analysis we do involve comparing parts of a whole and ranking them by value. For instance, when trying to make sense of total expenses (the whole), we often aggregate them by department (the parts) to see how much each department adds to overall expenses. Placing the departments in order based on expenses (from highest to lowest or vice versa), makes relative values easier to compare. It's remarkable how the minor act of sorting items by value simplifies the process of comparing them. In the first example below, departments are arranged alphabetically, which forces us to rearrange them in our heads to see how they rank—a difficult task because of the limits of working memory, which we discussed earlier.

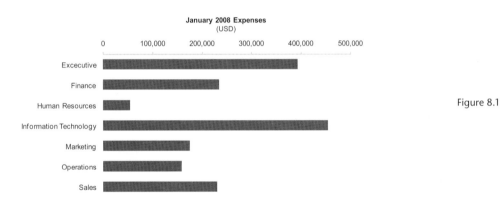

Figure 8.1

The other factor that complicates our ability to understand these departmental expenses as parts of the whole is the unit of measure that was used to express them. The dollar amount of each department's expenses is difficult to translate into a proportional measure (that is, some percentage of 100% in total). When we sort the expenses by amount and express the amounts as percentages, the part-to-whole and ranking relationships spring to life.

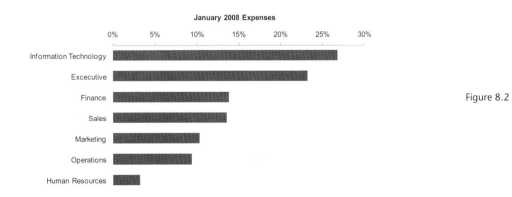

Figure 8.2

If these seven departments did not make up a whole, and we were examining their ranking only, it wouldn't be necessary to express them as percentages.

Part-to-Whole and Ranking Patterns

When we examine ranked values, whether they represent parts of a whole or not, the patterns that concern us are formed by differences in magnitude from one value to the next across the entire series. These patterns, which are fairly simple and limited in scope, include the following:

Pattern	Description	Visual Example
Uniform	All values are roughly the same.	
Uniformly different	Differences from one value to the next decrease by roughly the same amount.	
Non-uniformly different	Differences from one value to the next vary significantly.	
Increasingly different	Differences from one value to the next increase.	
Decreasingly different	Differences from one value to the next decrease.	
Alternating differences	Differences from one value to the next begin small and then shift to large and finally shift back again to small.	
Exceptional	One or more values are extraordinarily different from the rest.	

This is certainly not an exhaustive list of meaningful part-to-whole and ranking patterns; it's just a few that are common. What these patterns mean depends on the nature of the data we're examining. Unusual differences from one value to the next, sets of values that appear to be grouped based on similar values, significant breaks in a pattern, and obvious exceptions to the norm are a few characteristics that almost always deserve our attention.

Part-to-Whole and Ranking Displays

Part-to-whole relationships are commonly displayed as pie charts. This is unfortunate. Pie charts force us to compare either the 2-D areas formed by each slice or the angles formed by each where the slices meet in the center. Visual perception handles neither of these comparisons easily or accurately. If you had to put the slices of the pie chart on the following page in order by size from largest to smallest, or if you had to calculate the difference in percentage between any two slices, notice how much time it would take and how much you would rely on rough estimates.

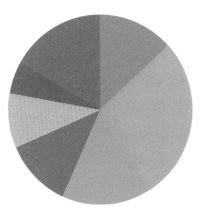

Figure 8.3

Pie charts are also especially time consuming to interpret when legends are used to label the slices because this forces our eyes to bounce constantly back and forth between the legend and the pie to make sense of it.

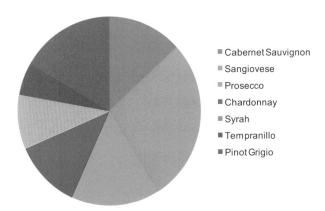

- Cabernet Sauvignon
- Sangiovese
- Prosecco
- Chardonnay
- Syrah
- Tempranillo
- Pinot Grigio

Figure 8.4

Even when slices are labeled directly, we're still disabled in our ability to estimate and compare their sizes. You might be tempted to object, "This could be solved by displaying the values as text next to each slice," as illustrated below:

- disagree, pie charts are easy to view visually

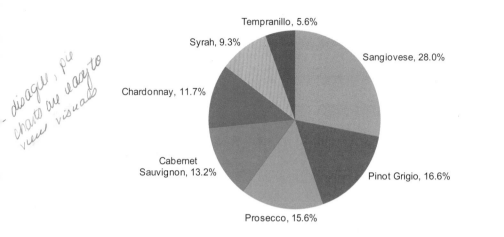

Figure 8.5

This is true, but what's the point of using a graph—a visual representation of the quantitative data—if we must rely on printed values to make sense of it? If the graph doesn't reveal most of what we wish to see directly and visually, without assistance from text, we would be better off using the table below.

Wine	Percent
Sangiovese	28.0%
Pinot Grigio	16.6%
Prosecco	15.6%
Cabernet Sauvignon	13.2%
Chardonnay	11.7%
Syrah	9.3%
Tempranillo	5.6%
Total	100.0%

Figure 8.6

Bar Graphs

Bar graphs are much more effective than pie charts for analyzing ranking and part-to-whole relationships. What is difficult to see and do using the previous pie charts is easy using the following bar graph.

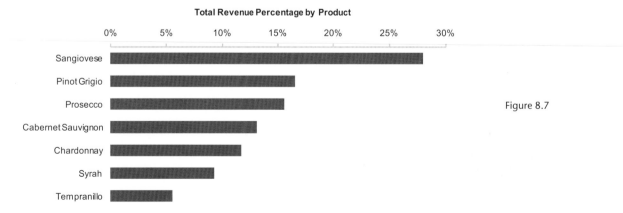

Figure 8.7

Stick with bar graphs rather than pie charts for analyzing part-to-whole and ranking relationships, and you'll reach more accurate conclusions and do so in a fraction of the time. There is one exception, however, which we'll look at next.

Dot Plots

When all the values in a bar graph fall within a fairly narrow range, and that range is far from zero, we might want to spread the values across more space in the graph to make it easier to see and compare their differences. In the following graph, because all the salaries are tightly grouped together between $42,000 and $53,000, the differences between them are harder to compare than they would be if these values were spread across more space.

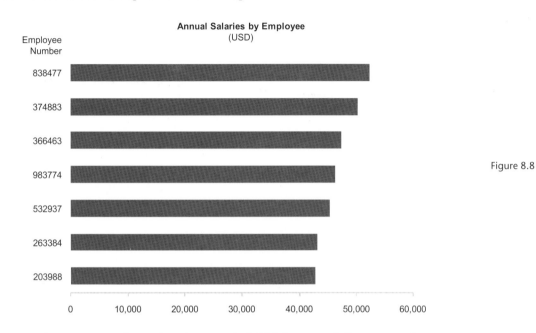

Figure 8.8

We can't just narrow the scale to begin at $42,000, because differences in the bars' lengths would no longer accurately represent the differences in the values. We can narrow the scale without creating this problem, however, by switching to a dot plot. Here's the same set of values with points in the form of a dot plot:

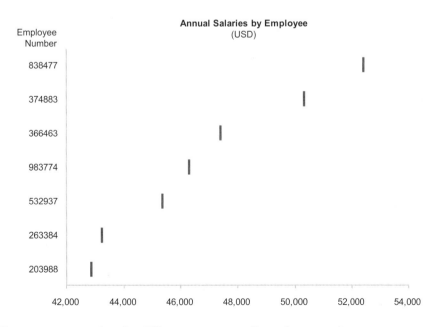

Figure 8.9. Dot plots usually encode values using dots (circles), but greater precision can be gained by using objects such as the short vertical lines shown here.

Now we can examine the differences more easily and accurately.

Pareto Charts

Sometimes, when we examine values that are ranked by size, it's also revealing to examine the cumulative contribution of parts to the whole, starting with the largest and working sequentially to the smallest. As illustrated below, if we're in the business of selling laptop computers, it would be worthwhile to know that the top four of the 12 reasons that laptops are returned to us by buyers account for 84% of total returns. Also, more than 60% of laptop returns are for two reasons alone: they are either too difficult to set up or, once set up, too difficult to use.

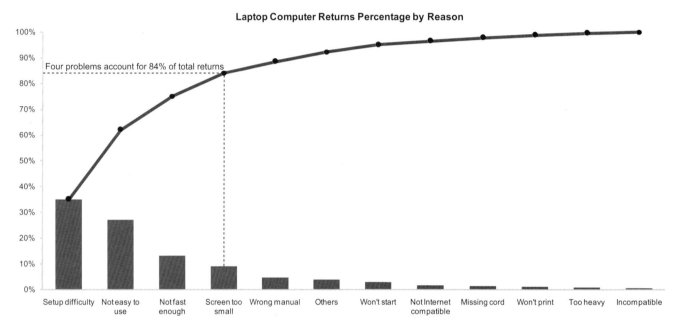

Figure 8.10

This type of display is called a *Pareto Chart*. To construct it, you simply rank the items by size from largest to smallest, display the individual values as bars, and display the cumulative values from one item to the next as a line. This is easily done with Excel by associating the individual values with vertical bars (what Excel calls *columns*) and the cumulative values with a line, which can be done in a single graph by associating a specific chart type with each set of values.

Pareto Charts were named after Vilfredo Pareto, the social scientist whose observations led to what we know as the Pareto Principle (also known as the 80/20 rule). He noted that 80% of Italy's wealth was possessed by 20% of the population, which has led others to point out that 80% of a company's sales are often associated with 20% of its customers.

Part-to-Whole and Ranking Techniques and Best Practices

We'll look at four techniques and best practices for part-to-whole and ranking analysis:

- Grouping categorical items in an ad hoc manner
- Using Pareto charts with percentile scales
- Re-expressing values to solve quantitative scaling problems
- Using line graphs to view ranking changes through time

Grouping Categorical Items in an Ad Hoc Manner

As I mentioned previously, it's helpful to work with information that has been segmented (grouped) in meaningful ways. A good data warehouse segments data in the ways that are frequently useful, but it can never anticipate all of the groupings that we might need when we're exploring and analyzing data. By its very nature, analysis takes us into undiscovered realms and requires that we adapt as needed in the moment. Consequently, the ability to group categorical items in an ad hoc manner is critical, especially when analyzing part-to-whole and ranking relationships. For example, the Pareto chart in Figure 8.10 includes several reasons for the return of laptops on the right side that don't add up to much. In such a case, we might want to lump everything from "Not Internet compatible" through the rest of the list into a single item called something like "Other," resulting in the following display:

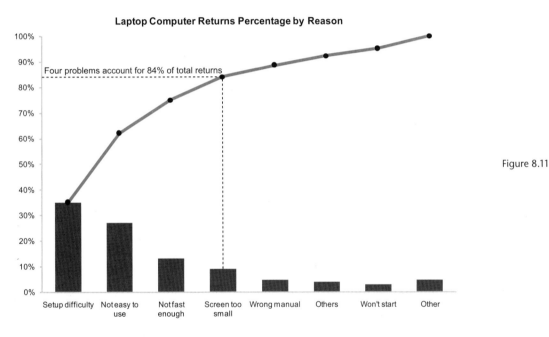

Figure 8.11

Other examples abound, which I'm sure you encounter from time to time. In the following example, I decided to take all the beverages that fall into the dessert category (on the left) and group them together (on the right).

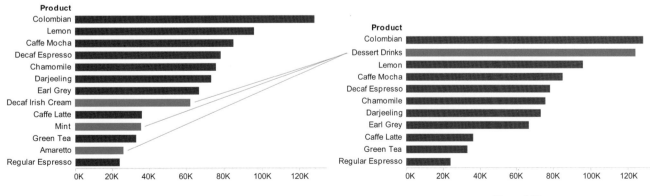

Figure 8.12

With some software, ad hoc groupings simply can't be created. You might be forced to rely on someone in the IT department to add another field to the data warehouse. God forbid, because this could take months, and you might only need to do it once.

Using Pareto Charts with Percentile Scales

Pareto charts can be useful even when the items we're comparing make up an interval scale rather than an ordinal scale of ranked items. The following example, which features an interval scale (the sizes of orders from largest to smallest, grouped into percentile intervals), shows a type of graph that I've found quite revealing at times. Each interval represents a range of 10 percentage points, starting at the left with the top 10% of orders ranked by size, proceeding to the next 10% of orders by size, and so on all the way to the 10% of orders that were the smallest.

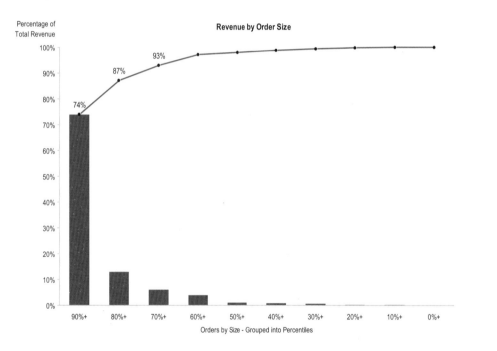

Figure 8.13

I created this particular example several years ago for clients, which led them to an "Aha!" experience. They were shocked to learn that 70% of their orders (everything to the right of the 70%+ bar) accounted for only 7% of their revenue even though these orders ate up a majority of their sales efforts. This same approach, using percentiles in a Pareto chart, can be used to examine many large data sets of various types.

Re-expressing Values to Solve Quantitative Scaling Problems

When a set of ranked values extends across a vast scale, sometimes the lowest values barely register on the graph and are, as a result, difficult to see and compare. In the previous example of a Pareto chart with a percentile scale, you might have found it annoying that the bars from 50%+ to the right through 0%+ were difficult to see and certainly could not be compared with even a modicum of precision.

One way to solve this problem—often the best way—involves viewing the low values independently in a separate graph, as shown below:

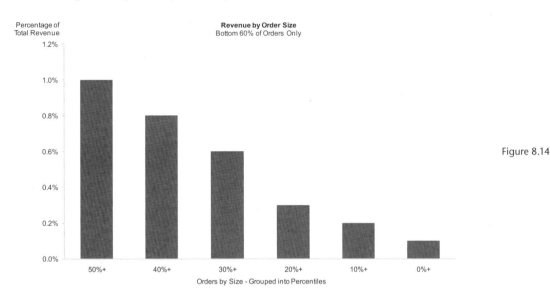

Figure 8.14

By keeping both graphs in front of our eyes, we can still see the low values in relation to those that are high (in the graph with all the values), but we can also compare the low values with ease and accuracy (in the graph that contains the low values only).

Another way to solve this scaling problem involves re-expressing the values so that they are more evenly distributed across the quantitative scale in a single graph. Re-expressions, such as those we'll look at now, should be used with caution. Although they make it easier to see the full set of values in a single graph, they alter the distances between the values in a way that distorts the actual magnitudes of those differences. If you keep this distortion in mind, however, this approach can be useful.

Three re-expressions are particularly good at solving our scaling problem in which the low values are hard to read on the large graph. Each type of re-expression accomplishes this by stretching the low values out across more space in the graph and compressing the high values into less space. They do this to varying degrees. The following list is sequenced by the amount of stretching and compression, from least to greatest:

- Square root re-expression
- Logarithmic re-expression
- Inverse re-expression

It's best to use the re-expression that solves the scaling problem with the least distortion to the differences between the values. If you start by re-expressing the values as their square roots, but the problem persists, move on to the next.

To illustrate how these re-expressions work, let's begin by expressing the example above in U.S. dollars rather than percentages.

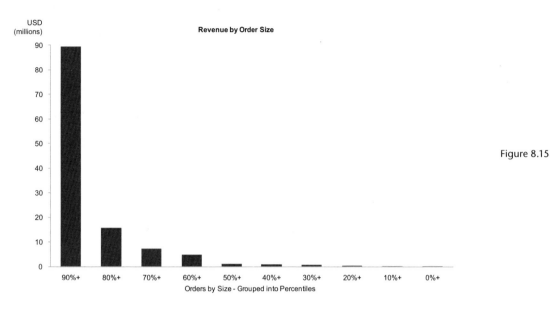

Figure 8.15

Now let's calculate the square root of each revenue amount and graph the results. To discourage ourselves from comparing the heights of the bars as a means of comparing these square root values, let's switch from a bar graph to a dot plot instead.

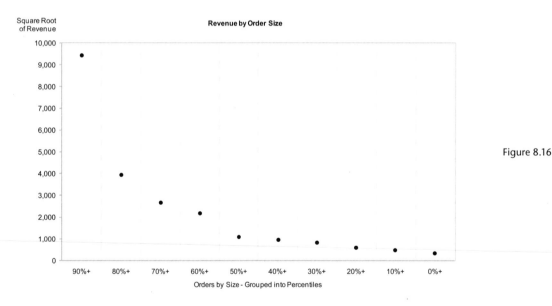

Figure 8.16

Notice how the distance between the highest and lowest values has been reduced. The dots that represent the lowest values, however, are still not far enough from the baseline to support easy comparisons. Despite this problem, we can now begin to see something that wasn't apparent before: the fact that particular percentile ranges seem to be grouped together with similar values. Notice that the 90%+ value stands alone, but that the next three percentiles, 80%+ through 60%+, seem to form a group that steps down in value gradually before a bigger drop to the 50%+ percentile. Everything from the 50%+ interval down appears to form a final group.

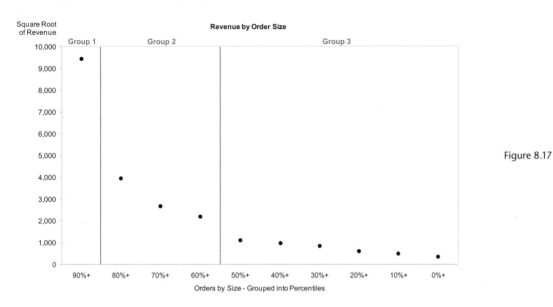

Figure 8.17

Perhaps these groupings will become more apparent if we move on to a logarithmic re-expression.

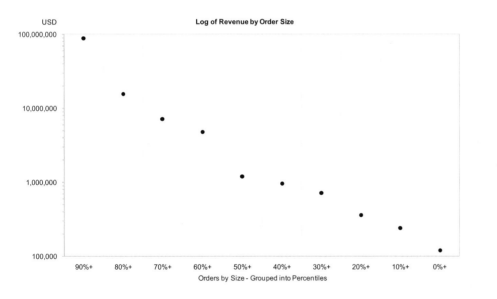

Figure 8.18

Notice that we've once again compressed the high values and spread the low values, which makes the spacing of all the elements in the set closer. The groupings that began to emerge in the square root re-expression are still visible and are now easier to identify and distinguish. If this analysis prompted us to consider a change in our sales efforts to eliminate low-value orders and focus exclusively on high-value orders, the gap below the 60%+ point might be a good place to draw the line.

Even though the log re-expression seems as if it's probably the best and that moving on to the inverse re-expression would reposition the values more than necessary, let's take a look at it anyway. An inverse re-expression reverses the rank order, making the highest value the lowest and the lowest the highest. It does this by dividing a number that is equal to or greater than the highest value by each of the values. In the following example, I have taken the highest value, $89,346,737, and divided it by each of the percentile values to produce the following inverse re-expression:

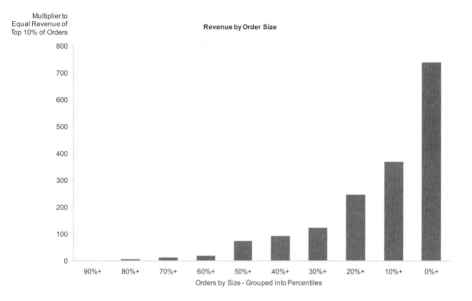

Figure 8.19

As you can see, we have now indeed taken re-expression too far and lost sight of the highest values by compressing them too much. Despite this problem, however, an inverse re-expression sometimes presents values in terms that are easier to wrap our heads around. If values in the millions of dollars were difficult to conceive, it might be helpful to think in terms of how many of the low-value orders it would take to equal what is earned by orders at the high end. In this example, we can see that it takes almost 800 times the amount of revenue earned by the bottom 10% of orders to equal the amount brought in by the top 10% of orders.

In his fascinating book, *Graphic Discovery: A Trout in the Milk and Other Visual Adventures*, Howard Wainer provides a good example of inverse re-expression. His example displays car prices for convertibles in 1997 (derived from a *New York Times* article) extending from a $487,000 Ferrari F50 at the high end (which Wainer includes in a class called "penis substitutes") to a $15,475 Honda del Sol at the low end. To solve the scaling problem and simplify the values, Wainer used an inverse re-expression, which measured how many of each car you could buy with a million dollars. This not only compared these cars in a less abstract manner, it also brought the values closer together in a single graph, scaled from two Ferrari F50's at the low end to 65 Honda del Sol's at the high end. Wainer's solution is elegant in its simplicity.

Using Line Graphs to View Ranking Changes through Time

Although we would never use a line graph to display a single ranking relationship, line graphs are useful when we want to see how a ranking relationship changes over time (that is, a combination of a ranking and a time-series relationship). This technique has been used for quite some time to display results of rowing competitions in the form of what's called a *bumps chart*. Because collegiate rowing competitions in England traditionally take place on narrow rivers that prevent crews from rowing side by side, crews are spaced with 1 ½ boat lengths between them at the start. When one crew rows so fast that it overtakes a crew ahead of it, the overtaken crew must pull over and allow the faster crew to pass. These races are called *bumps*, owing to the fact that a crew signals the fact that it has overtaken another by bumping it in some manner, often with an oar. Bumps competitions are spread across four days. The objective is to advance each day by overtaking one or more crews. The following is an example of a bumps chart, which records the results of these races:

Division 2	Tue	Wed	Thur	Fri	
19 X-Press 3					**Champs**
20 City 3					City 3
21 St Ives					X-Press 3
22 Max'm Entropy					Max'm Entropy
23 Champs					Cantabs 5
24 Cantabs 5					St Ives 1
25 Champs 2					Cantabs 6
26 X-Press 4					Champs 2
27 Isle of Ely					Isle of Ely
28 Cantabs 6					Champs 3
29 Simoco 2					X-Press 4
30 '99 5					Simoco 2
31 Champs 3					St Radegund 1
32 Camb Veterans					**City 4**
33 Cantabs 7					'99 5
34 St Radegund					Leys School
35 Sandwich boat					Sandwich boat

Figure 8.20. Created by Kelly O'Day of www.ProcessTrends.com

Each place where one line crosses another indicates that a boat has passed another. A line that slopes upwards represents the boat that overtook the other. In this example, the only crew that overtook another on every leg of the four-day competition was *Champs*.

A line graph of a similar design can be used to display changes over time in the ranking relationship among a set of items, such as sales people ranked by sales performance. The sole purpose in this case is simply to show changes in ranking, not the actual values (for example, sales amounts in dollars) associated with those changes.

Here's a simple example:

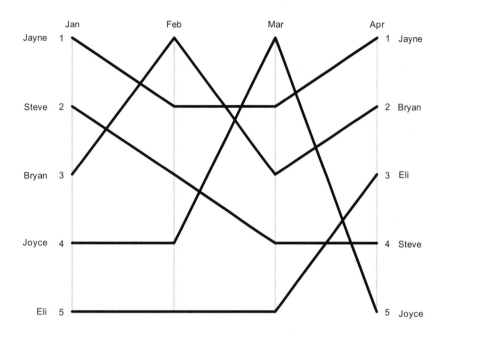

Figure 8.21

The slopes of the lines and their intersections are strong visual cues for changes in rankings. This is a simple graph to construct once you assign ranking positions (1, 2, etc.) to each of the items for each point in time. This example was constructed in Excel using a standard line graph.

9   DEVIATION ANALYSIS

Introduction

Examining how one or more sets of values deviate from a reference set of values, such as a budget, an average, or a prior point in time, is what I call *deviation analysis*. The classic example of deviation analysis involves comparing actual expenses to the expense budget, focusing on how and to what extent they differ. Unfortunately, the way people usually examine these differences doesn't work very well. Here's a typical example:

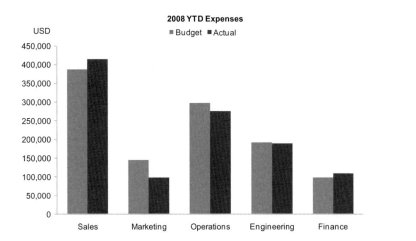

Figure 9.1

To focus on the differences using this graph, we must perform arithmetic in our heads to subtract actual expenses from the budget. This can be avoided by displaying the differences between actual expenses and the budget directly. Here's the same information, this time displayed to directly feature the differences:

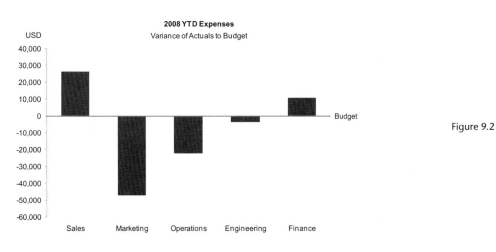

Figure 9.2

"Actuals versus budget" comparisons are the most common example of deviation analysis, but there are many other worthwhile examples. No task is more fundamental to analysis than the act of comparison. Focusing on simple deviations might seem mundane compared to some other types of analysis, such as correlations and distributions, but it is the bread and butter (or, for the health conscious among us, the fruits and vegetables) of quantitative data analysis. A few other useful, common deviation comparisons include:

Compared to	Example
Current target	Actual sales through today compared to what you were aiming for as of today
Future target	Current year-to-date website visits compared to your goal for the entire year
Current forecast	Actual sales through today compared to what you expected by today
Same point in time in the past	The number of riders on the bus system today compared to this day last year
Immediately prior period	The number of new hires this month compared to last month
Standard	The number of manufacturing defects today compared to the number that has been defined as acceptable
Norm	The number of post-surgical complications for a hospital compared to the national average
Other items belonging to the same category	Sales of one product compared to another
Others in the same market	Customers' satisfaction with our services compared to customers' satisfaction with competitors' services

Deviation Analysis Displays

Deviation analysis doesn't require fancy visualizations. The two best graphs for displaying deviations are bar graph and line graphs. In both cases, graphs that feature deviations should display as a reference line the set of values to which to other values will be compared (for example, the budget, when the comparison is between actual expenses and budgeted expenses). When used in deviation displays, reference lines are usually set to a value of 0 (left-hand example below), 0% (middle example below), or 100% (right-hand example below).

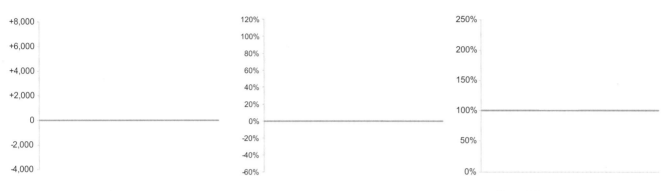

Figure 9.3

When the reference line represents $0, deviations are expressed as positive or negative values. For example, hardware sales of $3,583 in the year 2008 compared to $2,394 in 2007 would be expressed as a deviation of +$1,189. When the reference line is displayed as 0%, deviations are expressed as positive or negative percentages. The deviation described above would be expressed as +50% (that is, $3,583 ÷ $2,394 = 1.5 − 1 = 0.5 or +50%). When the reference line is displayed as 100%, deviations are expressed as percentages of the reference values. The same deviation mentioned above would in this case be expressed as 150% (that is, $3,583 ÷ $2,394 = 1.5 or 150%). The following graphs illustrate the same values displayed in these three ways:

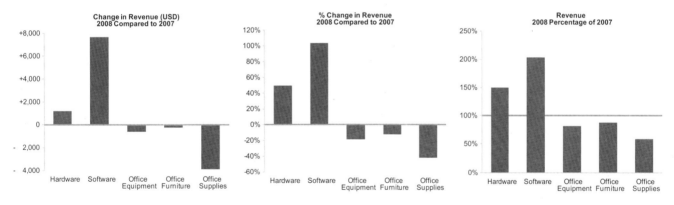

Figure 9.4

Bar Graphs

Bars can be used to encode data along nominal, ordinal (least change to greatest), and interval scales, as illustrated from top to bottom on the following page.

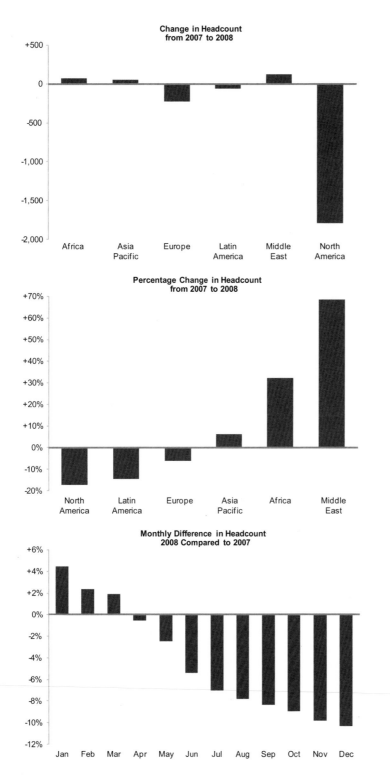

Figure 9.5

Notice how nicely the bars feature the deviations. In the case of the interval scale (the time series on the bottom), the bars focus our attention on each monthly deviation individually, but they don't paint the clearest possible picture of change through time. For this, we'll turn to line graphs.

Line Graphs

Lines should only be used to encode values along an interval scale, such as a time series, and are preferable to bars when you wish to focus on the overall shape of the change rather than on each individual value or comparisons of individual values, as we've previously discussed. In the following example, the same time-series values are displayed using bars above followed by a line below.

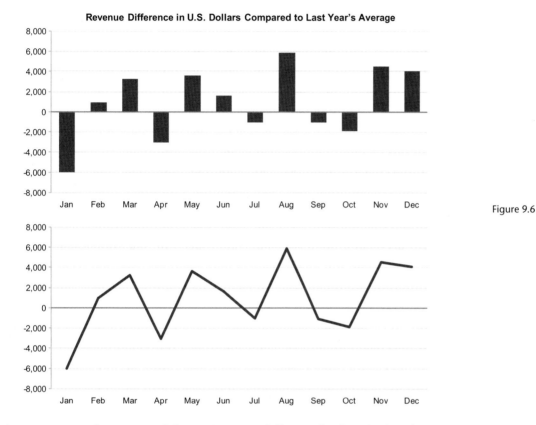

Figure 9.6

As you can see, the pattern of change is easy to follow with a line. Rather than comparing actual revenue to the budget, in the example above each month's revenue has been compared to the previous year's monthly average. In the following example of the same monthly revenue data, each month has been compared to the month of January to show how revenues have changed since the first month of the year.

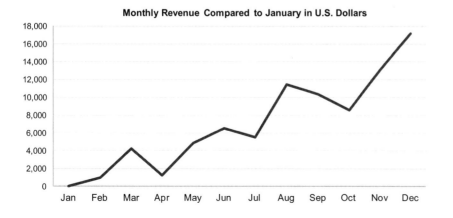

Figure 9.7

Deviation Analysis Techniques and Best Practices

Two practical techniques for squeezing the most from deviation analysis are worth knowing:

- Expressing deviations as percentages
- Comparing deviations to other points of reference

Expressing Deviations as Percentages

In some of the examples that we've examined in this chapter, deviations were expressed as percentages; in others, deviations were expressed as units such as dollars or counts. It's important to recognize that expressing deviations as percentages versus other units of measure can result in quite different pictures of what's going on. Both are useful, but we should know when to use one rather than the other.

One of the advantages of viewing deviations as percentages applies when comparing deviations of more than one set of values because percentages normalize the data sets in a way that can make comparisons easier. In the following graph, deviations between actual expenses and the budget are displayed in dollars for two sets of values: domestic expenses and international expenses.

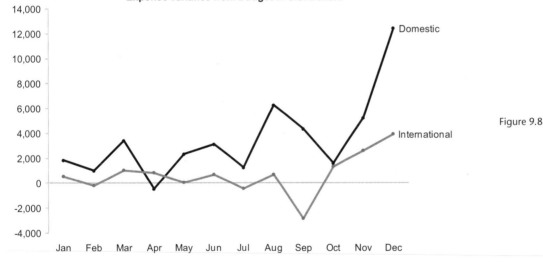

Figure 9.8

When we examine the deviations as dollars, both domestic and international expenses exceeded the budget at the end of the year, but the domestic deviation was much greater. Now, look at the same data, this time expressed as percentage deviation from budget.

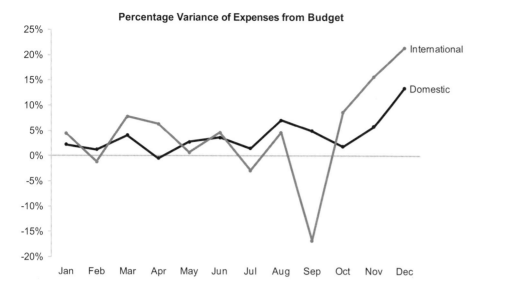

Figure 9.9

Domestic and international have now swapped places throughout much of the year, with international displaying the most extreme deviations at the end of the year. This has happened because the budget for international expenses is much smaller than the budget for domestic expenses, as shown in the following table.

Expenses (USD)	Jan	Feb	Mar	Apr	May	Jun	Jul	Aug	Sep	Oct	Nov	Dec
Domestic Actual	84,853	84,838	88,103	85,072	88,723	90,384	89,374	95,273	94,239	92,394	96,934	105,034
Domestic Budget	83,000	83,830	84,668	85,515	86,370	87,234	88,106	88,987	89,877	90,776	91,684	92,600
International Actual	12,538	12,438	14,934	14,033	13,945	15,938	14,086	15,934	13,945	17,338	19,384	22,394
International Budget	12,000	12,600	13,860	13,200	13,860	15,246	14,520	15,246	16,771	15,972	16,771	18,448

Figure 9.10

Because of the difference in budgeted amounts, a smaller deviation in the amount of international expenses produces a greater percentage deviation than for domestic expenses. If we were determining how well those who manage domestic expenses were doing compared to their international counterparts, percentages would give us a better measure of comparative performance. If we only cared about the excess dollars that were spent, however, the graph that displays dollar differences would better address our needs.

There are times when it is not practical to express deviations as percentages. For instance, if the values that you're comparing to a reference set of values fluctuate dramatically between small and large, this could result in percentages that are huge, such as hundreds or thousands of percent. Percentages work best when most of the values are less than or equal to 100% and exceptions do not exceed a few hundred percent.

Comparing Deviations to Other Points of Reference

It's often useful to see deviations in relation to other points of reference, such as defined standards or statistical norms. It's simple to visualize standards and norms as reference lines or reference regions. In the following example, the red line indicates the threshold of acceptable negative deviation from the revenue budget.

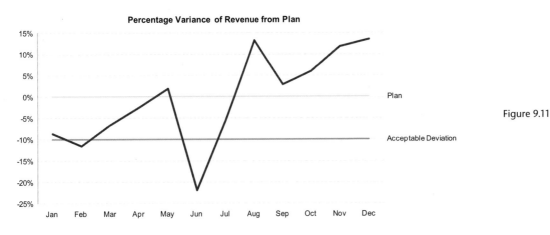

Figure 9.11

In Excel, a reference line such as this can be easily shown in a graph. In this case, in addition to each month's percentage deviation from the plan, the spreadsheet also contains monthly acceptable deviation entries of 10%.

The next example displays how the same set of revenue values deviates from the monthly mean and includes a region of fill color to display one *standard deviation* above and below the mean.

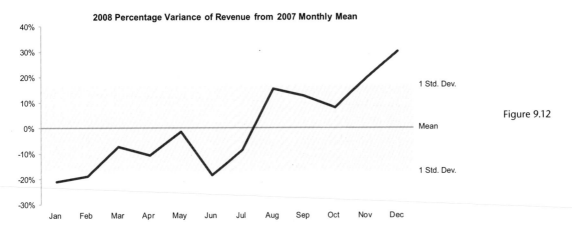

Figure 9.12

If your software doesn't include a simple way to highlight a region using fill color, which is currently the case with Excel, you can use reference lines to mark the top and bottom of the region instead.

10 DISTRIBUTION ANALYSIS

Introduction

Examining sets of quantitative values to see how the values are distributed from lowest to highest or to compare and contrast how multiple sets of values are distributed is a fundamental analytical process. Scientists and engineers analyze distributions routinely, but other organizations, especially businesses, tend to ignore them. This is unfortunate because distributions have important stories to tell. Consider for a moment what it would take for a company to understand how well it is handling shipments to its customers from various warehouses. Many companies would proceed by examining averages.

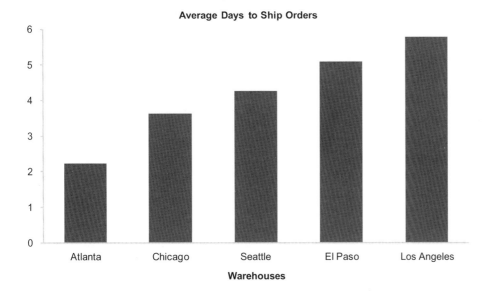

Average Days to Ship Orders

Figure 10.1

But an average, such as the statistical mean, tells us nothing about variability in the number of days these warehouses are taking to ship orders. The mean reduces each warehouse's story to a single number—a measure of center. With an average shipment timeline of 4.2 days, the Seattle warehouse could be keeping some customers waiting 10 days or more, but this fact would remain hidden in the graph above. Measures of average are not enough. The eminent biologist, Stephen Jay Gould, learned a very personal and poignant lesson about the limited view that's contained in averages alone, which he described in the article "The Median Isn't the Message." In July 1982, Gould learned that he was suffering from abdominal mesothelioma, a rare and serious form of cancer, usually associated with exposure to asbestos. After surgery, he asked his doctor to recommend what he could read to learn about his condition but was told that the literature wasn't very helpful. As soon as he could walk, he went immediately to Harvard's medical library to see for himself. After only an hour at the library, the reason for his doctor's attempt to discourage investigation became clear.

> *I realized with a gulp why my doctor had offered that humane advice. The literature couldn't have been more brutally clear: mesothelioma is incurable, with a median mortality of only eight months after discovery. I sat stunned for about fifteen minutes, then smiled and said to myself: so that's why they didn't give me anything to read. Then my mind started to work again, thank goodness.[1]*

Most people, lacking an understanding of statistics, would have remained stunned and slipped into resignation, assuming that they had only eight months to put their affairs in order. As someone who understood statistics, Gould realized that knowing that half the people with his condition survived only eight months or less was not enough, so he roused himself and continued his search for the full story. Later he wrote the following about our tendency to misinterpret measures of central tendency such as means and medians:

> *We still carry the historical baggage of a Platonic heritage that seeks sharp essences and definite boundaries…This Platonic heritage, with its emphasis in clear distinctions and separated immutable entities, leads us to view statistical measures of central tendency wrongly, indeed opposite to the appropriate interpretation in our actual world of variation, shadings, and continua. In short, we view means and medians as the hard "realities," and the variation that permits their calculation as a set of transient and imperfect measurements of this hidden essence. If the median is the reality and variation around the median just a device for its calculation, then "I will probably be dead in eight months" may pass as a reasonable interpretation.*
>
> *Variation itself is nature's only irreducible essence. Variation is the hard reality, not a set of imperfect measures for a central tendency. Means and medians are the abstractions.[2]*

His further investigation revealed a mortality distribution that was extremely skewed, extending to twenty years. After reading the conditions that favored longer survival, he realized that he was an ideal candidate for many more years of life. Revived by this hope, he in fact lived for 20 more very productive years and managed to publish his "Magnum Opus," *The Structure of Evolutionary Theory*, just prior to his death in 2002.

1. The story of Stephen Jay Gould's experience with cancer statistics was found in the CancerGuide, created and maintained by Steve Dunn, at www.cancerguide.org.

2. *Ibid.*

Now, back to the company that is trying to understand and improve its shipping performance. Many companies in this position, realizing that averages alone aren't enough, might use the following display to explore the facts:

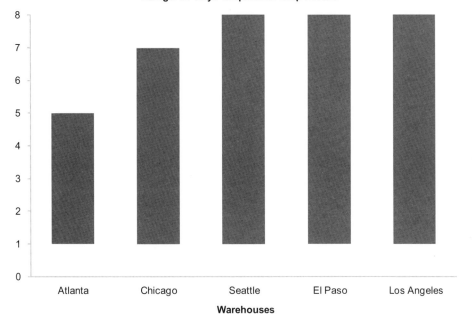

Figure 10.2

The range bars in the graph above tell us the range of days, from least to most, that each warehouse has taken to ship orders. Whereas the mean value only told us the center of the distribution, these range bars only tell us the spread. Something important is still missing. Based on these facts, either of the following lists of values—the number of days it took to ship 20 orders—would fit what we know about shipments from the Seattle warehouse:

1	4	4	4	4	4	4	4	4	4	4	4	4	4	4	4	4	4	4	8
1	1	1	2	2	2	3	3	3	3	4	4	5	5	5	6	7	7	8	8

Figure 10.3

What we lack is sufficient information about the shape of each distribution—where individual values are located throughout the range from lowest to highest. This is an ideal task for a graph. Considering just shipments from Atlanta and Seattle for the moment, notice how much more effectively we can evaluate and compare shipping performance using the two graphs on the following page.

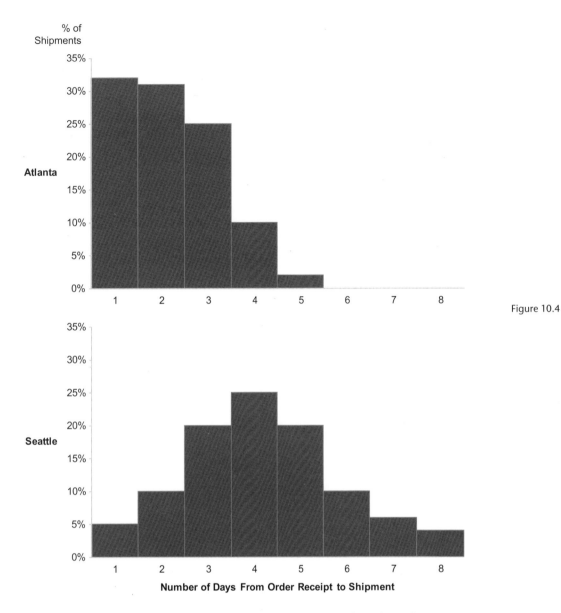

Figure 10.4

Even this simple example illustrates the insights we can glean from data sets by analyzing their distributions. For example, we can tell that most orders are shipped from the Atlanta warehouse on the same day that they're received, with a decreasing number of shipments as the number of days increases, compared to a fairly symmetrical distribution of shipments from Seattle across the range of days, with the greatest percentage occurring on the fourth day. As a data analyst, you can't afford to ignore these important stories. If you've avoided them until now because distribution analysis seemed complicated, you'll soon discover that the basics are easy to learn.

Describing Distributions

We'll begin by looking at the two primary ways of summarizing and describing distributions. The first involves visualization, which is our primary interest, but it is also useful for us to understand the second, which is the way that statisticians summarize and describe distributions using numbers alone. I'll illustrate these concepts using an example that is near and dear to all of our hearts: financial compensation. Here's a list of salaries that will serve as a simple example of compensation paid by a hypothetical company. If employees' names were shown next to the salaries, you would see that this list is arranged alphabetically by last name.

Salaries
35,394
23,982
15,834
88,360
43,993
21,742
19,634
79,293
42,345
35,376
25,384
98,322
17,945
31,954
33,946
23,777
26,345
32,965
49,374
23,596
19,343
32,063
18,634
26,033
34,934

Figure 10.5

This alphabetical list of salaries reveals little about the distribution. More is revealed when we sort the salaries in order from the highest at the top to the lowest at the bottom, as shown below.

Sorted Salaries
98,322
88,360
79,293
49,374
43,993
42,345
35,394
35,376
34,934
33,946
32,965
32,063
31,954
26,345
26,033
25,384
23,982
23,777
23,596
21,742
19,634
19,343
18,634
17,945
15,834

Figure 10.6

Now we can more easily see that these salaries extend from $15,834 to $98,322. Also, if we look a little more closely, we can also see that there's a significant gap that separates the three highest salaries from the fourth highest. In other words, we have some exceptions at the high end of the range that probably qualify as true statistical outliers. We'll continue with this and related examples as we proceed now to the key characteristics of distributions when visualized.

Key Visual Characteristics of Distributions

Three characteristics summarize the distribution of a set of values when the distribution is displayed visually:

- Spread
- Center
- Shape

SPREAD

Spread is a simple measure of dispersion, that is, how spread out the values are. It is the full range of values from lowest to highest, calculated as the difference between the two. The previous list of salaries has a spread of $74,488 ($98,322 minus $15,834). In the following example, I've increased the company's size to a few hundred employees but kept the same salary spread.

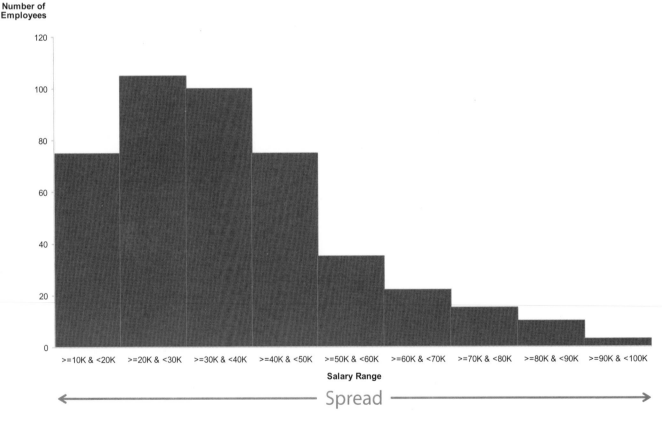

Spread is the easiest characteristic of a distribution to discern. From it we learn the lowest value, the highest value, and the distance between them.

Figure 10.7

CENTER

The center or central tendency is an estimate of the middle of a set of values, that is, an attempt to identify the value that is most typical. Sometimes called *location* by statisticians, it is an anchor of sorts for the set of values as a whole, a single number that summarizes the complete set of values. Most summaries of a distribution revolve around some measure of center, usually calculated as the median or the mean, which are both measures of average but are often quite different in value. Frederick Hartwig and Brian E. Dearing explain that "to be effective, measures of location should identify the value most characteristic of a set of cases, the one value which best describes the entire set of values, or, in other words, the value around which the other values are distributed."[3] A little later we'll look at the advantage that medians often have over means as a representation of what's typical when we analyze distributions.

3. *Exploratory Data Analysis*, Frederick Hartwig with Brian E. Dearing, Sage Publications, Inc.: Thousand Oaks CA, 1979, p. 13.

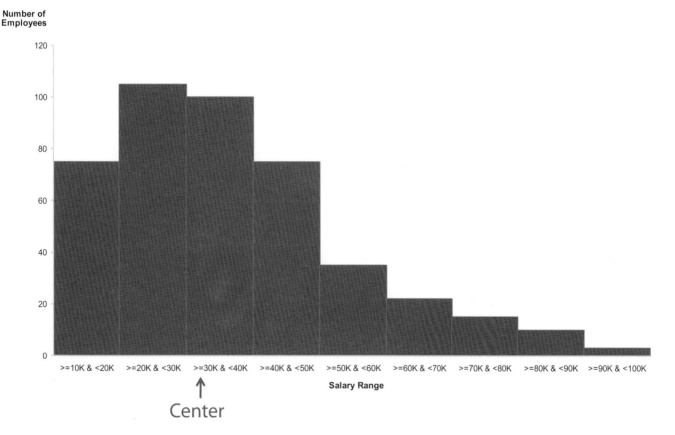

Figure 10.8

By identifying the center in a data set's spread, we can, even without viewing the data graphically, begin to guess the distribution's shape. In this particular salary example, because the center is closer to the low end of the spread than the high end, we know that the values tend to congregate closer to the low end. The graph shows us that in fact there is a clear peak closer to the low (left) end of the range.

SHAPE

The final primary visual characteristic of a distribution is its shape, which shows us where the values are located throughout the spread. Perhaps most are packed tightly nearer to the left end (the low values), as illustrated in our salary example. Or perhaps they are evenly distributed across the full range, with about the same number of people falling into each $10,000 interval.

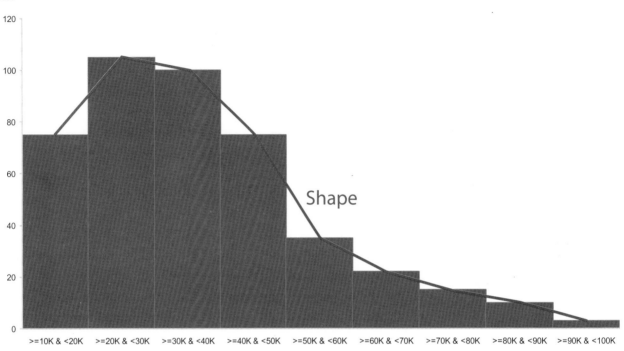

Figure 10.9

The shape of this salary distribution can be summarized using words alone as "single peaked near the low end of the spread and skewed to the right (that is, in the direction of the long tail, toward the higher values)." Words can't, however, come close to the description that a good picture provides.

Statistical Summaries of Distributions

Statisticians often summarize distributions using numbers alone. Just like graphical representations, these summaries revolve around a measure of center and include measures of dispersion that can be used to get a sense of shape.

A simple version is sometimes called a *3-value summary of distribution*. It consists of one number, which represents the center, and two numbers, which represent dispersion. For example, this could consist of the median, lowest, and highest values, as illustrated below:

Low	Median		High
15,834	31,954		98,322

Figure 10.10

A slightly more complex but much more informative version is called the *5-value summary of distribution*. Here's an example:

```
           25th      75th
        Percentile Percentile
    Low        Median                              High
    ├─────┼────────┼─────────────────────────────────┤
   15,834    31,954                                98,322
          23,596   35,394
```

Figure 10.11

This 5-value summary tells us much more about the shape of the distribution. The 25th percentile is the point at and below which 25% of the salaries (the lowest salaries) are located along the quantitative scale. The fact that the value of the 25th percentile is near the midpoint between the lowest value and the median tells us that the bottom half of salaries are fairly evenly distributed between the lowest and median values. The middle 50% of salaries, which are those on or between the 25th and 75th percentiles, called the *mid-spread*, are all located well below $57,078, the value that falls midway between the lowest and highest salaries.

The story told by the top half of salaries, however, is quite different. The long distance across which the top 25% of salaries are spread (from the 75th percentile to the highest value) indicates a great deal of variability in salaries at the top end. Usually when we see such a long distance associated with the bottom or top 25% of the values relative to the other sections, it is due in part to the presence of outliers. In this case, it is due to the three top salaries, which are well above the others.

Later, when we examine various ways to display distributions, especially box plots, we'll make use of both the 3-value and 5-value distribution summaries to construct them.

Rather than using the lowest and highest values to represent dispersion, statisticians often use standard deviations. I'm sticking with the full spread of low-to-high value and percentiles to illustrate the concept of dispersion, mostly because they're easier for non-statisticians to understand.

Distribution Patterns

The patterns that concern us when analyzing distributions fall into two main categories:

- Shape
- Outliers

Shape

If we examine distributions closely, the number of possible shapes they can form is infinite. Most distribution analysis, fortunately, is conducted at a summarized level where a finite number of meaningful patterns can be identified. We can identify these patterns by asking the following questions in order:

1. Curved or flat?
2. If curved, upward or downward?
3. If curved upward, single or multiple peaked?
4. If single peaked, symmetrical or skewed?
5. Concentrations?
6. Gaps?

CURVED OR FLAT?

The first and easiest characteristic to identify of a distribution's overall shape is whether it is curved or flat.

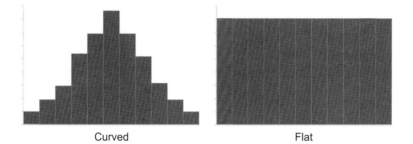

Curved   Flat

Figure 10.12

Most distributions are curved in some manner. Flat distributions, also called *uniform* distributions, maintain a nearly constant frequency from beginning to end. Consider a distribution along an age scale (0-9 years, 10-19 years, and so on), which we're using to describe purchases of a particular product by buyers' ages. If the frequency of purchases remains roughly the same across all age groups, we could say with a fair degree of confidence that age has no effect on purchases of this product. We can abandon age as a variable of interest when analyzing sales of this product.

The illustration of a flat distribution above is perfectly uniform, which you will probably never encounter in real data. Uniform distributions usually exhibit ups and downs, but they all fall within a fairly narrow range, such as the example below.

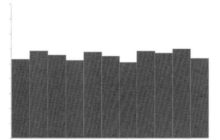

Figure 10.13

IF CURVED, UPWARD OR DOWNWARD?

If the distribution's shape is curved, the next thing to look for is whether it curves upward or downward.

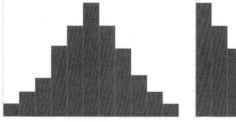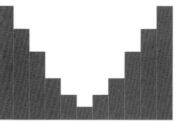

Upward   Downward

Figure 10.14

When the shape is curved upward, the number of items (also called the *frequency*) begins relatively low, increases to a peak, and then decreases until relatively low again. No distribution pattern is more common than this. A familiar example is the distribution of intelligence quotient (IQ) across the population. IQ's at both the low and high ends of the scale are found with less frequency than those in the middle. Using our product sales by age example from before, an upward curve would indicate that product sales start low with children but increase with age to a high point near the middle of life and then decrease from there as people grow into old age. The pattern that's illustrated above is perfectly symmetrical, but it need not be. As we'll see in a moment, this pattern can be symmetrical or skewed.

Distributions that curve downward—those that exhibit a relatively high frequency at the low end, followed by a dip in the middle, and then an increase to a higher frequency at the end of the scale—are less common, though certainly not rare. One example that comes to mind is the amount of leisure time that people enjoy throughout their lives, from infancy until their senior years. Children usually enjoy a great deal, but as they move into adulthood, leisure time usually diminishes and then increases again in old age with retirement. If product sales exhibited this pattern across age groups, this would mean that the product is unusual in that it is popular among children and old folks but not with those in the middle of life. It would be interesting to understand why those in the middle of life are uninterested when those on both sides of them seem to like the product.

IF CURVED UPWARD, ONE OR MORE PEAKS?

Patterns that curve upward rise to a peak, and usually only one, but distributions occasionally exhibit multiple peaks.

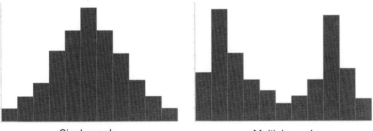

Single peak   Multiple peaks

Figure 10.15

Distributions with multiple peaks usually have only two although more are certainly possible. When two peaks are present, the distribution is called *bi-modal. Mode* is a statistical measure of central tendency, which refers to the interval along the categorical scale with the highest frequency. A bi-modal distribution has two intervals with high frequencies. They don't need to be equal in frequency, but must both stand out as significant peaks compared to the rest. If product sales by age exhibited the bi-modal pattern shown above, it would tell us that our product sells well among the young although a little less well among the youngest, declines during the middle years, grows again as people approach old age, and then declines again among the oldest.

IF SINGLE PEAKED, SYMMETRICAL OR SKEWED?

If the distribution is single peaked, as is most often the case, we should next look for the location of the peak. Is it near the center, the right, or the left?

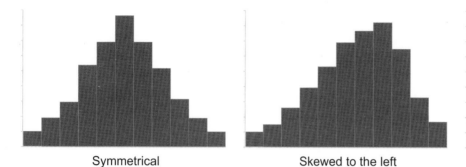

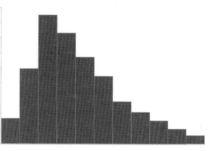

Symmetrical   Skewed to the left   Skewed to the right

Figure 10.16

If the peak is near the center, the distribution's shape is symmetrical, and we have what is usually called a *normal* or a *bell-shaped curve*. Many distributions exhibit this shape, including IQ scores, which peak at 100. Distributions are skewed when the peak is nearer to the right or left rather than the midway point. If the peak appears on the right we describe it, counter-intuitively, as skewed to the left, because skew refers to the direction of the long tail, not the peak. A right-skewed distribution often describes the pattern of a product's sales throughout its life: sales start off slow but increase rapidly as the product becomes known, and eventually reach a peak and then trail off gradually for the remainder of the product's life until it is finally discontinued.

CONCENTRATIONS?

Somewhat independent of the general patterns that we've examined so far, another meaningful feature of a distribution's shape involves the presence of concentrations: areas where the values are noticeably higher than others.

Concentration

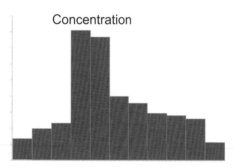

Figure 10.17

In the example above, the high concentration of values in the fourth and fifth intervals from the left obviously qualify as a peak, but concentrations don't always correspond to a predominant peak. In the following example, there is a predominant peak on the left, so the distribution is skewed to the right, but there are also high concentrations of values near the middle and near the end. Something is definitely going on here that ought to be investigated.

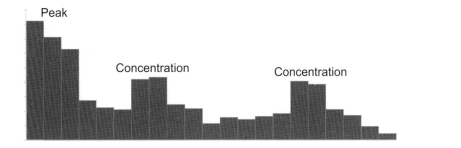

Figure 10.18

GAPS?

The last common pattern to look for is the presence of gaps in the values: areas where there are few or no values relative to surrounding areas.

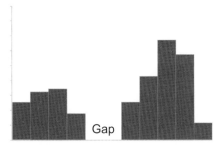

Figure 10.19

If the graph above represents product sales by age, a gap in the middle age group such as the one we see here should really arouse our curiosity. What could possibly account for this complete lack of sales to the age groups near the middle of the distribution?

Outliers

As with all types of analysis, outliers should always get our attention. Remember that outliers are values that fall beyond the statistical norm. The distance between these extraordinary values and those that are typical is too great to ignore. In the example below we see a gap, but beyond the gap at the high end of the distribution live a few values that are unusual. Outliers in distributions are almost always found near one end or the other.

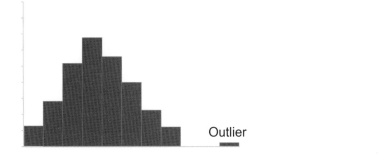

Figure 10.20

If the example above displays the distribution of salaries in a company, a few people obviously make a great deal more money than what's typical. Thresholds beyond which should be considered outliers can be calculated in several ways. One of the simplest, which serves as a good rule of thumb, involves taking the mid-spread—the distance between the 25th and 75th percentiles—multiplying it by 1.5, and then identifying the thresholds by subtracting that amount from the 25th percentile to mark the lower threshold and adding it to the 75th percentile to mark the upper threshold. Using our salary distribution example from before (shown again below), we can use this simple method to set an upper threshold of $53,091 for identifying outliers. The 75th percentile value of $35,394 minus the 25th percentile value of $23,596 equals a mid-spread of $11,798. Multiplying the midspread by 1.5 produces $17,697, which we then add to the 75th percentile to get the upper threshold of $53,091, which tells us that at least one outlier and probably more exist at the high end. Subtracting this same amount from the 25th percentile gives us a lower threshold of $5,899, which falls below the lowest value on our scale, which tells us that there are no outliers at the low end.

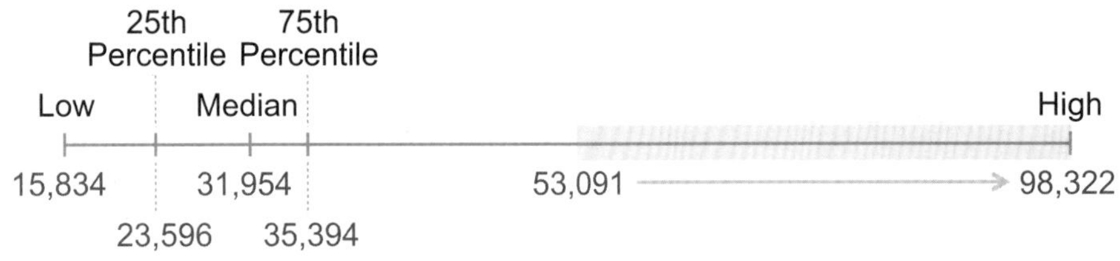

Figure 10.21. This simple rule of thumb for identifying outliers was suggested in *Understanding Robust and Exploratory Data Analysis*, Hoaglin, Mosteller & Tukey, editors, John Wiley & Sons, New York NY, 1983, p. 39.

Distribution Displays

Distributions can be displayed in several ways. Each has advantages for particular situations. We'll take a look at the different approaches and identify the proper use for each.

Distribution displays can be divided into two basic types: those used to view a distribution of a single set of values and those used to view and compare multiple distributions. We'll examine four of each type.

Single Distribution Displays

Three of the best ways to display distributions involve means that are already familiar. Even though each of these graphs has a special name when used to display a distribution, each makes use of old friends—bars, lines, or points. Only one, the stem-and-leaf plot, departs from this familiar territory, but it's simple to understand. Here are the four types of single distribution displays:

- Histograms
- Frequency Polygons
- Strip Plots
- Stem-and-Leaf Plots

HISTOGRAMS

When bars are used to display a distribution, the graph is called a *histogram*. The X-axis usually hosts a categorical scale (that is, a scale that labels what's being measured), which displays numeric intervals or "bins" of values. The Y-axis contains a quantitative scale, which counts the number of values (or measures the percentage of items) that appear in each interval. Here's a typical example, which counts the number of employees in a company by age along a scale that groups them into intervals of 10 years each:

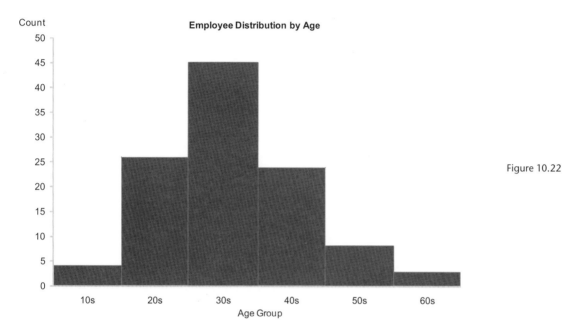

Figure 10.22

A histogram is the most common means to display a distribution. As you can see, it is nothing more than a bar graph, which in this case is being used to count the frequency of values that appear in a sequential series of quantitative bins (intervals). Unlike bar graphs that are used for other purposes, bars in histograms usually touch one another to suggest the contiguous connection between each sequential interval, that is, the fact that the intervals divide a continuous range of values.

Histograms do a good job of displaying the overall shape of a distribution while also making it easy to compare the magnitudes of individual intervals, such as the age groups above. Because histograms support both of these analytical tasks, they are preferred by most analysts.

What we can't see, however, is a measure of the distribution's center, nor can we precisely see the distribution's spread. By looking at this histogram, can you determine the median or the mean? What are the youngest and oldest employees' ages? It would be useful to have these values marked in some way on the graph itself, such as in the example on the next page, which includes the lowest value, the 25th percentile, the median, the 75th percentile, and the highest value.

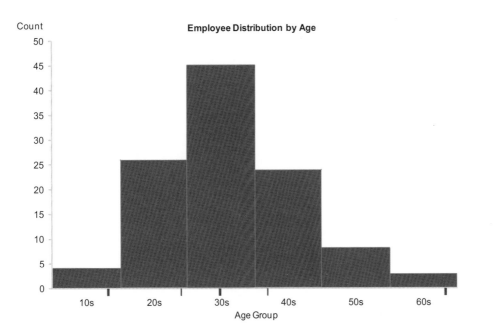

Figure 10.23

In this example, the three thick red lines mark the low, median, and high values in the distribution, and the thin red lines mark the 25th and 75th percentiles. If your software is able to enhance histograms in a similar manner, what you'll learn from them will increase.

FREQUENCY POLYGONS

When a line graph is used to display a distribution, it goes by the unfortunate name *frequency polygon*. This name is unfortunate because it puts an unfriendly and intimidating face on a simple display. Here's the same employee distribution by age that we saw above, this time displayed as a line:

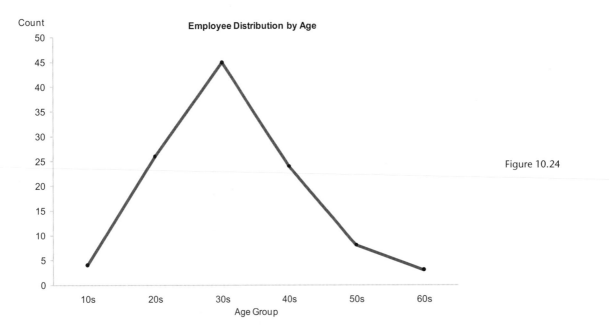

Figure 10.24

The strength of a frequency polygon is its ability to focus our attention almost exclusively on the distribution's shape. It does this well because there is only the line, which traces the shape, and nothing else to distract us. It does not, however, support magnitude comparisons between intervals as well as the histogram does, and it suffers from the same problems as the histogram in that its lacks a measure of center and an accurate measure of spread. Just as with the histogram, the frequency polygon's usefulness would be enhanced if we could see specific values such as the lowest, median, and highest.

STRIP PLOTS

Points such as dots can be used to display each individual value in a distribution, laid out along the interval scale, in a graph that's called a *strip plot*. Think of this graph as a one-dimensional scatterplot, that is, a scatterplot with only one scale rather than the usual two. The example below, which displays the same employee age data as above, was constructed using Excel, simply by selecting a scatterplot (what Excel calls an "XY Scatter") and selecting only one data set and associating it with the X-axis:

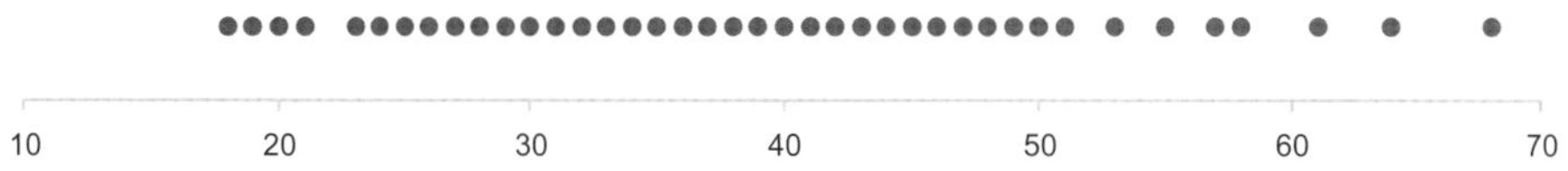

Figure 10.25

Strip plots provide details that most distribution displays lack. We can see each value, and, unlike histograms and frequency polygons, strips plots allow us to see the lowest and highest values. They provide these details at the expense of a clear overview of the distribution's shape, however.

If we want to lay out the distribution of a small set of values in a way that lets us see the values individually, strip plots can be quite useful. Not long ago, I had clients who needed to monitor the performance of about 10 hospitals on a dashboard. They needed to see how performance scores such as overall patient care were distributed across all the hospitals but in a way that made it possible to pick out the performance of individual hospitals, such as the worst performing and best performing. They also needed a way to compare individual hospitals to one another and to average performance overall. I introduced the strip plot to them, and they loved it. They use it not only to compare how hospitals are currently doing, but also how hospitals' performance in relation to one another has changed through time, using a time series of strip plots, which I'll illustrate a little later.

When multiple values in a distribution are the same or nearly the same, which is the case in the employee age example above, strip plots can suffer from occlusion, which is the inability to see some individual values because they are hidden behind others. This problem can be alleviated by (1) removing the fill color in the points, and (2) jittering the points. Remember that jittering separates overlapping values by slightly changing the values so they no longer occupy the same exact space. These steps have been applied to the strip plot below:

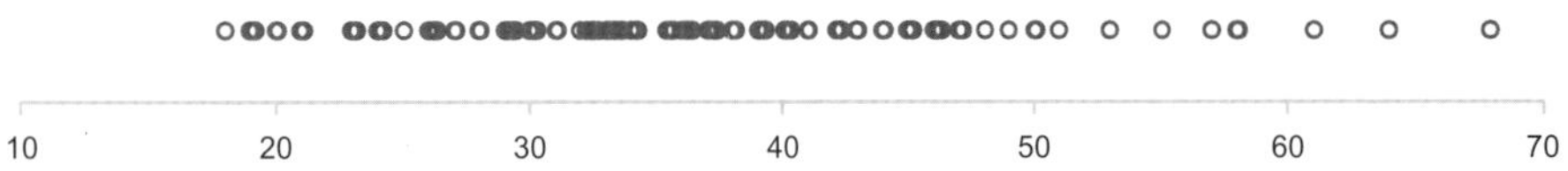

Figure 10.26

Just as with histograms and frequency polygons, when a measure of center and measures such as the 25th and 75th percentiles are shown on a strip plot, its usefulness is enhanced.

STEM-AND-LEAF PLOTS

And now for something completely different. Actually, *stem-and-leaf plots* only seem completely different at first glance, for they have much in common with histograms. Here's an example, once again displaying the employee age distribution:

```
1|8 9 9 9
2|0 0 1 1 3 3 3 4 4 4 5 6 6 6 6 6 7 7 8 8 9 9 9 9 9
3|0 0 0 0 1 1 2 2 2 2 2 2 3 3 3 3 3 3 3 3 4 4 4 4 5 5 5 5 6 6 6 6 7 7 7 7 8 8 9 9 9 9
4|0 0 0 0 1 1 2 2 2 3 3 4 4 5 5 5 6 6 6 6 7 7 8 9
5|0 0 1 3 5 7 8 8
6|1 4 8
```

Figure 10.27

Stem-and-leaf plots were invented by John Tukey, the brilliant Princeton statistician who in the 1970s introduced visual analysis methods that go by the name *exploratory data analysis* (EDA). Tukey invented the stem-and-leaf plot as a quick means to examine a distribution that could be produced with nothing more than pencil and paper. It combines summary and detail information in a single display. Here's how it works. The digits to the left of the line are called the stem and those to the right are the leaf.

Stem Leaf
```
1|8 9 9 9
2|0 0 1 1 3 3 3 4 4 4 5 6 6 6 6 6 7 7 8 8 9 9 9 9 9
3|0 0 0 0 1 1 2 2 2 2 2 2 3 3 3 3 3 3 3 3 4 4 4 4 5 5 5 5 6 6 6 6 7 7 7 7 8 8 9 9 9 9
4|0 0 0 0 1 1 2 2 2 3 3 4 4 5 5 5 6 6 6 6 7 7 8 9
5|0 0 1 3 5 7 8 8
6|1 4 8
```

Figure 10.28

Each individual value is recorded as a combination of stem and leaf digits. For example, the first employee's age, which appears in the top row on the left, is 18. This is formed by taking the stem digit "1" and combining it with the first leaf digit "8". Each stem value in this example represents an interval of 10 years: 1 represents employees who are in their teens, 2 represents employees who are in their 20s, and so on. The second value in the first row is 19, as are the third and fourth values. In other words, there are four employees who are in their teens. One is 18 years old, and the other three are 19 years old. Moving down to the second row, the first employee is 20, and so on.

Stem-and-leaf plots work well for relatively small data sets, but, as you can imagine, become unwieldy with large data sets. If you turn a stem-and-leaf plot on its side, it looks a lot like a histogram, using columns of numbers to form what appear in a histogram as bars.

Figure 10.29

To construct a stem-and-leaf plot, we begin with a sorted list of values and determine an appropriate place to divide them into stem intervals. With the employee age data, because all ages are only two digits, there was a simple, logical choice: to divide ages between the first and second digits, with each stem representing an interval of ten years. With larger numbers, we must decide where to split the values to form the best interval ranges. In the following example of interest rates, each consisting of a whole number followed by three decimal digits, I chose to use the whole number as the stem and the decimal digits as the leaf:

```
3 | 375 500 625 750 750 875 875 875
4 | 125 125 250 250 250 375 375 500 500 500 625 625 750 750 750 875
5 | 125 125 125 250 250 250 250 375 375 500 500 500 625 625 625 750 750 875 875
6 | 125 125 125 125 250 250 250 250 375 375 500 500 625 625 750 750 875
7 | 125 125 125 125 250 250 250 250 250 250 375 500 625 750
8 | 125 125 125 125 125 250 250 250 250
```

Figure 10.30

Regardless of how large the values are, I advocate a simple approach to constructing stem-and-leaf plots that makes them easy to interpret. This approach works as follows:

- Assign from 1 to 2 digits to the stem
- Assign from 1 to 3 digits to the leaf
- Use the line to represent the decimal point
- Round numbers to a level indicated by a multiplier (for example, "x1,000", which instructs the reader to interpret the actual value by multiplying the combined stem and leaf number by 1,000)

In the employee age example, the multiplier is 10 (that is, intervals of 10 years). For example, you can take the first value of 1.8 (the stem digit, followed by a decimal point where the line appears, followed finally by the leaf digit) and multiply it by 10 to get the value 18. The interest rate example has a multiplier of 1. Below is an example that has much larger numbers: dollars in millions. Each value represents sales revenue in a particular state.

Revenue per State
(x1,000,000 USD)

```
0 | 7 8 8 9 9 9
1 | 0 0 1 3 4 4 5 7 7 8 9
2 | 1 1 2 3 3 4 5 5 6 6 7 8 9
3 | 0 0 1 2 3 3 5 8
4 | 0 1 3 5 8
5 | 1 6 9
6 | 2 2 4
7 | 1
```

Figure 10.31

The state with the lowest revenue only earned $700,000, while the one with the highest earned $7,100,000. Rather than including every digit of the sales revenue numbers to show the exact dollar amount, for distribution analysis purposes I chose to round state revenues to the nearest $100,000.

When you want to examine a distribution that consists of 100 values or less in a way that summarizes it without losing sight of the details, and especially if you must construct the display by hand (such as on a napkin in a restaurant), a stem-and-leaf plot is a handy tool.

Multiple Distribution Displays

When we need to examine and compare multiple distributions, such as salary distributions for several years, we can either use multiple instances of one of the graphs we've just examined, something I call a distribution deviation graph, or another one of Tukey's inventions: the *box plot*. We'll consider each of the following graphs for displaying multiple distributions:

- Box plots
- Multiple strip plots
- Frequency polygons
- Distribution deviation graphs

BOX PLOTS

The simplest possible way to display multiple distributions uses *range bars*, illustrated below.

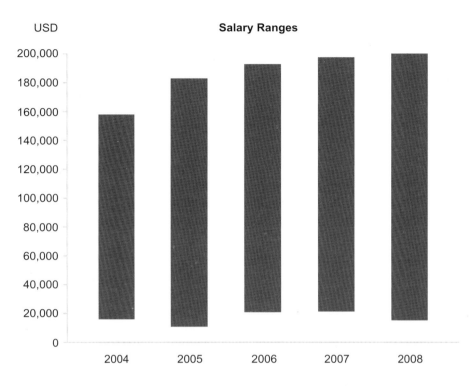

Figure 10.32

Range bars are never adequate, however, because they reveal only the distribution's spread while ignoring its center and shape. Box plots are a rich extension of range bars, which anyone can learn to use with a little instruction and practice. Below is an example of a box plot, which I've kept simple for now by encoding a single distribution, of the salary data we looked at previously.

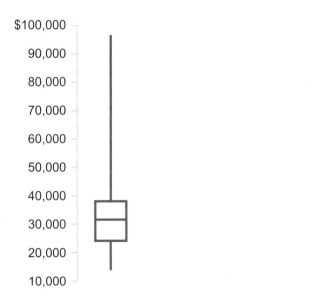

Figure 10.33

Here's an example of one of these boxes with its parts labeled:

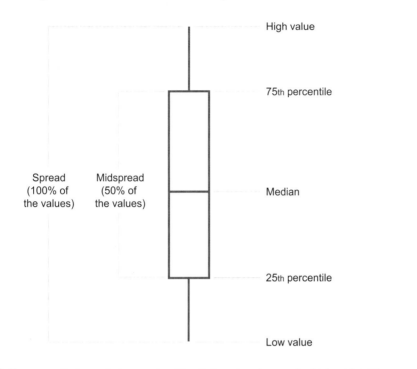

High value

75th percentile

Spread
(100% of
the values)

Midspread
(50% of
the values)

Median

Figure 10.34

25th percentile

Low value

The full name of a box plot, as coined by Tukey, is a *box-and-whisker plot*. The lines that encode the top and bottom ranges of values are called whiskers, and the rectangle in the middle, which encodes the midspread, is called the box. If box plots are foreign to you, and perhaps a bit intimidating, I guarantee that it will only take a moment to learn how to read them. Given how much they can tell us about distributions, they are quite elegant yet simple in design. This particular example graphically displays the equivalent of a 5-value distribution summary.

Returning briefly to the salary example (Figure 10.33), take a moment to list the various facts that it reveals about the distribution of salaries.

· · · · · · · ·

Let's see how you did. First, this graph tells us that the full range of salaries is quite large, extending from around $14,000 on the low end to around $97,000 on the high end. Second, we can see that more people earn salaries toward the lower rather than the higher end of the spread. This is revealed by the fact that the median, which is approximately $32,000, is closer to the bottom of the spread than the top. The middle half (midspread) of employees earn between $25,000 and $38,000, which is definitely closer to the lower end of the overall range. The 25% of employees who earn the lowest salaries are grouped tightly together across a relatively small $10,000 range. But look now at the great distance across which the top 25% of salaries are distributed. This tells us that, as we proceed up the salary scale, there are probably fewer and fewer people in each interval along the scale, such as in the intervals from $60,000 to $70,000, $70,000 to $80,000, and $90,000 to $100,000. Overall, salaries are not evenly spread across the entire range; they are tightly grouped near the lower end and spread more sparsely toward the upper end where the salaries are more extreme compared to the norm. Not too shabby for a display that consists of a simple box and a couple of lines.

Using a box plot to view a single distribution isn't very useful. Other distribution displays do this better. In most instances, however, no form of distribution display supports the examination and comparison of several distributions better than box plots. The following example illustrates how rich a story a good box plot can tell:

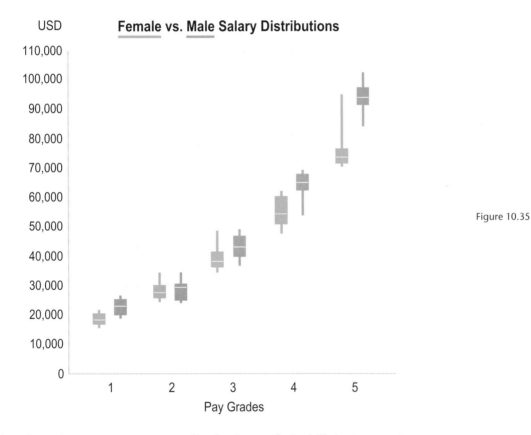

Figure 10.35

Take a few minutes now to test your distribution analysis skills by interpreting this story about male versus female salaries in five different pay grades. Make a list of the facts, and then try to put into a sentence or two the story about pay equity that lives in this graph.

· · · · · · ·

Here are three facts that I noticed:

- Women are typically paid less than men in all salary grades.
- The disparity in salaries between men and women becomes increasingly greater as salaries increase.
- Salaries vary the most for women in the higher salary grades.

Sometimes doing something as simple as changing the order of categorical items in a graph makes a difference in what we see. Below are two versions of the same box plot: the one on the left is what we just looked at above. In the one on the right, the order of males and females has been switched.

Figure 10.36

The graph on the left displays a pleasing curve, beginning in the left bottom corner and sweeping up to the right top corner. Our eyes love nice continuous lines and curves. Because of this, the disparity between male and female salaries is not nearly as noticeable and startling as it is in the graph on the right because of the jaggedness of the curve. Just as with bar and line graphs, it is often useful to compare distributions in a box plot to ranges of the norm or defined standards. In the next example, the actual distribution of salaries is compared to prescribed salary ranges for each pay grade. This allows us to see that some men in pay grades 1 and 5 are being paid salaries that exceed the prescribed ranges.

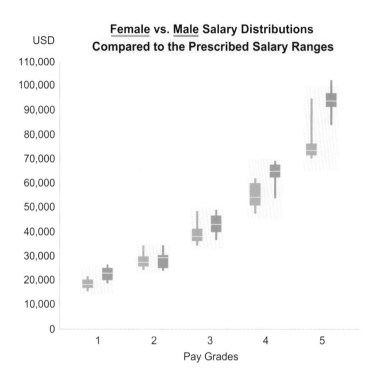

Figure 10.37. This graph is based on a winning design that was submitted by Christopher Hanes to a data visualization competition that I judged in 2005 for *DM Review* magazine.

Before ending our look at box plots, I should mention that most software products that support box plots add another element to the display: the separation of outliers from data in the normal range, which was part of Tukey's original design. Going back once more to the single salary distribution example, a box plot might look like this:

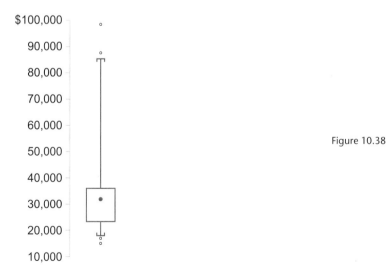

Figure 10.38

The ends of the whiskers are often capped using something like the ⊔ shapes that appear in this example. I personally think that end caps are unnecessary and that box plots are cleaner without them, but they are conventional and certainly acceptable. The center is often marked with a dot rather than a short line, which is not ideal, because a line can mark the value more precisely, but a dot is sufficient. The most significant addition to this box plot involves the small dots that are located beyond the whiskers, which mark the outliers. In this example, outliers have been defined as all values that fall either below the 5th percentile on the low end or above the 95th percentile on the high end, resulting in two outliers on each end. This means that the whiskers, which represented the lowest and highest 25% of the values in previous examples, now only extend to the 5th percentile at the bottom and the 95th percentile at the top, with each representing 20% of the values.

Although it isn't always necessary to display outliers separately in a box plot, it is generally useful for analytical purposes despite the complexity that it adds to the display. Software products that support box plots usually allow us to select various ways to calculate measures of center (such as the median or mean), ends of the box (such as the 25th and 75th percentiles or one standard deviation below and above the mean), and ends of the whiskers (such as the 5th and 95th percentiles or two standard deviations below and above the mean).

MULTIPLE STRIP PLOTS

When describing strip plots before, I mentioned an example that used multiple strip plots to show how the health-care performances of 10 hospitals differed from one another and changed through time. Here's how this might look across four quarters:

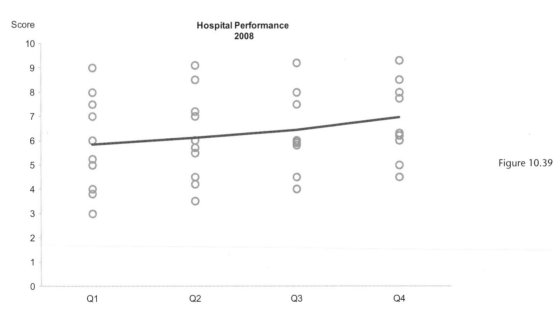

Figure 10.39

In this example, the mean of each quarterly distribution of health-care scores is displayed as a line, so we can see how overall performance has changed. At a glance we can tell that the distribution's spread from the lowest to the highest values in Q4 is less than it was in Q1. This has happened because the lowest scores have risen. The fact that we haven't connected the scores of each hospital with a line eliminates clutter and encourages us to focus on the distributions in given quarters and how they've changed. If we do want to track the changing performance of a particular hospital, however, connecting that hospital's values with a line would do the job, as I've done below.

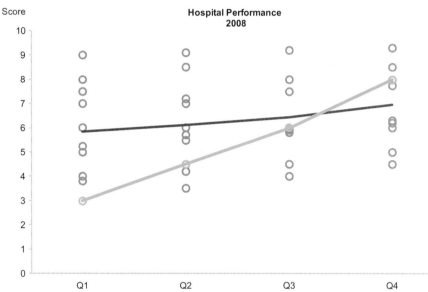

Figure 10.40

The ability to click on any dot and have the full series of values for that hospital automatically connected and highlighted in this manner would be a nice feature. You can simulate this effect somewhat in Excel by using a regular line graph with fairly large data points, all of the same color, and removing the lines (or making them very light and thin). In Excel, when you click on any data point, the entire series of data points is selected (as shown in the screen capture on the following page, indicated by the four light blue dots around each of the points in the selected series), and when you hover over a data point with the mouse, a pop-up box appears, which lists the name of the data series, the categorical item (Q1 in this case), and the value. Although the level of highlighting is subtle in Excel when a data series is selected, it works well enough to let us track how the series of values changed through time.

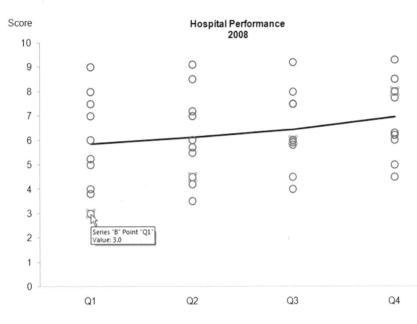

Figure 10.41

When we want to analyze the distribution of a small set of values as they change through time in a way that lets us maintain sight of the individual values in the distribution, strip plots are a simple and effective solution.

FREQUENCY POLYGONS

When we want to compare the shapes of multiple distributions, line graphs can often support this process nicely—either with multiple lines (one per distribution) in a single graph or as a trellis arrangement of multiple line graphs. This first example allows us to compare the timeliness of shipments from five warehouses:

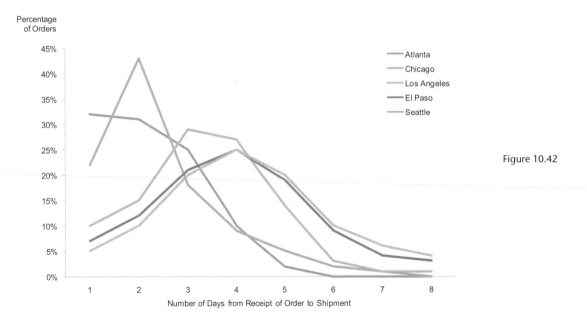

Figure 10.42

As long as there aren't too many lines, this display works fairly well although it is a little difficult to isolate any one line from the others to study its shape exclusively because the presence of the other lines is distracting. To solve this problem, a trellis arrangement of line graphs can be used, as illustrated below:

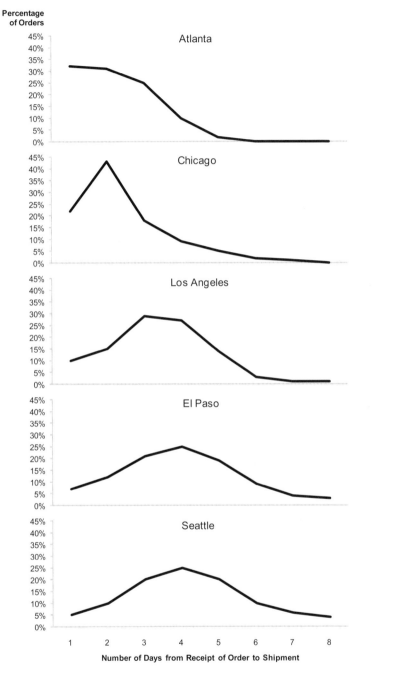

Figure 10.43

As you can see, it is much easier to compare the shapes of these distributions using a trellis arrangement. It is more difficult, however, to compare the magnitudes of values that appear in separate graphs. So, for distribution shape comparisons, nothing beats a trellis arrangement of line graphs (or bar graphs as a series of histograms), but for shape and magnitude comparisons, a single graph will usually do the job better.

DISTRIBUTION DEVIATION GRAPHS

When we want to focus on how two distributions differ, we can display the differences directly in the form of what I call a distribution deviation graph. The following example displays the differences in percentage of shipments per day using two of the warehouses from the previous page.

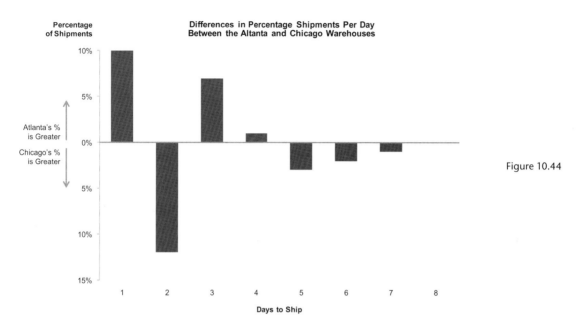

Figure 10.44

In this case, we don't care about the shapes of the two distributions; we only care how they differ. This type of graph can be easily constructed in Excel by calculating the differences between two sets of distribution frequencies (for example, Atlanta ships 32% of its orders in one day while Chicago only ships 22%, resulting in a difference of 10% in favor of Atlanta.) Essentially, this is nothing more than a regular bar graph that displays the differences between two distributions rather than the actual distributions of each.

Distribution Analysis Techniques and Best Practices

We'll cover three best practices in this section:

- Keeping intervals consistent
- Selecting the best interval
- Using measures that are resistant to outliers

All three are essential to good distribution analysis.

Keeping Intervals Consistent

The first rule regarding the sizes of intervals along the categorical scale is that they must be equal. Each of the following three histograms displays the same data, but in two the intervals are inconsistent in size.

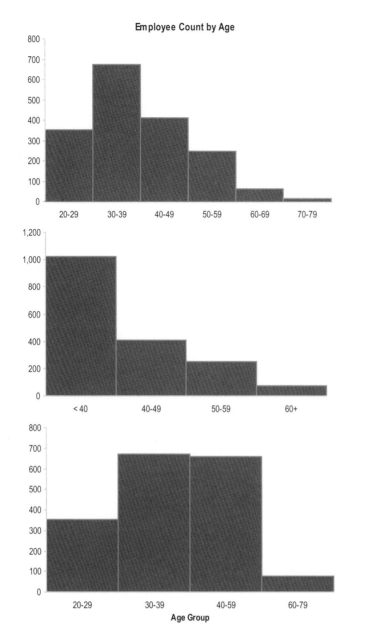

Figure 10.45

The top histogram is the only one with consistently sized age intervals. The second histogram begins and ends with 20 year age groups but has 10 year groups in the middle. The third histogram begins with two intervals that are 10 years in size and then switches to intervals that are 20 years in size. Notice how much different these distributions appear when they do not use a consistent set of intervals.

It is acceptable to break this rule when the vast majority of values fall within a particular range but a few outliers extend the overall spread far into the distance. Consider an example involving sales orders that usually fall within a range of $100-200 but occasionally amount to as much as $1,000. Intervals of $10 each would work well for the $100-200 range, but it would be absurd to extend them all the way to $1,000. In this case, we have two options: we can either eliminate the outliers and focus only on those values that fall between $100 and $200 or we can group all values over $200 into a single final interval.

Selecting the Best Interval

The second practice involves determining how large to make the intervals, or, stated differently, the number of intervals into which we should divide the full range of values. Too many intervals results in a raggedly shaped distribution picture, which displays too much detail and makes it difficult to discern the essential pattern. Too few intervals summarize the data to a level that is too generalized, resulting in a loss of meaningful variations in the distribution's shape.

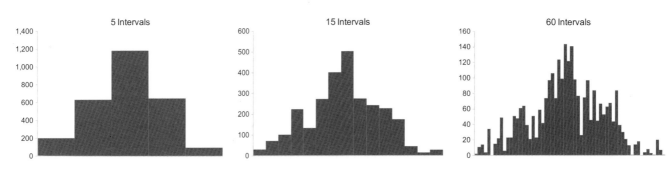

Figure 10.46

Cleveland describes our dilemma:

> *When a histogram is made, the interval width of the histogram is generally greater than the data inaccuracy interval, so accuracy is lost. As we decrease the interval width of a histogram, accuracy increases but the appearance becomes more ragged until finally we have what amounts to a one-dimensional scatterplot. In most applications it makes sense to choose the interval width on the basis of what seems like a tolerable loss in the accuracy of the data; no general rules are possible because the tolerable loss depends on the subject matter and the goal of analysis.[4]*

4. *The Elements of Graphing Data*, William S. Cleveland, Hobart Press, 1994, p. 135.

The goal is to find the right balance between too many and too few intervals to display the best possible picture of the distribution's overall shape without losing sight of useful details. Unfortunately, there is no simple formula for doing this; there is never just one right way to view data. It pays to experiment a bit, trying different interval sizes and viewing the distribution shapes that emerge in an effort to gain insight into the data.

A few products, such as Spotfire Decisionsite, allow us to view a distribution in the form of a histogram and vary interval sizes at will simply by manipulating a slider control. This makes it extremely quick and easy to view various versions of a distribution based on different interval sizes and to make rapid adjustments until the view is ideally suited to the purpose at hand. I hope that this simple feature will soon become standard in visual analysis software.

Using Measures that are Resistant to Outliers

Some measures of center and dispersion are highly influenced by outliers in the data and some are highly resistant. When outliers exercise too much influence over a distribution display, the resulting patterns do a poor job of describing the distribution as a whole. Hartwig and Dearing describe the situation and state the goal as follows:

> When statistical summaries are used, the exploratory approach relies more heavily than other approaches on what are called resistant statistics. Because they are more sensitive to the bulk of the data than are non-resistant statistics, they are less affected by a few highly deviant cases. As a result, they can do a better job of describing the smooth and, having done this, they make it possible to identify the rough more clearly.[5]

5. *Exploratory Data Analysis*, Frederick Hartwig with Brian E. Dearing, Sage Publications, Inc.: Thousand Oaks CA, 1979, p. 12.

Here's the distribution of salaries that we examined previously, displayed as a horizontal box plot:

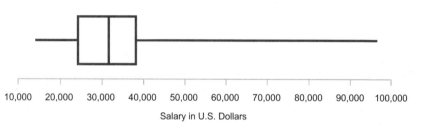

Figure 10.47

In this display, the center represents the median, and the ends of the box represent the 25th and 75th percentiles. The median, which is nothing more than the 50th percentile, and all other percentiles, are highly resistant to outliers. The median is determined by sorting the entire set of values by magnitude and selecting the value that falls in the middle of the set. Because it is highly resistant to outliers, it provides a good measure of center when we wish to see what's typical. Notice that the extremely high salaries, which produce the long tail formed by the right whisker, have neither influenced the position of median nor the ends of the box, which mark the 25th and 75th percentiles.

Now look at another distribution display of the same data, which this time uses measures of center and dispersion around that center that are highly susceptible to outliers:

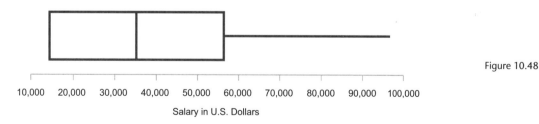

Figure 10.48

In this case, the center represents the *mean*, which is calculated by adding up the values in the entire set and dividing the result by the number of values. The ends of the box represent one standard deviation below and above the mean. This picture of the distribution is quite different than the previous one above.

The mean is highly susceptible to outliers; a single outlier can shift the mean significantly in the direction of that outlier. If we want to summarize the total financial impact of salary expenses per employee with a single measure of center, the mean does the job well. If we want to express the salary that is most typical, however, the mean isn't a good measure.

Standard deviation is a measure of dispersion that, because it's based on the mean, is also heavily influenced by outliers. In the example above, one standard deviation below the mean actually extends below the lowest salary in the data set. Because the dispersion of salaries above the mean is so great as a result of the outliers, the standard deviation has been stretched too far to properly represent values below the mean. Medians and percentiles, because they are resistant to outliers, are usually better measures on which to base distribution displays.

Another approach that makes use of means and standard deviations in an acceptable way eliminates the influence of outliers by removing them from the data set before displaying the distribution. This approach displays a distribution that looks much more like one formed by the median and percentiles, but it sacrifices the outliers to achieve this result.

I hope that, if you were not familiar or comfortable with distribution analysis before reading this chapter, you find it friendlier now that we have cast a little light on it. Potential insights that you can only experience by examining distributions are worth the mental effort of these simple lessons, which you can now reinforce and enhance with a little practice using information that matters to you.

11 CORRELATION ANALYSIS

Introduction

Correlation analysis looks at how quantitative variables relate to and affect one another. Like distribution analysis, correlation analysis is routinely performed by statisticians, scientists, and engineers but done less often by business analysts. This is unfortunate because correlation analysis is our best means to track down causes. Causation is one of the essential concerns of analysis. When a problem occurs, you can't begin to fix it until you understand the cause. When something good happens, you can't hope to keep it going or reproduce it unless you understand the cause.

When we understand correlations, we can do more than describe what happens. We can anticipate or even create what happens. Perhaps more than any other quantitative relationship, correlations open our eyes to the future, giving us the ability to mold it in the best of cases, and, when that's not possible, to at least prepare for what's likely to happen.

Correlation analysis involves comparing two quantitative variables to see if values in one vary systematically with values in the other, and if so, in what manner, to what degree, and why. For example, price is correlated with demand in a negative sense when increases in a product's price correspond to decreases in demand for that product. Another example that is easy to understand is the relationship between how tall people are and how much they weigh. Here's a sample list of 20 men, sorted in order of height from shortest to tallest:

Height (inches)	Weight (pounds)
61.2	134.8
63.5	150.8
64.4	157.6
65.7	167.9
67.4	182.4
67.5	183.3
68.1	188.8
68.3	190.6
69.2	199.2
69.4	201.1
70.2	209.1
70.9	216.4
71.9	227.2
71.9	227.2
73.4	244.5
73.9	250.5
74.3	255.4
75.0	264.3
75.8	274.8
78.8	318.1

Figure 11.1

When two variables correlate—that is, there's a relationship between their behaviors— the nature of that relationship is not necessarily causal. Correlation can indicate any of the following four situations:

- One variable causes another's behavior.
- Neither causes the other's behavior; both are caused by one or more other variables (for example, the correlation between age and income, which is caused not by age but by earning capacity, which happens to be related to age).
- Neither causes the other's behavior, but another variable connects them (for example, the correlation between death rates and sunshine, which is likely a result of old folks often choosing to live in sunny locations when they retire).
- The apparent correlation is erroneous because of an insufficient or biased sample.

When a correlation is found, it's up to us to determine its nature. First, we must investigate further to confirm that our data sample is sufficient and unbiased. If the data sample passes muster, we should next check to see whether other variables are also correlated, which could enlarge our understanding of the relationships we're observing.

In his book *Don't Believe Everything You Think*, Thomas Kida illustrates the problem of insufficient and biased samples by recounting the case of a politically conservative commentator who argued against expenditures on education by citing research that claimed a negative correlation between spending and performance on SAT scores. Kida exposed a flaw in this commentator's reasoning:

> *However, the states that he pointed to as having high scores—Iowa, North Dakota, South Dakota, Utah, and Minnesota—had SAT participation rates of only 5 percent, 6 percent, 7 percent, 4 percent, and 10 percent, respectively. These numbers are quite low given that about 40 percent of all high school seniors take the SAT in the United States. He used New Jersey as an example of low SAT scores and high educational expenditures, but 76 percent of high school seniors take the SAT in New Jersey...Some state university systems do not require the SAT, they use the American College Testing (ACT) program. Thus, only students who plan on attending college out-of-state take the SATs, and those students are likely to have higher academic achievement than the average student in the state. In addition, states with better educational systems typically have more students who want to go to college, so a greater proportion of students take the SAT, resulting in more students with average abilities sitting for the exam.[1]*

1. *Don't Believe Everything You Think*, Thomas Kida, Prometheus Books, Amherst, New York NY, 2006, p. 131.

For those of you who are concerned with business correlations, Kida points out that a correlation between advertising and product sales does not necessarily indicate that advertising is the cause of increasing sales. It could be the result of improvements to the product or the beginning of a seasonal upswing in sales.

A variable that is caused by one or more other variables to behave in particular ways is called a *dependent variable*, and the others are called *independent variables*. When a causal relationship exists, this doesn't necessarily mean that a particular independent variable is solely responsible for the behavior of the dependent variable. It's entirely possible that the effects are influenced by multiple variables.

When two variables are correlated, and neither causes the behavior of the other, but both are caused by one or more other variables, we have what's called a *spurious correlation*. There is indeed a correlation between the first two variables; it's just not a direct cause and effect relationship. If you enjoy mystery novels, you might appreciate that a third, unseen variable that can cause an effect observed in two other variables is called a *lurking variable*. It affects the other variables but was not included in the analysis that discovered a correlation between the other two, so it remains lurking in the shadows. In his textbook *Elementary Statistics*, Mario F. Triola cites an example:

> One study showed a strong correlation between the salaries of statistics professors and per capita beer consumption, but those two variables are affected by the state of the economy, a third variable lurking in the background.[2]

2. *Elementary Statistics*, Eighth Edition, Mario F. Triola, Addison Wesley Longman, Inc., New York NY, 2001, p. 513.

Describing Correlations

Similar to distributions, correlations can be summarized and described graphically or with numbers. We'll look first at how they are described graphically, and what defines a correlation as linear or non-linear. Then we'll look at how statisticians define correlations numerically.

Key Characteristics of Correlations

When a correlation between two quantitative variables exists, it can be described in the following terms:

- Direction
- Strength
- Shape

Each of these characteristics can be displayed visually.

A correlation's direction can be positive or negative. When variables are correlated in a positive manner, this means that as the values of one variable increase, so do the corresponding values of the other. When displayed in a scatterplot, if the overall pattern represented by the values slopes upward from left to right, the correlation is positive. That is, as values of the variable on the X-axis increase, values of the variable on the Y-axis also tend to increase. If the overall trend slopes downward from left to right, the correlation is negative. That is, as values of the variable on the X-axis increase, values in the variable on the Y-axis tend to decrease. The following two examples illustrate both correlation directions: positive on the left and negative on the right. These are both *linear correlations* because the shape of the graphed values approximates a straight line.

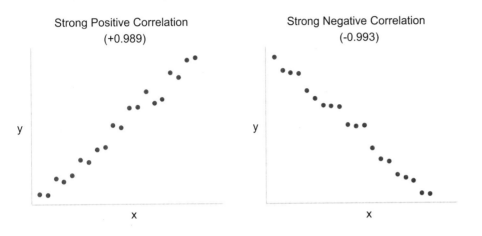

Figure 11.2

Typically, correlations are either positive or negative, but they can be more complicated, beginning in one direction and then changing directions one or more times.

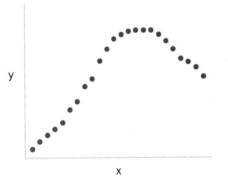

Figure 11.3

If the values are tightly grouped in association with a particular trend, this means that the correlation is strong. The following example illustrates something rare: perfect linear correlations that are as strong as possible.

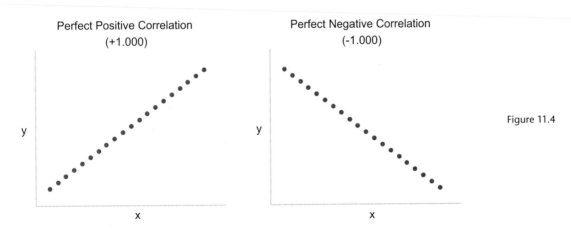

Figure 11.4

The stronger the correlation, the more precisely we can predict how much one variable will increase or decrease in relation to specific increases or decreases in the other variable. The more scattered the values are in relation to the overall trend, the weaker the correlation is. In the left-hand example below, we see a correlation that is fairly weak. On the right, we see variables that are not correlated. When properly graphed, the absence of a correlation appears as a random distribution of values without a particular shape and direction.

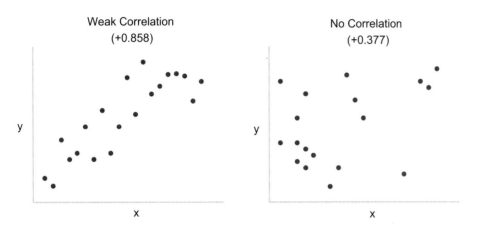

Figure 11.5

Correlations come in two fundamental shapes. Some are straight, which, as noted before, we call *linear*. Some are curved, which we call *curvilinear*. One of each is illustrated below.

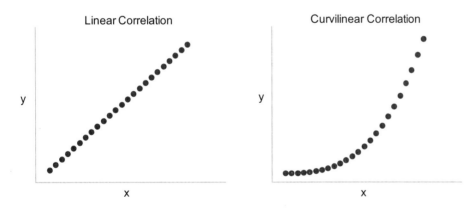

In the curvilinear example above, the correlation begins as only slightly positive and then becomes increasingly positive through the remaining values. Other patterns can also be found in correlations, including concentrations or clusters of values in particular areas, and gaps where we would expect values to ordinarily appear.

Statistical Summaries of Correlations

Statisticians describe correlations using two mathematical measures, which, despite their technical names, are relatively easy to understand.

- *Linear correlation coefficient* (expressed in formulas as *r*)
- *Coefficient of determination* (expressed in formulas as r^2)

Figure 11.6

Technically, statisticians only use the term "correlation" when referring to linear relationships. It's not that they don't acknowledge that relationships between quantitative variables come in shapes that aren't linear, or that they don't find curvilinear relationships meaningful; they simply don't call them correlations. They restrict use of the term correlation to relationships that can be described using a mathematical expression called the correlation coefficient, which we'll soon examine. For our purposes and to keep things simple, however, I see no need to restrict the term correlation in this manner. To take liberties with the words of Shakespeare: "A correlation of any other shape would work as well."

Even though we're focusing on visual methods for discovering and examining correlations, these statistical measures come in handy, especially as a way to confirm the strength of correlations.

The linear correlation coefficient (r) describes both the direction and strength of a correlation, but it can only be applied to correlations that are linear (that is, those with a shape that is relatively straight). The value of r ranges from +1 to -1. The sign (positive or negative) indicates the direction of correlation. A value of zero indicates the complete non-existence of a linear correlation. A value of +1 indicates a perfect positive correlation and -1 a perfect negative correlation, as illustrated below.

Another name for the linear correlation coefficient is the *Pearson product-moment correlation coefficient*, named for the person who initially devised the measure. Knowing this might be useful for gaining entry into private statistical clubs.

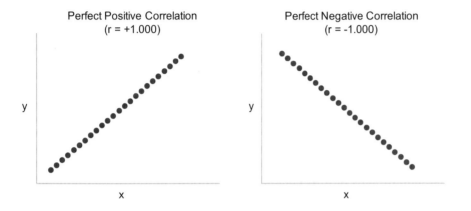

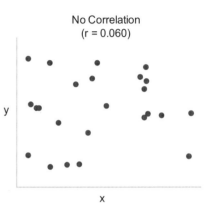

Figure 11.7

In Excel, the function *CORREL()* can be used to calculate the linear correlation coefficient of two paired sets of values.

Whether a particular value of r is considered strong or weak can't be determined in general, but only in relation to particular data and analytical purposes. A value of r that is considered strong in one branch of science regarding one particular phenomenon or topic might not be considered strong in a different context.

The coefficient of determination (r^2) describes the strength of correlation but not its direction. The coefficient of determination is equal to the linear correlation coefficient squared, which is why it's expressed as r^2. For example, a linear correlation coefficient expressed as r = +0.993 can also be expressed as the coefficient of determination r^2 = 0.986 (that is, 0.993 × 0.993 = 0.986049, rounded to 0.986). Values of r^2 are always positive, ranging from 0 to 1.

One advantage of r^2 is that it can be meaningfully expressed as a percentage, which makes it a bit easier to understand. For instance, an r^2 value of 0.986 indicates that 98.6% of the change in the dependent variable (a man's weight in the current example) can be determined by the value of the independent variable (his height).

The Excel function *RSQ()* can be used to calculate r^2, the coefficient of determination, although Excel doesn't call it by this name.

While we can use r and r^2 to test a linear correlation's strength, we shouldn't rely on them as an exclusive means to describe correlations. Visual representations tell a richer story. This can be illustrated with the *Anscombe Quartet*, which consists of four sets of values, each containing 11 paired sets. The data sets each appear in the following four scatterplots:

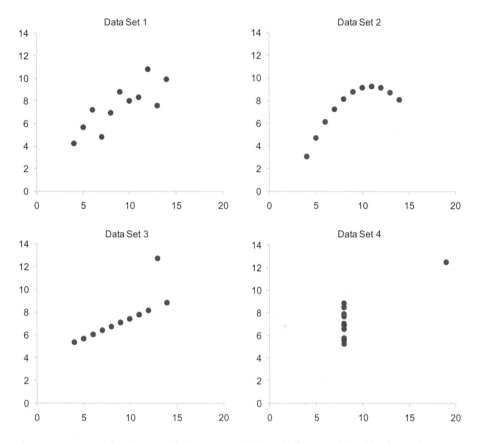

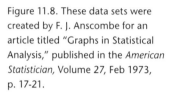

Figure 11.8. These data sets were created by F. J. Anscombe for an article titled "Graphs in Statistical Analysis," published in the *American Statistician,* Volume 27, Feb 1973, p. 17-21.

As you can see, the shapes of these correlations differ considerably, but when they're described using statistical summaries alone, they don't differ at all. The following statistical values describe several aspects of these data sets identically despite the clear differences that we can see in the scatterplots.

N (number of values)	11
Mean of the X-axis values	9.0
Mean of the Y-axis values	7.5
r	0.82
r^2	0.67
Sum of the squares	110.0
Trend line equation	$(y = 0.5x + 3)$

This example demonstrates that even the best statisticians, no matter how sophisticated, must use their eyes to fully understand data.

Correlation Patterns

Correlation analysis is concerned with two classes of patterns: (1) a correlation's shape, which defines the nature of the relationship, and (2) outliers, because their existence informs us of exceptions to the relationship and what causes them.

Shape

Meaningful patterns formed by a correlation's shape can be identified by asking the following series of questions:

- Is it straight or curved?
- If curved, is it curved in one direction only or both?
- If curved in one direction only, is it logarithmic, exponential, or some other shape?
- If curved in both positive and negative directions, does it curve upward or downward?
- Are there concentrations of values?
- Are there gaps in the values?

STRAIGHT OR CURVED?

When a correlation exists, data points are arranged roughly in a shape that is either linear or curvilinear. When a linear correlation is displayed in a scatterplot, differences between pairs of data points along the X-axis are roughly associated with proportional differences between the same pairs of data points along the Y-axis. For instance, if there is a linear relationship between men's heights and weights, and a one-inch increase of height from 60 to 61 inches corresponds to a five-pound increase in weight, then a one-inch increase in height from 70 to 71 inches should also roughly result in a five-pound increase in weight.

If there is a linear correlation between the amount of money spent on ads and the number of orders a company receives in any given week, a scatterplot of this relationship with a linear trend line (straight line of best fit) might look like this:

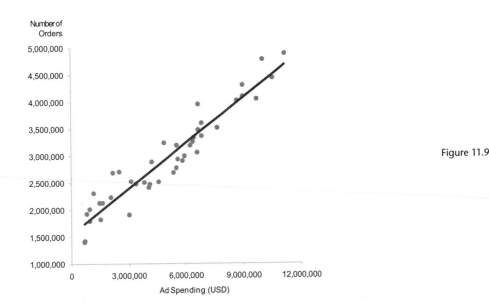

Figure 11.9

When a correlation is curvilinear, the relationship between values along the X-axis and corresponding values along the Y-axis is not fixed to a consistent amount; it varies. There is still a predictable correlation between the two variables, but it fits a non-linear shape. Going back to the height-versus-weight example, if a 5% increase in height consistently corresponds to a 3% increase in weight, the pattern that we would see in a scatterplot would curve upward like this:

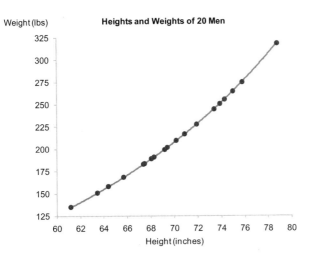

Figure 11.10

ONE DIRECTION OR TWO?

Now we'll consider the shape of the curve. The shape of a curvilinear correlation displayed in a scatterplot can move upward from left to right (positive correlation), downward from left to right (negative correlation), or both upward and downward at various places. The question that we're asking now is whether it curves in one direction only (either upward or downward) or in both directions. A correlation that curves in one direction only, always positive or negative, can still vary in the rate at which it curves along the way. One that curves in both directions (sometimes positive and sometimes negative) does so because one or more influences along the way cause the nature of the correlation to change.

Hartwig and Dearing do a nice job of describing various correlations and, in the process, introduce a few technical terms.

> *Nonlinearity can take a wide variety of forms, but the distinction between monotonic and nonmonotonic relationships is most important. A monotonic relationship is one in which increases in X are associated either with increases in Y or with decreases in Y through the entire range of X. In other words, monotonic relationships do not double back on themselves. In contrast, nonmonotonic relationships do double back on themselves, such as occurs whenever increases in X are associated with increases in Y up to some point, after which increases in X are associated with decreases in Y. Since all linear relationships are monotonic and all nonmonotonic relationships are nonlinear, three general classes of relationships exist: linear, nonlinear monotonic, and nonmonotonic. Nonlinear monotonic relationships differ from linear relationships in terms of the rate of increase or decrease. In linear relationships, the rate at which Y increases or decreases with increases in X remains the same throughout the entire range of X; hence, a straight-line relationship. In nonlinear but monotonic relationships, the rate at which Y increases or decreases along X changes. Increases in X may be associated with increases (or decreases) in Y at an increasing (or decreasing) rate, or even a combination of rates, but the direction of the relationship never changes. In contrast, nonmonotonic relationships are ones in which the direction itself changes.[3]*

3. *Exploratory Data Analysis*, Frederick Hartwig with Brian E. Dearing, Sage Publications, Inc.: Thousand Oaks CA, 1979, p. 49.

LOGARITHMIC OR EXPONENTIAL?

Correlations that curve in one direction only (monotonic) often exhibit shapes that are either logarithmic or exponential. Logarithmic curves look like the following examples:

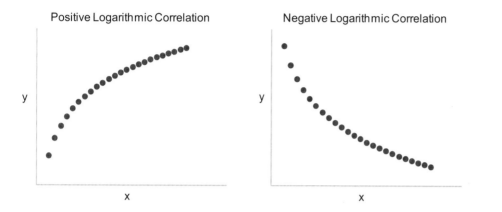

Figure 11.11

Along a logarithmic curve, values in a scatterplot go up or go down (that is, when we read them from left to right) at an ever decreasing rate of change. The degree of change starts out great but then steadily decreases and eventually levels off. This logarithmic growth pattern is often seen when correlating the number of people who are assigned to a project with the amount of work they produce. Expanding the team from one person to two usually produces a high degree of additional productivity, but with each new person the degree of additional productivity that's gained decreases. At some point it would no longer make sense to add more people because the insufficient increases in productivity would result. A sample project might exhibit the following correlation between the number of people working on it and the amount of work produced by them:

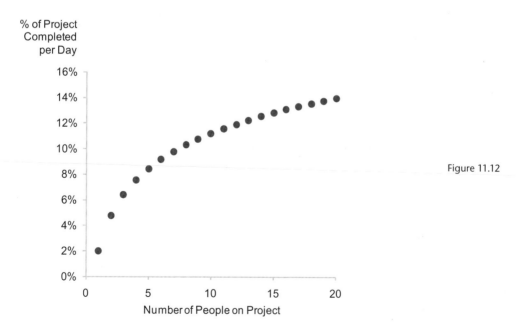

Figure 11.12

Exponential curves look like the following examples:

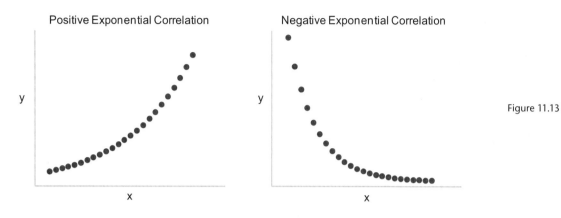

Positive Exponential Correlation

Negative Exponential Correlation

Figure 11.13

From one value to the next along an exponential growth curve (positive correlation), values in a scatterplot go up by a steadily increasing degree. Along an exponential decay curve (negative correlation), values go down by a steadily decreasing degree. Compound interest that banks pay grows exponentially through time. Here's what the pattern looks like when $1,000 is deposited into an account that pays 8% interest, compounded daily:

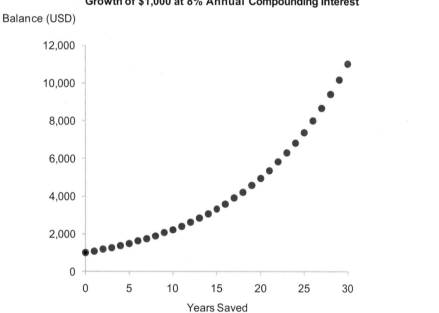

Growth of $1,000 at 8% Annual Compounding Interest

Balance (USD)

Years Saved

Figure 11.14

Populations also often exhibit this pattern of growth during spans of time when space and other resources are abundant.

Correlations that go up (positive) or go down (negative) at varying rates of change aren't always logarithmic or exponential. Nevertheless, if we can identify a pattern in the way the rate changes, these correlations are just as meaningful and predictable. Fortunately, most software products that support scatterplots, including Excel, provide ways to associate trend lines with a series of values and do the math to produce them for us. This includes lines that fit logarithmic and exponential models as well as others, such as polynomial models, which we'll touch on later when we take a closer look at trend lines. Thankfully, we don't need to rely on our eyes alone to determine whether a correlation is logarithmic, exponential, or one of several other types of trend lines that these products support. We can tell the software to fit a trend line of a specific type to the data as closely as possible and then use our eyes to confirm how well it fits the data. Finding the mathematical model that best fits the data is a fundamental operation of statistics.

CURVED UPWARD OR DOWNWARD?

When correlations move in more than one direction (non-monotonic), they often curve upward or downward. Here's an example of each:

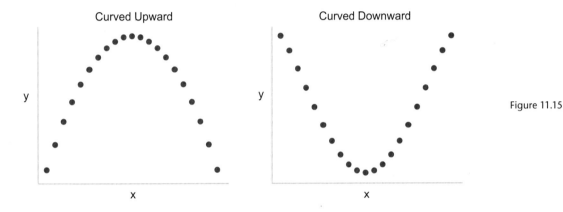

Figure 11.15

Correlations that curve upward work in the opposite fashion to those that curve downward. Those that curve upward begin with a positive correlation but gradually turn around to become negative. Those that curve downward, which we encounter less often, begin with a negative correlation but gradually turn around to become positive. A product that increases rapidly in sales during its early life but gradually slows down during middle age and eventually begins decreasing in sales as it walks somberly toward obsolescence exhibits a curvilinear correlation that curves upward. Remember the example from before of the correlation between the number of people working on a project and resulting productivity? What I didn't mention previously is that by adding more and more people, not only can productivity gains slow down, they can actually turn around at some point when additional people only get in one another's way, resulting in productivity losses.

Some correlations are shaped like an "S" and are therefore called *S-curves* (also called *logistic curves* or *growth curves*). For example, here is one that shows increasing sales until the product's popularity reaches its peak and then levels off.

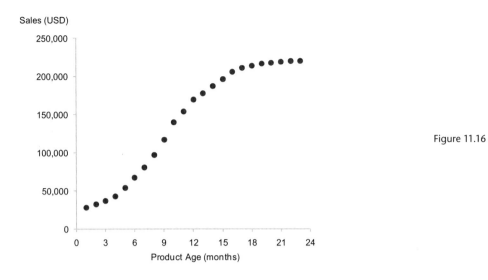

Figure 11.16

It's quite possible that, given time, a correlation shaped like this will eventually begin moving in the negative direction. Patterns that curve in more than one direction require a different type of trend line to fit the data than those that I've already mentioned; we'll come back to this topic later.

CONCENTRATIONS?

Correlations often exhibit groups of values that are close to one another, that is, concentrations of values, which are easy to spot in a scatterplot because the data points are clustered together. The scatterplot below illustrates the concentrations of values in a correlation.

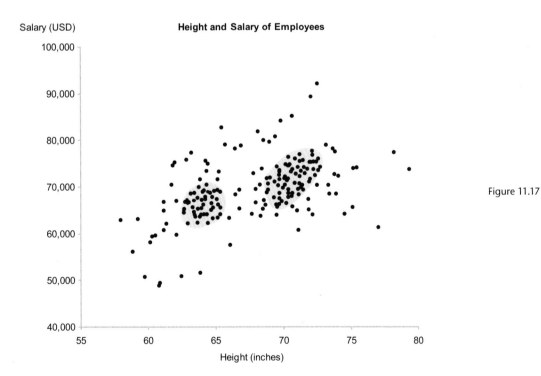

Figure 11.17

Here we see a concentration of values around 64 inches in height and another around 70 inches in height. Can you guess what might be causing this? The answer would be crystal clear if I used data points of different colors to distinguish men and women. The average height of women is around 5'4" and of men is around 5'9". A frequency polygon with separate lines for men's and women's heights reveals peaks at these approximate locations, as shown below.

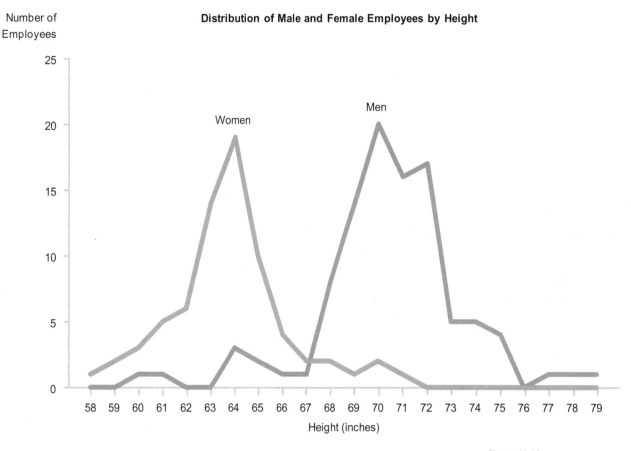

Figure 11.18

GAPS?

Just as meaningful as concentrations, correlations sometimes exhibit what appear as gaps in the values: empty regions where we would expect to find values. When two variables are not correlated, values appear to be randomly distributed. In such cases, particular regions of the plot area can be empty of data points without being meaningful. However, when a correlation exists, values form a particular pattern, so when points are missing where the pattern suggests they ought to appear, the omission is almost always meaningful.

The following scatterplot shows how the amount of time between eruptions of Old Faithful geyser in Yellowstone Park correlates to the duration of eruptions. Notice the gap at around 70 minutes between eruptions.

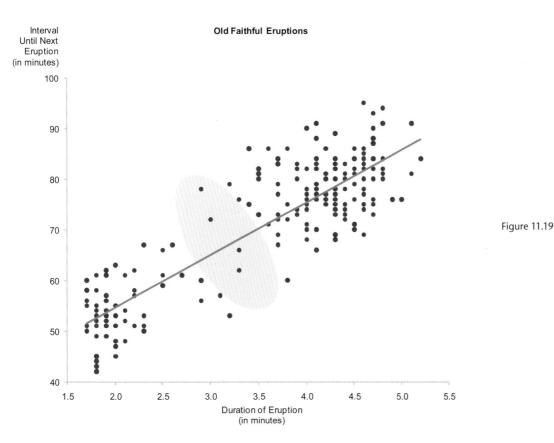

Interval Until Next Eruption (in minutes)

Old Faithful Eruptions

Duration of Eruption (in minutes)

Figure 11.19

It's tempting to interpret the pattern formed by this correlation as two clusters of values—one in the lower left and one in the upper right—but what appear on the surface as concentrations actually consist of values that are fairly evenly distributed. What makes these two regions look like clusters is a gap in the correlation's linear trend. Why are there so few eruptions that last between 3 and 3.5 minutes in length? We would expect longer eruptions, during which more thermal pressure has dissipated, to result in longer intervals between eruptions, but what causes this gap? I don't know the answer, but I suspect that scientists have examined this closely and probably know why.

OUTLIERS

Even when two variables are correlated, there are often a few values that don't fit the basic shape formed by the majority. Such values, which seem to have gone astray, are outliers. When we have determined the shape of a correlation and found a trend line that describes its shape well, values that appear relatively close to the trend line are said to *fit the model*. In fact, the values that are adequately represented by the trend line, taken together, are called the *fit*. In a scatterplot, outliers are values that are vertically distant from the trend line compared to the majority of values, which are closer. Statisticians call the vertical distance of a value from the trend line the *residual*, illustrated below:

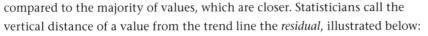

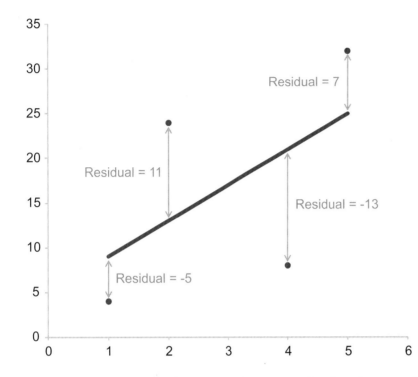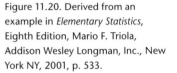

Figure 11.20. Derived from an example in *Elementary Statistics*, Eighth Edition, Mario F. Triola, Addison Wesley Longman, Inc., New York NY, 2001, p. 533.

We don't fully understand our data until we've examined and made sense of the values that don't fit. It's important to understand under what circumstances values stray from the flock.

Correlation Displays

No graph is more useful for examining correlations than a scatterplot. No other graph displays the correlation of two variables as well—not even close. The one limitation of a scatterplot, however, is that it is designed to compare two quantitative variables only. When we want to search for possible correlations between many quantitative variables, rather than using scatterplots to test each pair one at a time, we can use another visualization, the *table lens*, to detect possible correlations between many variables all at once in a single display. And, located between the rich display of two variables provided by a single scatterplot and the broad view across several variables provided by a table lens, resides, the *scatterplot matrix*, which displays several scatterplots in a way that we can use to bounce rapidly back and forth among several pairs of variables. We will look at scatterplots and scatterplot matrices first, and then at table lenses.

A single scatterplot can in fact be used to compare three variables, but this requires the addition of a third axis, called the Z-axis, which complicates analysis considerably; 3-D scatterplots are hard to read. They are sometimes used by scientists and engineers to examine particular data sets but a great deal of training and practice is required to spot and make sense of particular patterns that are meaningful in those data sets.

Scatterplots for Comparing Two Variables

Scatterplots are wonderful. They simply and elegantly display two quantitative variables and how these variables are related, using single data points to represent both variables by placing them on a plane (a two-dimensional space) defined by two axes, each with its own quantitative scale. This method of displaying data using two-dimensional coordinates was originally invented by the mathematician and philosopher René Descartes.

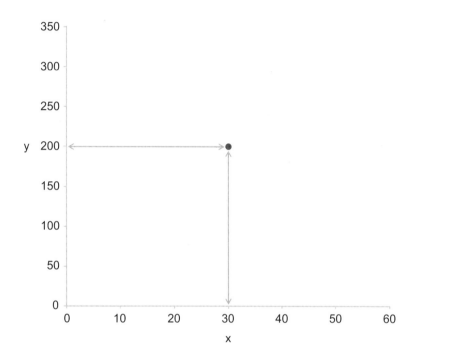

Figure 11.21

I've seen scatterplots that contain thousands of data points and can actually be used to make sense of data. All of the meaningful patterns that correlations can exhibit as well as the presence of outliers are superbly displayed in scatterplots. Later, in the *Techniques and Practices* section of this chapter, we'll learn some guidelines for using scatterplots effectively.

Scatterplot Matrices for Comparing Multiple Pairs of Variables

A scatterplot works so well for comparing two variables that it shouldn't come as a surprise that one way we can compare several variables is to combine multiple scatterplots. A scatterplot matrix allows us to explore how several variables interact with one another even though we can only see the relationship of two particular variables per scatterplot.

Here's a well-known example, which William Cleveland features in his book *The Elements of Graphing Data*.

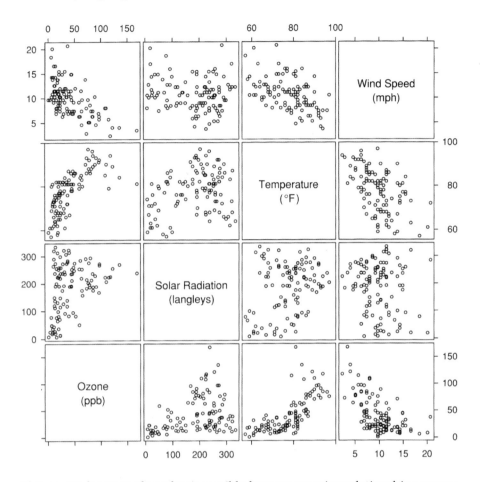

Figure 11.22. *The Elements of Graphing Data*, William S. Cleveland, Hobart Press, 1994, p. 257.

This particular example makes it possible for us to examine relationships among four atmospheric variables: ozone (an air pollutant when at ground level), solar radiation, air temperature, and wind speed. How do these four variables interact? To find out, let's begin by learning how to read the display. The variable names serve as labels for both their row and their column in the matrix. To compare two variables, simply find the scatterplot where the row of one variable intersects the column of the other. For example, the scatterplot in the top left corner compares ozone levels on the X-axis to wind speed on the Y-axis. As you can see, there appears to be a negative correlation between ozone and wind speed: the faster the wind blows the less ozone there is in the air. This makes perfect sense. The scatterplot in the bottom right corner compares the same two variables, but this time wind speed is measured on the X-axis and ozone on the Y-axis.

Fairly quickly, by moving from one scatterplot to the next, we can construct the story of how these variables interact. Wind speed correlates to ozone negatively. Temperature correlates to ozone positively. Solar radiation appears to correlate positively to ozone, but this relationship is weak. So far, we know that wind speed and temperature both seem to correlate fairly well to ozone. We don't know, however, whether either causes ozone to increase or decrease. How do they relate to one another? Wind speed appears to correlate negatively to temperature as well as to ozone. Perhaps decreases in ozone and temperature are both caused by increases in wind speed. We could go on, but you get the point. Rather than constructing each scatterplot separately, and examining each one independently while relying on memory to hold findings in our minds, a scatterplot matrix allows us to construct a rich understanding of the interrelationships among these variables, rapidly and easily.

Even if we don't have software that will automatically construct a scatterplot matrix for us, we can construct one on our own. In Excel, we can do this by creating the first scatterplot, copying and pasting it to each position to form a matrix, and then changing the data in each new scatterplot to address every possible combination of two variables.

Table Lenses for Comparing More than Two Variables Simultaneously

A *table lens* provides a simple way to look for correlations among several variables all at once. It uses horizontal bars to encode values, arranged like a table, with a separate column for each variable, and a separate row for each item that has been measured. The example below will clarify what I mean, which is difficult to explain in words alone.

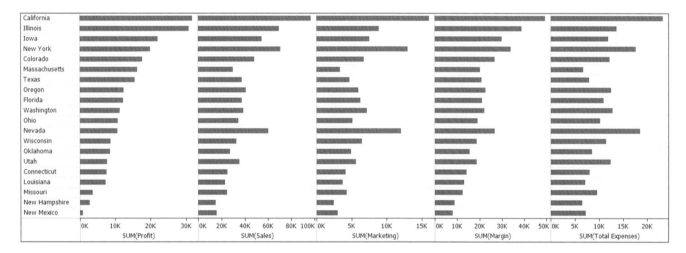

I constructed this example of a table lens using Tableau Software. The table lens displays, for 20 states, five variables related to sales: profits, revenues, marketing expenses, profit margin, and total sales-related expenses. The quantitative scales for each of the variables are independent from one another. There is no reason to keep them consistent because we are not comparing the magnitudes of values across variables, only the patterns formed by each column of bars. By sorting the states in order from the highest to the lowest values in a particular column (the profit column in this example), we can easily search for other columns that roughly exhibit either the same pattern of high to low values or the opposite pattern of low to high values. If the pattern in a particular column is roughly arranged from high to low values similar to the profit column, the variable in that column is positively correlated to profits. If the bars in another column roughly exhibit the opposite pattern, arranged from low at the top to high at the bottom, then the variable in that column is negatively

Figure 11.23. Created using Tableau Software

correlated with profits (that is, as profits decrease the values in the other column increase). In this particular example, we can see that all of these variables are roughly correlated in a positive manner, with margin exhibiting the strongest correlation to profit.

As you can see, a table lens does not display correlations as richly or as precisely as scatterplots do, but it does provide a great way to look for possible correlations among many variables all at once. When you begin to explore data, looking for whatever correlations might exist between many variables, using a table lens is a great way to begin.

The table lens was originally created by Ramana Rao. A commercial version of his design was implemented by a company that he founded named *Inxight Software*. Ramana once wrote a guest article for my newsletter (the *Visual Business Intelligence Newsletter*), which featured the following screen shot of a table lens from Inxight Software.

"TableLens: A Clear Window for Viewing Multivariate Data," Ramana Rao, *Visual Business Intelligence Newsletter*, Perceptual Edge, Berkeley CA, Jul 2006.

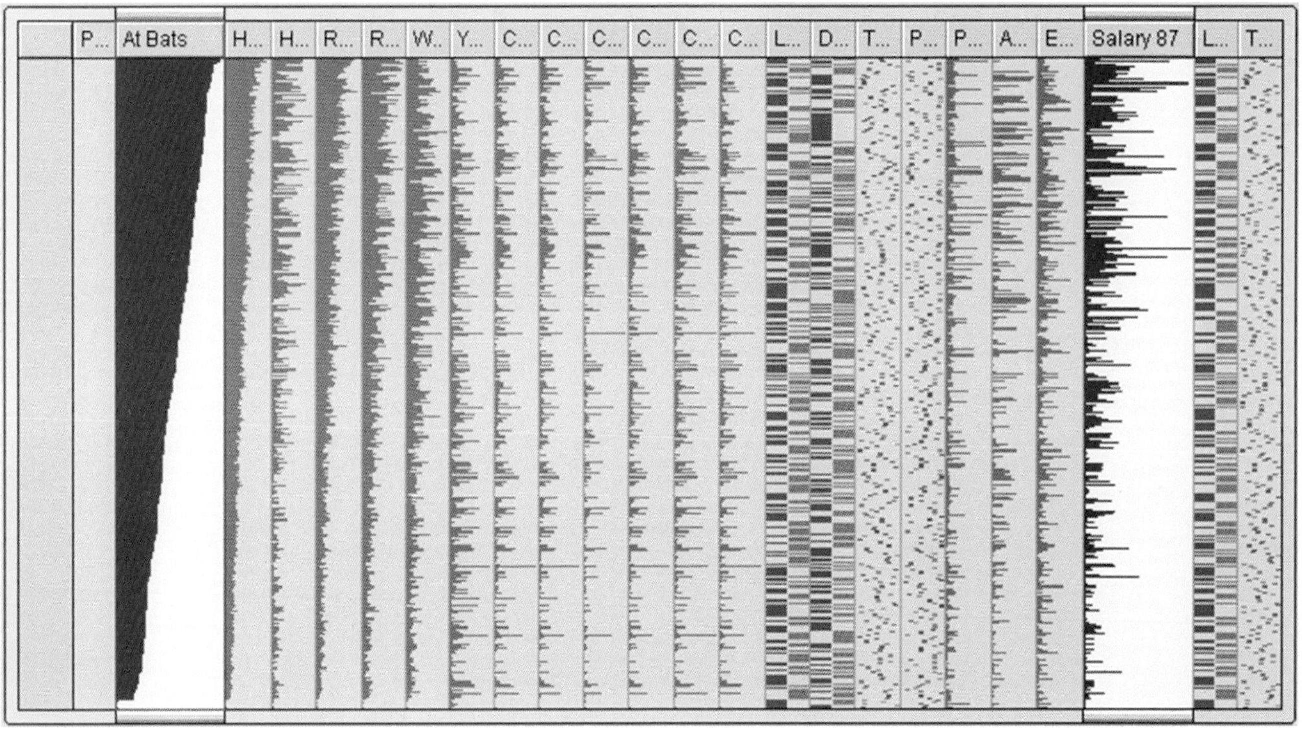

Figure 11.24. Created using Inxight's Table Lens software

This example displays baseball statistics from 1987 for 323 baseball players. Each row represents a different player. It compares 25 variables, one per column. Variables include season and career at-bats, hits, home runs, and runs batted in (RBIs), as well as categorical properties (the columns with colored dots rather than bars) including team and field position. I'm not assuming that you're all baseball fans and find these statistics interesting. But I am hoping that the ability to search for correlations among this many variables at once is a prospect that you'll find exciting.

You might be wondering how, with so many small bars packed together so tightly and no visible labels, we can tell which baseball player is represented in a particular row. With the Table Lens product from Inxight Software, this is done by clicking one or more rows to expand them, as shown on the following page.

	Players	A...	H...	H...	R...	R...	W...	Y...	C...	Career ...	Career ...	Career ...	C...	C...	L...	D...	T...	P...	P...	A...	E...	S...	L...	T...
75	Reggie Willi...									87	4	39												
76	Reggie Jac...									2510	548	1509												
77	Ray Knight									1102	67	410												
78	Randy Kutc...									44	7	28												
79	Randy Bush									344	43	178												
80	Rance Mulli...									614	43	295												

Because the product works in this way, you can focus on patterns in the data without distraction from details until you want them. And, when you do, details on demand are only a mouse-click away. Displays can be constructed with other products, such as Tableau Software, to simulate the appearance and basic functionality of a table lens, but they don't necessarily offer all the functionality that exists in this dedicated table lens product from Inxight Software.

A table lens conventionally encodes values as bars, but data points work also, as illustrated below.

Figure 11.25. Created using Inxight's Table Lens software

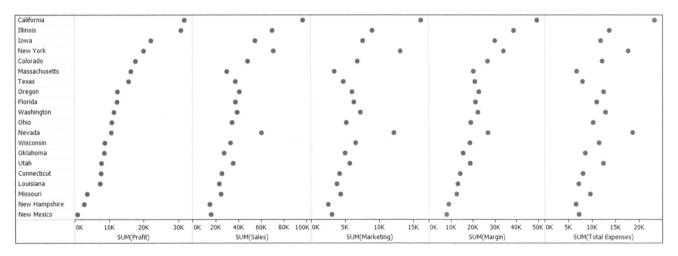

Figure 11.26. Created using Tableau Software

Notice that with data points, it is not as easy for your eyes to track across and compare the values in a single row (which corresponds to a single state in this example), but it is perhaps easier in some cases to see the shapes formed by the entire set of values in a single variable and to compare the overall shape of one variable to another.

Correlation Analysis Techniques and Best Practices

As one of the more complicated types of analysis, correlations can be under-stood most effectively when we're careful to follow a few best practices and techniques. We'll take a look at the following nine:

- Optimizing aspect ratio and quantitative scales
- Removing fill color to reduce over-plotting
- Comparing data to reference regions
- Visually distinguishing data sets when they're divided into groups
- Using trend lines to enhance perception of the correlation's shape, strength, and outliers
- Using multiple trend lines to see categorical differences
- Removing the rough to see the smooth more clearly
- Using trellis and crosstab displays to reduce complexity and over-plotting
- Using grid lines to enhance comparisons between scatterplots

Optimizing Aspect Ratio and Quantitative Scales

When we use a scatterplot, the shape of the data and the visibility of meaning-ful patterns are influenced by the graph's aspect ratio (the relative sizes of the plot area's height and width) and the range of quantitative values along each axis. It is almost always best to make the plot area roughly square in shape, with equal height and width. Doing so favors neither quantitative variable over the other but treats them as equal. Notice how the shape of the data differs between the following three scatterplots that contain the same data but have different aspect ratios.

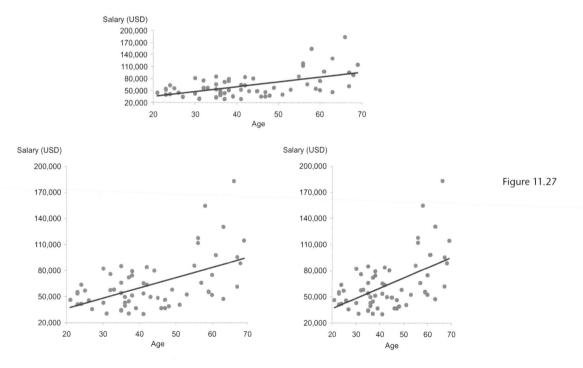

Figure 11.27

When scaling a scatterplot, it is best to begin each scale just a little below the lowest value and end it just a little above the highest. Doing so makes full use of the plot area and spreads the values across as much space as possible to give meaningful patterns the best chance of being seen. Even though the information looks quite different in the two graphs below, both contain the same values. The difference in appearance is a result of the quantitative scales in the graph on the right being adjusted to fill the plot area with the data, while the scale along the left graph's X-axis extends well below the highest value, resulting in a large part of the plot area being empty.

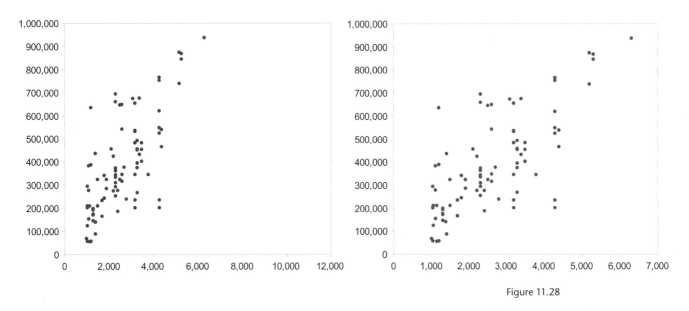

Figure 11.28

Removing Fill Color to Reduce Over-plotting

When many data points are close together and overlap one another in a scatterplot (what I described earlier as over-plotting), this problem can be reduced by removing the fill color from the points, leaving only their outlines. This makes it a little easier to see when data points overlap.

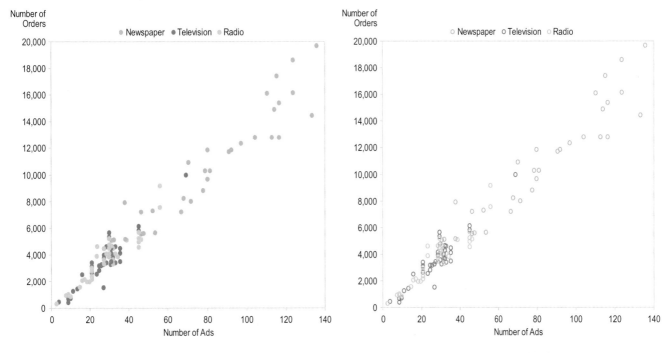

Figure 11.29

Rather than repeating the other over-plotting reduction techniques that we looked at in *Chapter 5: Analytical Techniques and Practices*, I refer you back to that section and encourage you to review it now with scatterplots in mind.

Comparing Data to Reference Regions

Another technique that we covered in *Chapter 5: Analytical Techniques and Practices* involves the use of reference lines, which can make it much easier to compare data to a reference set of values, such as an average or a defined performance standard. When using scatterplots, because there are two quantitative scales, it is sometimes useful to delineate entire reference regions. Reference regions serve the same purpose as reference lines, but instead of marking a linear (one-dimensional) set of values, a reference region marks a two-dimensional set of values. Here's an example:

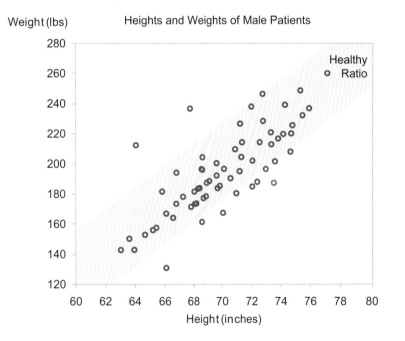

Figure 11.30. Don't worry if your own height and weight do not fit into the "Healthy Ratio" region of this graph. This example was created using made-up data to illustrate the use of reference regions and does not display actual health data.

In this case, the reference region makes it exceptionally easy to see when men's weights fall outside the healthy range. This display allows us to examine height to weight ratios so that we can see the number of men who fell outside of the healthy range as well as the overall correlation of height and weight.

Visually Distinguishing Data Sets When Divided into Groups

When a scatterplot displays distinct groups of values, such as newspaper, television, and radio ads in the following example, groups can be visually distinguished from one another by either assigning different shapes (such as dots, triangles, and squares in the left-hand example) or different colors to the data points (orange, blue, and green in the right-hand example).

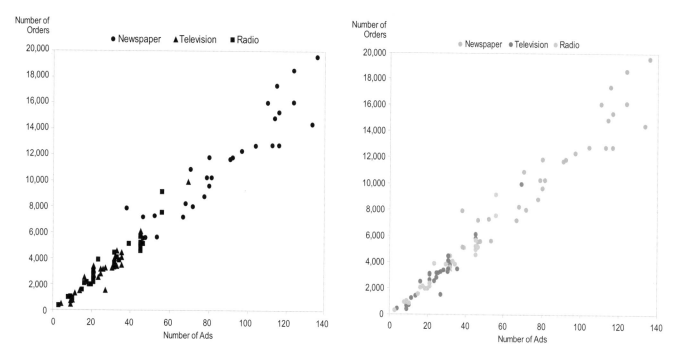

Figure 11.31

Both methods work, but for people with normal color perception, groups stand out more clearly as distinct from one another when different hues are used. Just make sure that the hues you select are different enough from one another to be easily distinguished. If you have difficulty distinguishing particular hues, however, you can either use only those hues that you can tell apart, or use different shapes.

Some of the shapes that are easiest to distinguish from one another are the following:

All but the "X" shape are available in Excel, but you can replace the X with a – (a long dash) when you need more than four symbols. These symbols are easier to distinguish if you keep the ones with interiors (circle, square, and triangle) empty.

Using Trend Lines to Enhance Perception of a Correlation's Shape, Strength, and Outliers

When applied to a scatterplot, a trend line traces the basic shape of the data from left to right. It draws a line, either straight or curved, through the full set of values from left to right in a way that comes as close as possible to passing through the center of them. Expressed statistically, it is a line that produces a set of residuals (the vertical distances of each data point from the trend line) that, when squared and summed, is the least possible amount. For this reason, a better term for a trend line in a scatterplot is a *line of best fit*. It both summarizes

Technically, statisticians refer to curved lines that are fitted to the shape of the data not as lines but as curves. For our purposes, I'm using the term line ("trend line" and "line of best fit") whether the line is straight or curved.

the data's shape and visually supports us in determining the strength of the correlation based on how closely values come to the line. It also helps us identify outliers, values that are located far from the line. Cleveland wrote:

> When the purpose of a scatter plot is made to study how one variable, a response, depends on another variable, a factor, noise in the data often makes it difficult to visually assess the underlying pattern. A smooth curve can show the pattern much more clearly.[4]

4. *The Elements of Graphing Data,* William S. Cleveland, Hobart Press, 1994, pp. 119 and 120.

In the following example, the line of best fit makes it easier to see the correlation's linear shape and positive slope as well as its meager strength.

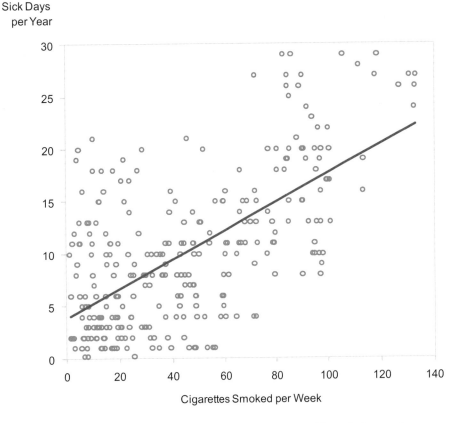

Figure 11.32

Because correlations can form different shapes, lines of best fit for tracing various shapes are needed. When software draws a line of best fit in a scatterplot, it isn't using its eyes to do so; it's using math to calculate the shape. So it can only draw the line within the constraints of particular mathematical models, and it's up to us to choose the appropriate model. The correlation shapes that we examined earlier can be produced using the following models of best fit:

Shape	Fit Model	Examples

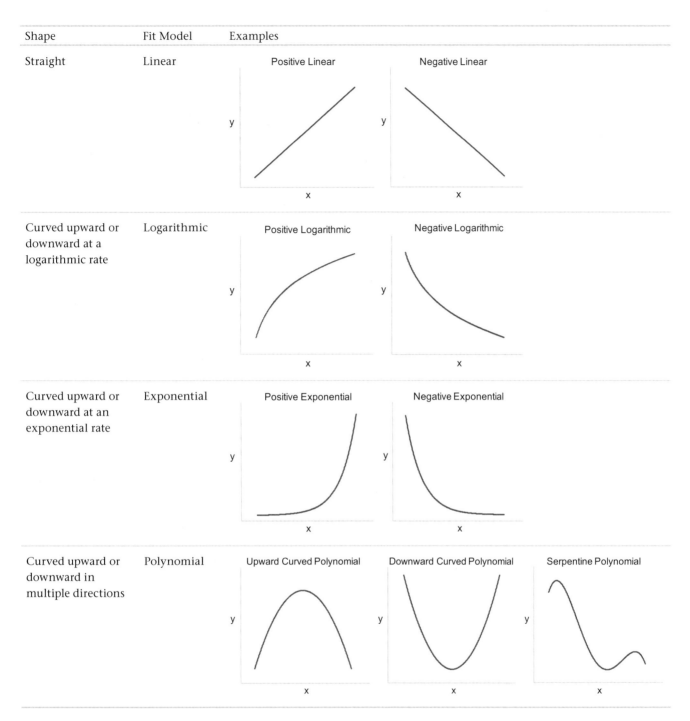

The first three models—linear, logarithmic, and exponential—are relatively easy to use and understand. If the shape looks straight or curved at a steadily increasing or decreasing rate of change (exponential or logarithmic), we simply ask the software to display the line of best fit that seems appropriate and check its r^2 (coefficient of determination) to see how closely the values fit the model.

It's also easy to create curves that curve upward or downward in multiple directions if the software we're using supports polynomial (or quadratic) trend lines, but be careful to not overuse polynomial lines. In theory, you could make a polynomial line curve so much that it fits every value perfectly, no matter how random the values might be. Getting a trend line to fit every value, as illustrated in the example below on the right, doesn't meaningfully summarize the shape of the data, so it's not useful for predicting values.

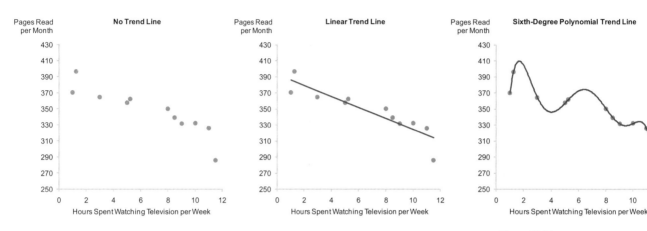

Figure 11.33

To use a polynomial trend line, we must first select a number that indicates its *order* (sometimes called its *degree*). The lowest order is 2 for a line that curves once. The highest order of a polynomial line is sometimes limited by software to prevent us from going crazy and producing a line that is excessively curvy and therefore useless. For example, Excel limits polynomial lines to an order of 6.

When we find a line of best fit that has a high r^2 value, that means it describes the correlation's shape well and can be used to predict values that don't actually exist in our data set, although they could. For example, if we have a straight line of best fit that does a good job of describing the relationship between men's heights and weights, but no one in our data set is 63 inches tall, we could use it to predict how much a man of that height would probably weigh. What we can't always do, however, is use it to predict values that fall beyond the range in our data set. This might work for the predicting weights from known heights of especially short or especially tall men, but would it work for the example I mentioned earlier of a correlation between the number of years a product has been on the market and sales of that product? What if the product that we're examining has reached its peak, but we don't know it? The correlation so far might look like an "S" curve. If we extended the line of best fit out into the future, continuing the current trend of gradual increases in sales, we would predict higher sales two years from now. If it's now at its peak and sales will soon begin to curve downward, our prediction would be wrong. When we use what's known as a basis for predicting the future, the better we know our information and how it behaves, the better we'll be able to anticipate possible changes we should take into account.

Using Multiple Trend Lines to See Categorical Differences

So far, each example of a trend line that we've seen involved a single line of best fit to describe the entire set of values in a scatterplot. There are times, however, when it is useful to see how different groups of data vary in the shape of their correlation. The scatterplot below displays the relationship between the distance traveled by airline flights and the total flight times during a particular span of months. What it reveals is the nice linear correlation between these two variables that we would expect.

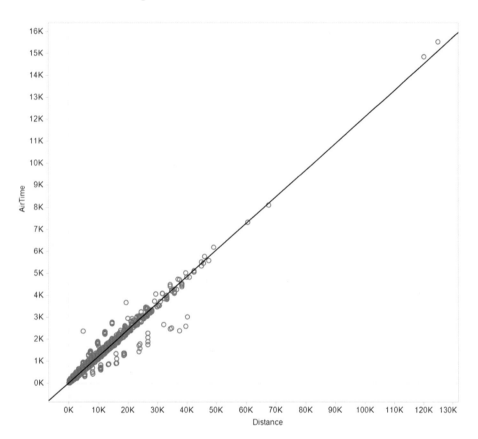

Figure 11.34. Created using Tableau Software

Looking closer, however, we can see that there is a series of values in the lower left corner that exhibit a slightly steeper linear pattern and another series that follows a path below that is less steep than the dominant trend. Differences like this should arouse our curiosity. Are the flights that take longer per distance traveled (the set with the steeper incline) different from the other in some identifiable way? How about those that cover the same distance in much less time (the lower series)? Let's experiment to see if we can find a categorical variable (airline, airport, etc.) that's associated with these differences. In the scatterplot on the next page, I've distinguished the different airlines using color, including a separate trend line for each airline. (Airline names, which would ordinarily be visible, have been intentionally hidden.)

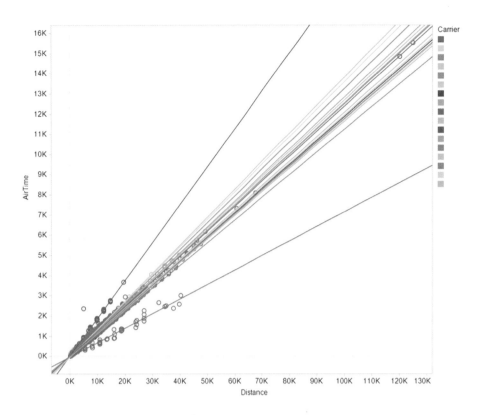

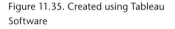

Figure 11.35. Created using Tableau Software

We can now see that all of the flights that took longer belong to a single airline (the brown dots) and all those that took less time belong to a single airline as well (the lavender dots). Although the cause of airline in brown's longer than normal flights isn't obvious and needs further investigation, we might speculate that flights by the airline represented by the lavender dots took less time because this particular airline mostly flies routes over open ocean and consequently encounters less traffic and fewer restrictions associated with regulated air space. The separate trend lines make it easier to see the magnitudes of difference in flight times based on the slopes of the lines. As long as there is sufficient information to justify the use of separate trend lines per group, displays like this can be very enlightening.

Removing the Rough to See the Smooth More Clearly

As I mentioned before, statisticians refer to values that are associated with the line of best fit as the *smooth* and outliers as the *rough*. The act of finding the mathematical model that best describes a correlation—that is, fitting a line to it that describes its shape—is called *smoothing* the data. Once the distinction between the smooth and the rough can be seen, we usually want to examine the rough and the smooth independently. Outliers in a scatterplot can cause a great deal of space in the plot area to be empty of data, forcing other values—the smooth—into a much tighter space than is ideal for examining them. Notice in the example below how much the presence of a few outliers has corralled the smooth into a relatively small section of the scatterplot.

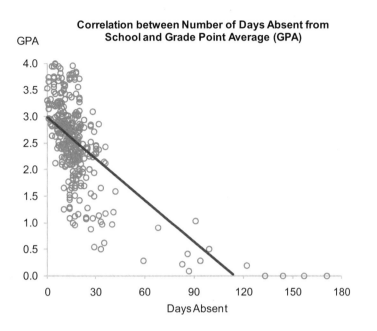

Figure 11.36

In such cases, it is often helpful and acceptable to temporarily remove the rough from the picture, so the patterns in the smooth can be examined more clearly. Here's the same information, this time without the rough.

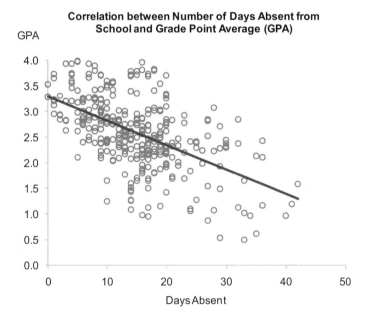

Figure 11.37

Not only is it easier to see the smooth, but the line of best fit can more accurately describe the smooth now that it's not being influenced by those pesky outliers.

Using Trellis and Crosstab Displays to Reduce Complexity and Over-Plotting

When a large number of values appear in a single scatterplot, over-plotting often results, and when those values are split into multiple groups, it can be difficult to focus on them separately. Trellis and crosstab displays of scatterplots can alleviate both of these problems. Values in the following scatterplot are grouped into three types of products (furniture, office supplies, and technology) by symbol shape and three regions (central, east, and west) by color.

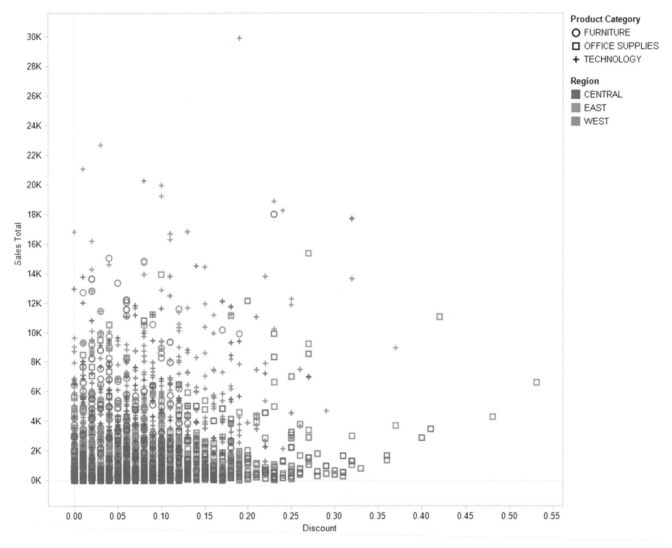

Figure 11.38. Created using Tableau Software

The problem of over-plotting is obvious in the lower left corner of the plot area. Even putting the over-plotting aside, it's hard to make sense of the data because too many different dimensions of meaning must be parsed—the meaning of each color (regions) and symbol shape (product category), in addition to the usual meanings of the X and Y positions of the data points. If we wish to understand the data in light of different product categories and regions, perhaps there's a better way to do it. Look at how the crosstab arrangement of scatter-plots below displays the same information with less complexity by breaking it into multiple graphs.

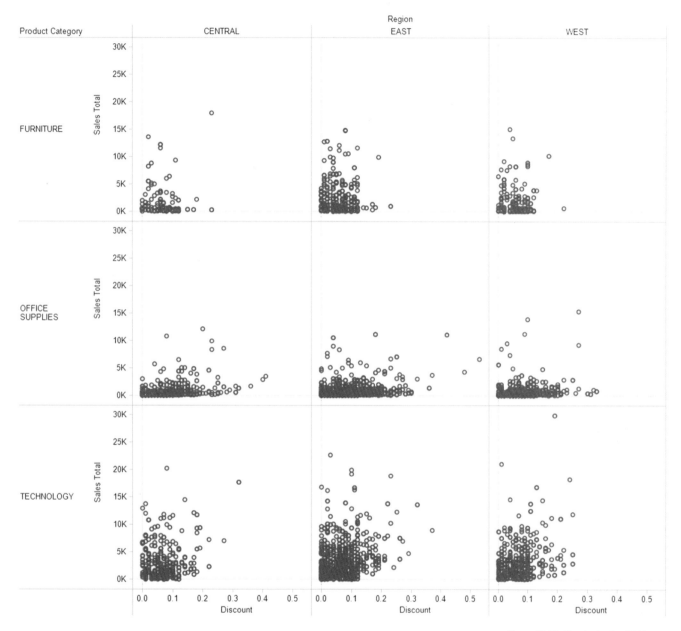

By separating each region and product category, we can now compare the correlation patterns formed by each group and more easily spot the differences. Having simplified the display, we could now introduce more meaning to the scatterplots using colors to split the values into market segments (see following page) if this enhanced breadth of view is worth the increased complexity that results.

Figure 11.39. Created using Tableau Software

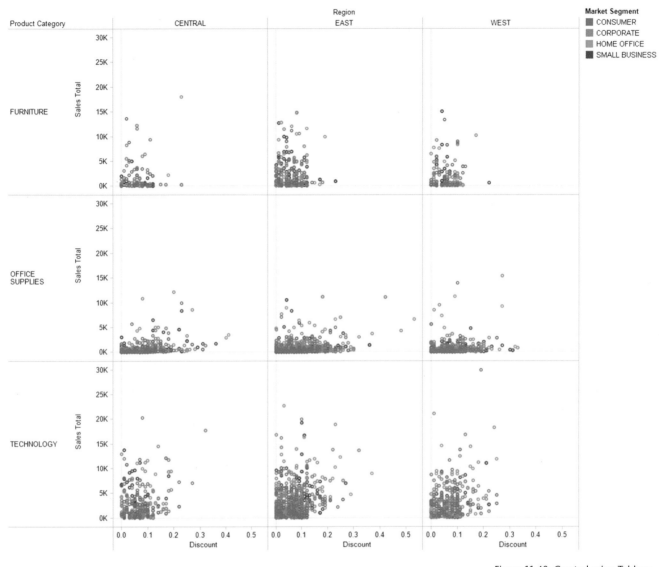

Figure 11.40. Created using Tableau
Software

Using Grid Lines to Enhance Comparisons between Scatterplots

Comparing multiple scatterplots calls for a technique to make the comparison
easier and more accurate. Imagine we're examining the relationship between
employees' annual raises and their performance ratings, and we want to see if
there's a difference between males and females. Here's how this might look in a
set of two scatterplots:

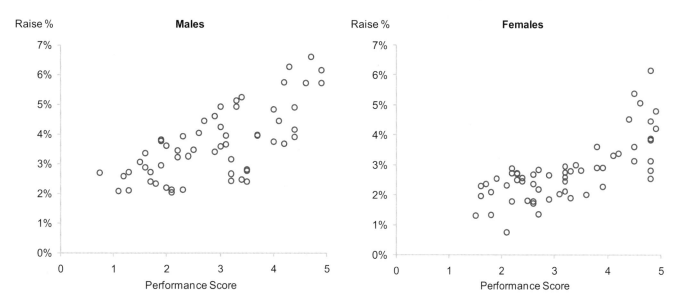

Figure 11.41

We notice that there appears to be a significant difference, especially around performance ratings of 3 and raises from 3% to 5%, which suggests that we should examine this set of values more closely. We could filter out all other performance ratings to focus exclusively on this region, but if we don't want to lose sight of the whole while attending to this one area, the simple addition of light grid lines makes it easy to isolate this section, as illustrated below.

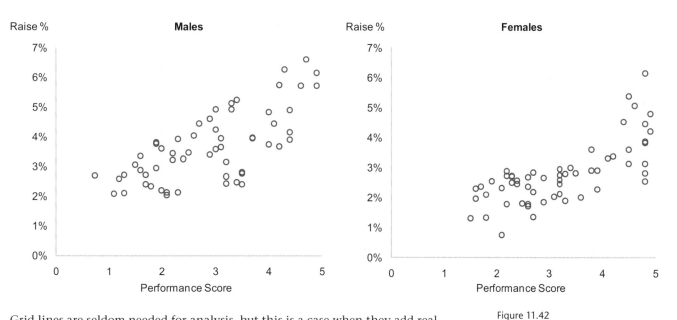

Figure 11.42

Grid lines are seldom needed for analysis, but this is a case when they add real value.

As you can see, even if you've never analyzed correlations in the past, you can venture into this territory with confidence and assurance that the journey will be worth the effort.

12 MULTIVARIATE ANALYSIS

Introduction

Multivariate analysis is a bit different from the other types we've examined. As with all types of quantitative data analysis, the fundamental activity is comparison, but the comparison in this case is more complex than for other types. Other forms of analysis usually compare multiple instances of a single quantitative variable, such as sales revenues per region, or one variable to another, such as revenue to profit. In contrast, multivariate analysis compares multiple instances of several variables at once. The purpose of multivariate analysis is to identify similarities and differences among items, each characterized by a common set of variables.

A simple example involves automobiles. Imagine that we work for an automaker, and we're trying to determine which characteristics contribute most to customer satisfaction for particular types of buyers. Our database includes the following variables, which we'll use to characterize and compare each of the cars:

- Price
- Gas mileage
- Top speed
- Number of passengers
- Cargo capacity
- Cost of insurance
- Repair costs
- Customer satisfaction rating

The values of all these variables for each car combine to form its multivariate profile. We want to compare the profiles of cars to find which ones best characterize each type of buyer, from those looking for a basic commuter vehicle to those looking for thrills. To do this effectively, we need a way to see how the cars compare across all selected variables at once. We must compare these variables as whole sets, not just individually. Multivariate analysis revolves around the following questions:

- Which items are most alike?
- Which items are most exceptional?
- How can these items be combined into logical groups based on similarity?
- What multivariate profile corresponds best to a particular outcome?

The patterns that answer these questions are the ones that are most meaningful in multivariate analysis.

Multivariate Patterns

In multivariate analysis, we examine patterns formed by several values that measure different attributes of something, which exhibit its *multivariate profile*. To do this, we must find ways to represent several variables worth of information about something as a single composite pattern. To pursue the questions listed above ("Which items are most alike?", and so on), multivariate profiles must be displayed in a way that makes it easy for us to spot similarities and differences among them even when hundreds of items are in play. The form that these patterns take is determined by the type of visualization that we use, which is what we'll take a look at now.

Multivariate Displays

I'll introduce three quite different displays that people have attempted to use for multivariate analysis. Only one is truly effective; of the other two, one does the job poorly (I've included it only so you know to avoid it) and one works satisfactorily when a better means isn't available.

These three types of displays go by the following names:

- Glyphs
- Multivariate heatmaps
- Parallel coordinates plots

The method that works well is the parallel coordinates plot, but be forewarned: it will probably seem absurd and overwhelmingly complex at first glance.

Glyphs

You can guess, based on the fact that it's part of the word "hieroglyphics," that a glyph is a picture of something. Egyptian hieroglyphics were pictures that formed a written language. In the context of information visualization, the term "glyph" has a particular meaning: "A glyph is a graphical object designed to convey multiple data values."[1] A glyph is composed of several visual attributes, each of which encodes the value of a particular variable that measures some aspect of an item. To illustrate how glyphs work, I'll construct one from scratch that I doubt has ever been used for multivariate analysis (and I hope will never be). I'll use stick drawings of people to represent multiple variables that describe or measure aspects of human physiology and health. Each of the following three glyphs represents the health of a different individual:

1. *Information Visualization: Perception for Design*, Second Edition, Colin Ware, Morgan Kaufmann Publishers, San Francisco CA, 2004, p. 145.

Figure 12.1

The variables are encoded as follows:

Visual Attribute	Variable
Color	Body temperature
Shape of the head	Blood type
Thickness of the torso	Body mass index
Position of the arms	Heart rate
Position of the legs	Blood sugar level

If we memorized the meanings of each visual attribute and learned how to decode particular expressions, such as a square versus a round head or a wide versus a narrow stance, we could theoretically use these glyphs to examine and compare the health of many individuals.

The best known example of a glyph was created by Herman Chernoff in 1972. He used simplified line drawings of the human face and mapped different variables to particular facial features (size of the eyes, curvature of the mouth, shape of the head, and so on). Here's a sample collection, each a little different.

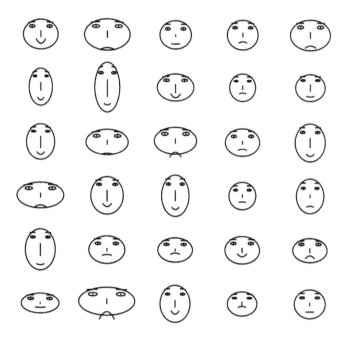

Figure 12.2. Chernoff introduced this idea in an article, "Using faces to represent points in k-dimensional space," *Journal of the American Statistical Association,* 68, 1973, pp. 361-368.

Chernoff chose the human face because human perception has evolved to rapidly read and interpret facial expressions. From early childhood we learn to recognize faces and respond to subtle facial expressions although much more is communicated by facial expression than we usually learn to recognize, such as whether or not someone is telling the truth. Despite a great many research studies that have used Chernoff faces, I have never seen any convincing evidence that they work effectively for multivariate analysis.

Two other glyphs that have also been used for multivariate analysis are called *whiskers* and *stars*. Whisker glyphs, illustrated below, consist of multiple lines that radiate out from a center point. Each line represents a different variable and its length encodes its value.

Figure 12.3

Star glyphs, illustrated below, are similar to whiskers in that variables are encoded as distance from a center point. This time the endpoints of the radiating lines are connected to form an enclosed shape.

Figure 12.4

I mentioned before that we could theoretically use glyphs to examine and compare multivariate profiles. But what works in theory does not always pan out in practice, and I believe that this is one of those cases. If you ever encounter a product that promotes glyphs for multivariate analysis, don't let the novelty of the display entice you. Put it to the test, attempting to use real data to solve real problems, and see if it works. Until glyphs can prove their worth in the realm of real-world data analysis, I recommend that you avoid products that are based on this approach.

Multivariate Heatmaps

In general, heatmaps are visual displays that encode quantitative values as variations in color. Sometimes when we speak of heatmaps, we're referring to a matrix of columns and rows, similar to a spreadsheet, that encodes quantitative values as color rather than text. Heatmaps, such as the following example, can be used to display multivariate data. In this case the items on display are products (one per row) and the quantitative variables (one per column) consist of the following:

- Price
- Duration (length of time on the market)
- Units Sold
- Revenue
- Marketing Expenses
- Profit

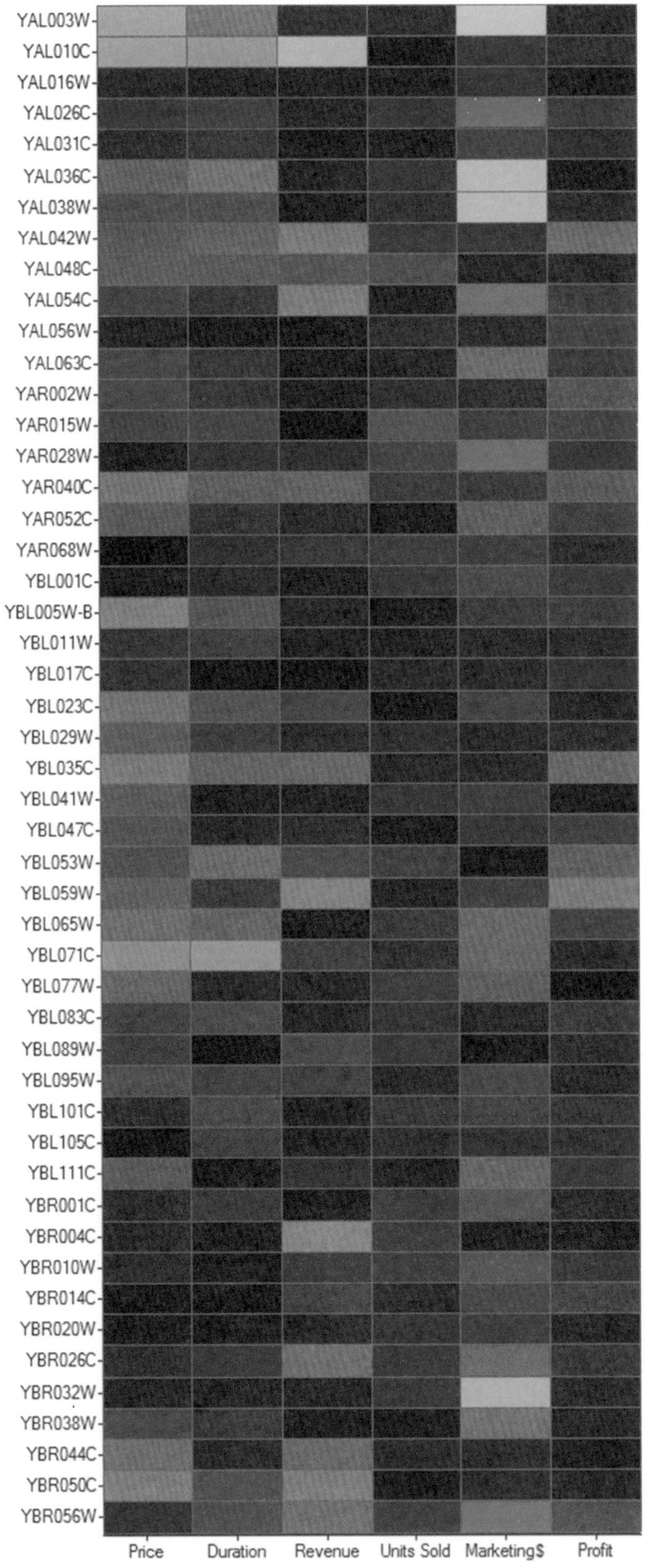

Figure 12.5. Created using Spotfire

The combination of colors across a single row displays a product's multivariate profile. In the previous example, higher-than-average values appear as green (the darker the higher), near-average values appear as black, and lower-than-average values appear as red (the darker the lower).

As you can see, heatmaps alone can be difficult to use when searching for similar profiles, but they can be used to reveal exceptions, such as the bright green and bright red values in the Marketing$ column, and predominant multivariate patterns, such as the fact that product YAL026C (the fourth row) exhibits all lower-than-normal values (red), except for Revenue.

Whether they're being used to display multivariate data or for other purposes, heatmaps suffer when colors haven't been chosen wisely. The previous example illustrates two common problems:

- The distinction between red and green cannot be seen by the 10% of males and 1% of females who suffer from the most common form of color blindness.

- When multiple hues are appropriate for encoding continuous values, such as positive and negative numbers, a dark color such as black usually shouldn't be used to encode values in the middle (in this case values near average), because it is much too salient (that is, visually prominent). Assuming it's appropriate to encode these values as above and below a particular value (in this case as above and below the average value for all products), the colors in this next version work better. Positive values are blue, negative values are red, and values near zero (average) fade from blue and red to light gray. No form of color blindness that I know would prevent people from seeing the difference between red and blue. The light gray that has been used to represent numbers close to zero intuitively represents low values and grabs our attention less than the vibrant reds and blues that have been used to draw our attention to extremes on both ends of the continuum.

Better colors have improved the following heatmap, but its usefulness for multivariate analysis is still limited, because it's difficult to see the combination of colors for particular products as a pattern. Because multivariate profiles are complex by nature, no visualization can display them with perfect clarity or be analyzed with utter ease, but the one we'll examine next stands a full head above the others.

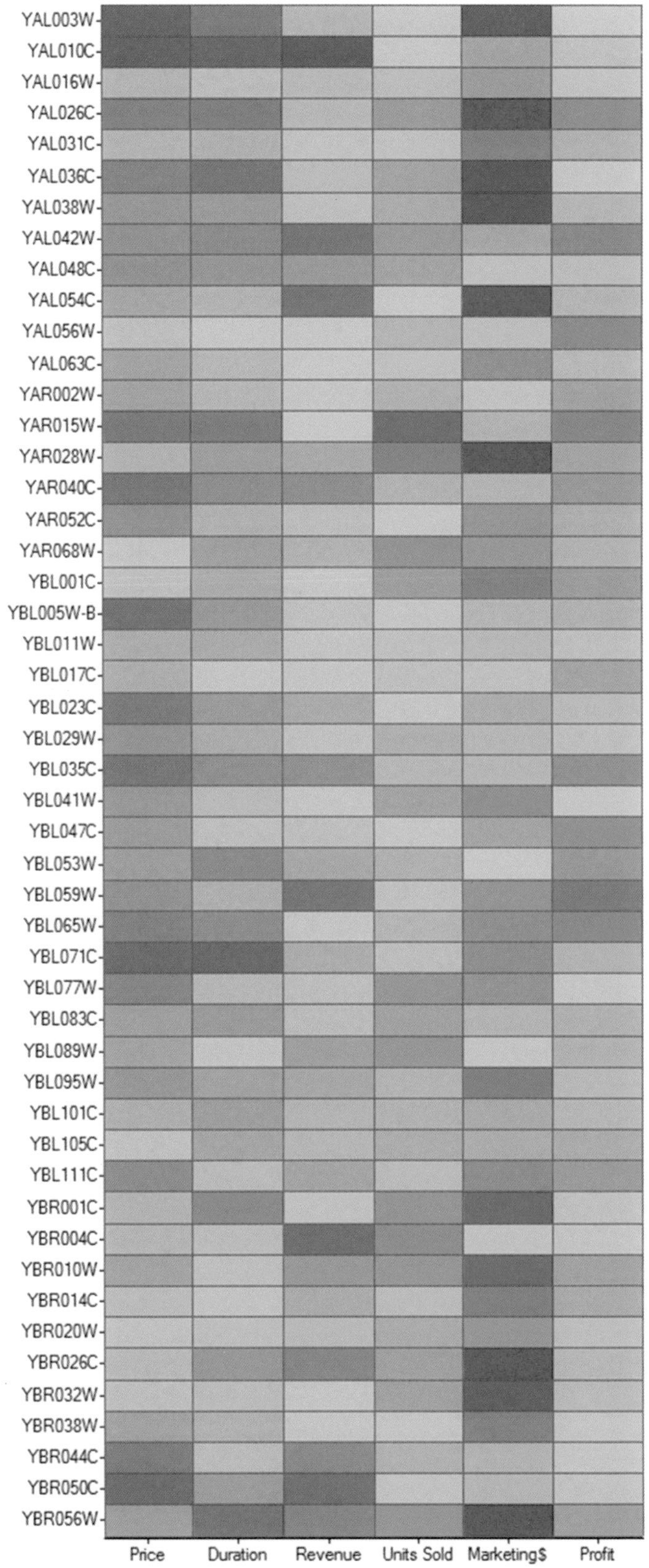

Figure 12.6. Created using Spotfire

Parallel Coordinates Plots

The first time I laid eyes on a parallel coordinates plot, I laughed and cringed simultaneously because it struck me as a ridiculously complex and ineffective display. Ordinarily, if graphs that use lines to encode data include more than a few, they deteriorate into useless clutter. Parallel coordinates plots, however, can include hundreds of lines, which in most cases would boggle the senses. Even the example below, which includes only 49 lines, will likely strike you as absurd.

Parallel Coordinate plots were invented by Alfred Inselberg in the late 1970s.

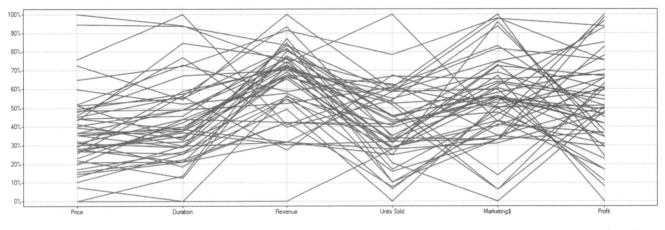

Figure 12.7. Created using Spotfire

However, this frenzy of intersecting lines, when used properly for multivariate analysis, can actually lead to great insight. It includes six variables (price, duration on the market, revenue, units sold, marketing expenses, and profit) for 49 products, one product represented by each of the lines that extends from left to right across the graph. The values for each variable in this particular example are laid out along percentage scales, which all begin at 0% at the bottom and extend to 100% at the top. For example, product prices, rather than being expressed in dollars, have been converted to percentages, with the highest priced product equal to 100% and the lowest equal to 0%. Parallel coordinates plots can be set up this way, using a common scale for all variables, or so that each variable is scaled independently using the original values, such as dollars, counts, and so on. Either way, the display looks and works in basically the same way.

Unlike regular line graphs, which should only be used to connect values along an interval scale such as time, parallel coordinates plots connect values associated with entirely different variables. In this example, measures of six different variables for a single product are connected with a line that intersects each axis at the point where the product's value for that variable is located along the scale. Although it's unusual to display values across multiple variables using a line to connect them, the shape formed by the line is meaningful because it forms a multivariate pattern that describes a particular product. The individual patterns formed by different lines can be compared to determine similarities or differences among products. That is, they could be compared if it were possible to distinguish one line from another, which we can't do with the display above.

Unlike line graphs, which use lines to connect values along an interval scale such as time, patterns formed by individual lines in a parallel coordinates plot contain less inherent meaning. If we change the order of the variables in the plot, the patterns will change, so we usually shouldn't become too attached to particular patterns, such as by taking time to memorize them as significant, but should use them only to examine and compare multivariate profiles in the moment.

What we can do with this parallel coordinates plot in its current state is glimpse the big picture: predominant patterns and exceptions. For example, we can see that one of the products (YAL010C), represented by the line that I've highlighted below, has a revenue amount that is much lower than the others. We can speculate that this is due to its short lifespan (notice its duration value) and perhaps, in part, to its low price.

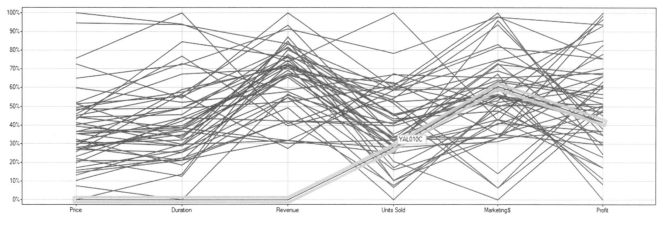

Figure 12.8. Created using Spotfire

We can make a few other observations at this point:

- One product has sold quite a bit more than its closest rival.
- Most products have been on the market from between 20% and 60% of the full range of time for all products.
- There is a heavy concentration of revenues between 65% and 85% of the full range, from least to greatest.

Even in the midst of clutter, predominant patterns and exceptions are visible. More detailed understanding will, however, require interaction with the data to cut through the clutter.

Most often when analyzing multivariate data, we look for multivariate profiles that correspond to a particular condition. For instance, if we were examining the current example, we might want to find out which multivariate profiles most correspond to high profits. It helps to position the primary variable of interest, such as profits in this case, as the last axis, as I've done in the example above, because this makes it easier to focus on that variable. To investigate multivariate conditions associated with high profits thoroughly, however, we'll need to focus on the products that intersect the profit scale near the high end, for example those with profits of 80% and above. Although we can easily distinguish those lines where they meet the profit axis, it is still difficult to follow them across the other axes because all products are displayed as dark gray lines, which are hard to distinguish from one another. So, for our analysis, we need some way to clearly separate products with high profits from the others. This can be accomplished using brushing and filtering, two of the methods that we examined in *Chapter 4: Analytical Interactions and Navigation*.

In the following example, all products with profits above 80% have been brushed, changing their color to red to make them stand out:

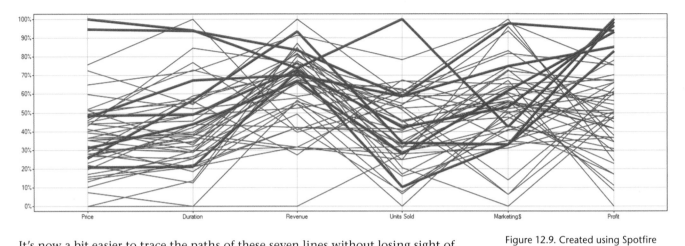

Figure 12.9. Created using Spotfire

It's now a bit easier to trace the paths of these seven lines without losing sight of the other data. In this case, the lines that aren't selected are still a little too distracting. If the unselected lines were lighter, this would probably work just fine. Or we can rely on the other method for focusing on the seven high-profit products only: filtering out all products but those with high profits, as I've done in the next graph below. Now that only seven lines remain, it's easy to check for a predominant multivariate pattern associated with highly profitable products.

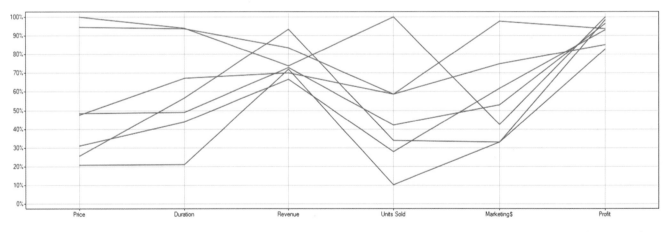

Figure 12.10. Created using Spotfire

We can now see that products with high profits exhibit a great deal of diversity in their overall multivariable profiles. A few significant patterns can be discerned, however. For instance, all products with high profits also have high revenues, which is no surprise. Also, in no case do marketing expenses fall below 30%. If we're hoping to produce high profits, the most we can say based on these particular variables is that we should try to generate high revenues and always invest more than a little in marketing.

To use parallel coordinates plots to best advantage, we need software that offers this kind of display along with good filtering and brushing functionality, but we can so something similar—identifying exceptions and predominant patterns in a set of multivariate data—using a tool as simple as Excel. By using a line graph with a line for each item that connects its value for each variable, you can create a display that looks like a parallel coordinates plot. Because a normal line graph uses the same quantitative scale for all values, however, you must normalize the quantitative scale associated with each variable so they are all the same. This can be done by converting each value of a particular variable to a percentage ranging from 0 to 100% so that all the variables share a common scale.

Multivariate Analysis Techniques and Best Practices

Visual data analysis works best in some cases when assisted by behind-the-scenes data crunching, rather than relying on our eyes alone. When we want to analyze multivariate data, computers can assist by performing the following two tasks:

- Ranking items by similarity
- Clustering items by similarity

Ranking Items by Similarity

Sometimes we examine multivariate data to find items that come close to matching a particular multivariate profile. For example, we might be interested in finding, among a pool of many thousand products, those with relatively low prices that have been on the market for an average amount of time, generate high revenues but have sold a relatively small number of units, and have lower-than-average marketing expenses yet high profits. It would be useful if we could describe this pattern and ask the software to find all products that come close to it. To illustrate how some software products do this, I'll use the same data set as above. The product that I'm using to illustrate this process, *Spotfire DecisionSite*, can search for patterns based on a multivariate profile that actually exists in the data set (including one that you enter specifically for this purpose), so I've selected one that comes close to the pattern described above, which I've highlighted in the example below.

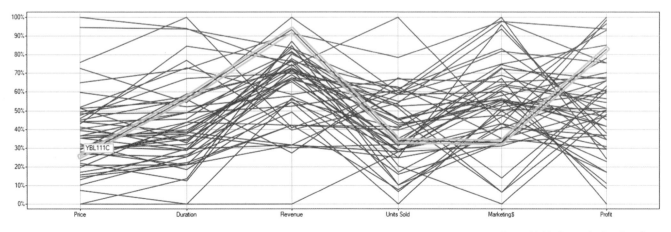

Figure 12.11. Created using Spotfire

After selecting this particular profile, I took advantage of Spotfire's pattern-detection functionality and asked it to search for similar profiles. In response, it automatically ranked every one of the 49 products from lowest to highest, based on how closely each corresponds to the selected profile. It also assigned a correlation coefficient value ranging from -1 (perfect negative correlation) to +1 (perfect positive correlation) to each. In the example below, I filtered out all but the selected profile (the highlighted line) and the one that is most similar to it.

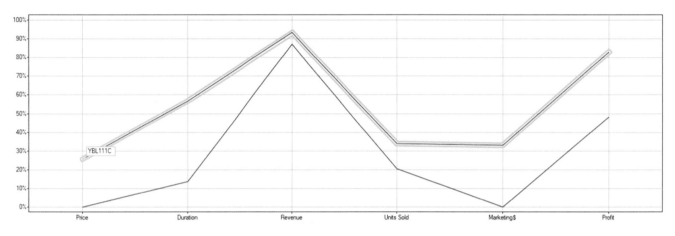

12.12. Created using Spotfire

The overall correlation coefficient of these two profiles is 0.90, which indicates a high positive correlation. When we're dealing with hundreds or perhaps thousands of items, our eyes aren't the best tools for spotting items that fit a particular multivariate profile. On such occasions, it makes sense to rely on computers to do what they do well—rapid and accurate calculations—and then let our eyes take over to examine the results.

Clustering Items by Similarity

Clustering is the process of segmenting data into groups whose items share a similar feature or features. In the example that we've been examining, similarity is determined by how much products are alike based on the total set of variables that we're examining (price, duration, and so on). Once again, computers are well equipped to do this work using a statistical clustering algorithm, which would be difficult and time consuming to do using our eyes. I asked the software to cluster the products for me, and it produced the six groups that appear below, each with its own color:

Clusters
☑ 1
☑ 2
☑ 3
☑ 4
☑ 5
☑ 6

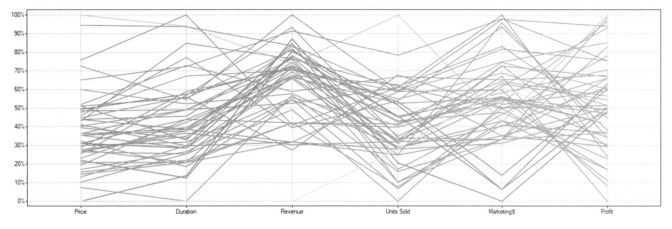

Even though the groups are distinguished by color, it's hard to see their similarities in the midst of this visual clutter. To make it easier, I asked the software to separate the groups using a trellis display, with one group one per graph.

Figure 12.13. Created using Spotfire

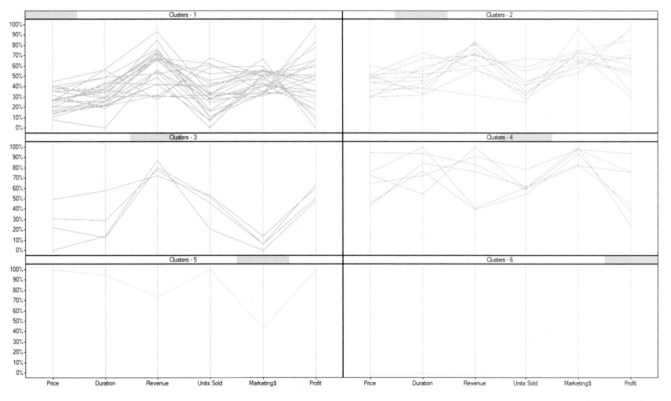

Figure 12.14. Created using Spotfire

Two of the products have such unique multivariate profiles (clusters 5 and 6), they've been placed in groups of their own. The product in cluster 5 has the highest profits of all. A total of 25 products were placed in cluster 1. The fact that this many products were this much alike wasn't obvious when viewing all the products together. Notice how similar to one another the products in the third group appear to be. The consistent midrange profits and low marketing expenses make these products worth further examination.

Statistical clustering algorithms are mathematically complicated. I won't pretend to be able to judge the relative merits of the many that are available. I trust that each is capable of doing the job and recommend that you use whatever method your software supports. If several similarity-matching methods are available, stick with the default method unless you've taken the time to learn their differences and the circumstances that make one better than the others.

This introduction to multivariate analysis and to parallel coordinates plots in particular is brief and designed to whet your appetite just enough to interest you in learning more. I hope you've recognized the rich potential of multivariate analysis.

PART III FURTHER THOUGHTS AND HOPES

I've tried to keep in mind while writing this book that its readers will use many different data analysis tools, some of which are far from ideal. I've tried to feature visualizations and analytical techniques that are supported by a broad range of products. I haven't neglected, however, to also introduce powerful visualizations and analytical techniques that aren't yet supported by most products because I want you to know how much more you can accomplish with the right tools.

Information visualization is still relatively new; what it offers has only made its way into a few commercially available products. Fortunately, many vendors that have fallen behind are beginning to recognize this fact. Given time, they'll learn enough about information visualization to add the capabilities that are really needed and really work, rather than the superficial and ineffective fluff that many have been inclined to offer so far. Despite information visualization's young age and the faltering steps that most vendors have taken toward helping us all maximize its benefits, a few vendors have developed products that can open our eyes to a rich data landscape and give us the means to explore it.

Today, with the right products, you can approach your data using the entire toolset that I've described. You can begin to experience what I call analytical flow: immersion in data, working at peak cognitive performance to make sense of it. Milhaly Csikszentmihalyi, a brilliant psychologist, coined the term flow to describe the experience of optimal performance, clear focus, and timeless absorption in an activity. You might consider me a data nerd for admitting without shame that I love wading into a river of information and giving myself up to the flow of discovery. This flow can only happen when software supports analysis so effectively that the tools recede from our awareness, allowing our eyes to see and our minds to explore, query, and understand without distraction.

What about the future of information visualization and why should we care? What's in store for those of us who seek to reveal the mysteries and insights that lie waiting in data? What can we hope to achieve? I hope that, when we look back in 10 years, the analytical flow that we can experience with the best tools of today will seem like viewing the world through a bug-splattered windshield on a dark and foggy night compared to the clarity of vision and fullness of understanding that we'll be able to experience then. I and many others will no doubt have to clean a lot of dirty windshields between now and then to get us there. Many bright and passionate people are already doing their part to make this happen. In the final two chapters of this book, I'll give you a glimpse into the future of information visualization that is now being created and then tell you why I think it matters.

Chapter 13—Promising Trends in Information Visualization

Chapter 14—Wisdom in the Age of Information

13 PROMISING TRENDS IN INFORMATION VISUALIZATION

In this chapter, we'll take a peek at eight current trends in information visualization research and development that will soon help us take greater advantage of the information age.

- Built-in best practices
- Integrated support for geo-spatial analysis
- Integrated support for network analysis
- Integrated support for collaborative analysis
- Custom analytical applications
- Illuminating predictive models
- Integrated data mining
- Improved human-computer interface devices

We'll take a brief look at each.

Built-in Best Practices

An encouraging trend that is near and dear to my heart can be seen in the efforts of a few software vendors who work to build analytical best practices right into their products. We know from experience and a great deal of research that some practices are usually effective and others are not. Good products make it as easy as possible for people to do things well and difficult to do things poorly. I agree with Richard H. Thaler and Cass R. Sunstein, the authors of *Nudge: Improving Decisions About Health, Wealth, and Happiness*, who argue that products and systems, especially those with which people interact to make decisions, ought to be designed to nudge them in the direction of what best serves their true interests. Yes, I believe software vendors bear a responsibility to nudge us in the right direction. We rightfully expect vendors to be the experts and to build products that reflect that expertise.

Consider this example. Most people never change software defaults, even when those defaults serve their needs poorly. They assume, as they ought, that the software vendor made good choices for them. But this is often not the case. Something as simple as well-thought-through defaults can go a long way toward improving our experience and the quality of results. An important example involves the use of color when visualizing data. Knowing which colors to use for particular purposes requires a level of expertise that most of us who analyze data shouldn't be required to have. Why not provide a few well-designed color palettes for particular purposes and make them easy to select and use? Why not engage the services of a color expert to design these palettes? It's shocking how rarely such obviously useful steps are taken when products are developed.

Another fine example of building intelligence about best practices into software would make it easy for us to select appropriate graphs given the nature

Nudge: Improving Decisions About Health, Wealth, and Happiness, Richard A. Thaler and Cass R. Sunstein, Yale University Press, New Haven CT, 2008.

The color palettes that are available in Tableau Software were designed by Maureen Stone, an expert in color and how it can be used most effectively to visualize data. The colors that are available in an Excel add-in product that I designed named *Chart Tamer* (from *Bonavista Systems*) were also provided by Stone. I've used some of these colors in visualization examples throughout this book.

of the data we're examining. For example, if the information we're examining doesn't involve time or something else that divides a continuous range of quantitative values into intervals of equal size (for example, ages 10-19, 20-29, and so on), we should be discouraged from using a line graph. If we choose graphs from a list or set of icons, the line graph should be dimmed to indicate its unavailability. To date, I've only seen this level of nudge built into one visual analysis product, but this will surely change in time. Software should only ask us to choose from viable options.

One final example appears to currently exist in one product, but work is going on among information visualization researchers to come up with better ways to support the practice. Remember that in *Chapter 7: Time-Series Analysis*, I briefly mentioned that patterns of change are often easiest to examine and compare using a line graph when the slope of change is banked to 45°, a practice that was originally promoted by William Cleveland. Given the usefulness of this approach, why not build into software an automated means to adjust the aspect ratio of a graph such that patterns of interest or the data set as a whole are banked to 45°? Apparently, the statistical analysis language R has provided this functionality for years. Now that improved algorithms for banking to 45° are available based on recent work by Maneesh Agrawala and Jeffrey Heer of the University of California, Berkeley, it would be a great time for vendors move these useful methods from the research laboratory to the real world by incorporating them into their products. Far too many good ideas like this one are gathering dust in stacks of academic journals.

Integrated Support for Geo-spatial Analysis

The original outline of this book included a chapter on geo-spatial analysis. I didn't omit it because it isn't worthwhile but because I felt that I couldn't do it justice in a few pages even if my goal was to introduce it and nothing more. Quantitative analysis is sometimes meaningful only if we can see where things are located; fortunately for us, what was previously the domain of a few analysts whose employers could afford expensive geo-spatial software is now becoming widely available. Google Maps and the mash-ups that can be displayed on them have sparked people's imaginations about what we can learn when examining data geo-spatially. Google Maps weren't designed for quantitative analysis, but more and more visual analysis products are now taking geographical displays seriously and providing functionality that takes advantage of the analytical potential of these displays. The flip side of this coin, unfortunately but not unexpectedly, is that almost every business intelligence software vendor out there now claims to support geo-spatial analysis even though most of them have done nothing more than provide the means to place crude quantitative displays on poorly designed maps.

Just because you can now display quantitative data on a map doesn't mean you should in every case. The location of something or its proximity to something else is not always useful information for analysis. But in some cases, it is critical to display data on a map. The example below nicely illustrates a case in which the data couldn't be understood without a geospatial display.

Figure 13.1. E. W. Gilbert, "Pioneer Maps of Health and Disease in England," *Geographical Journal*, 124, 1958.

Dr. John Snow created this display in an attempt to figure out the cause of a cholera epidemic in London in 1854. Each death is marked by a dot, and each of central London's water pumps is marked by an X. By viewing the data in this way, Snow was able to determine that the Broad Street pump (the one in the center of the map) was probably the source of the disease; he confirmed his hypothesis by removing the handle so the pump could not be used, which ended an epidemic that had taken over 500 lives.

In contrast, placing traffic lights to indicate the state of sales in four regions on a map of the United States as shown in next example adds no value. A simple table with a sales total for each region would have provided the information more directly.

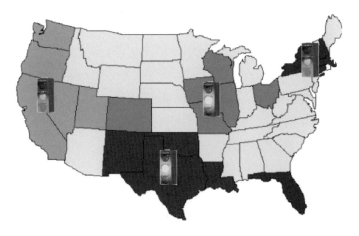

Figure 13.2. Derived from a dashboard found on the website of Hyperion Solutions Corporation, which has since been acquired by Oracle Corporation

To deliver something useful, software vendors must take advantage of what cartographers have learned through centuries of study, and marry this knowledge with what vendors already know about quantitative analysis. Here's a geo-spatial display of incidents requiring emergency response in a part of Seattle, Washington: assaults in dark gray, fires in red, and medical emergencies in green. Notice that the map has been designed to provide a platform for the quantitative data without distracting details, showing just enough geographical information to provide meaningful context.

Figure 13.3. Created using Tableau Software

If we zoom into a smaller section of this display to examine it in greater detail, we would ideally like a finer level of geographical detail to appear automatically, such as the names of major streets, as shown in the following example.

Figure 13.4. Created using Tableau Software

Another zoom should cause more geographical details to automatically appear, based on some intelligence about what most analysts would find useful, such as the additional level of street information that appears in the next example.

Figure 13.5. Created using Tableau Software

Notice, however, that it's not as easy as it should be to see the quantitative data in the midst of the geographical information. At this point, it would be useful to reduce the salience of the geographical information until it's visible enough to do its job without being so visible that it competes with the quantitative data. Having a convenient means to fade the map further into the background, such as a simple slider control, would be ideal, which is precisely what I used to produce the following example.

Figure 13.6. Created using Tableau Software

The best design guidelines for effective geo-spatial displays that I've found to date are available in *Designing Better Maps: A Guide for GIS Users*, Cynthia A. Brewer, ESRI Press, Redlands CA, 2005.

This is the level of attention to design that is required to support effective geo-spatial analysis, as a few vendors are beginning to figure out.

Integrated Support for Network Analysis

For many years information visualization researchers have focused a great deal of attention on the development of network visualizations. By network, I mean a set of entities that relate to one another in a manner that isn't structured as a neat hierarchy. For example, the World Wide Web, with its millions of websites, is a network. Websites are related to one another through a multidirectional set of links. The following example illustrates a popular use of network visualizations today for examining social networks. It uses nodes (the things, which in this case are people) and links (the relationships, which in this case indicate social connections).

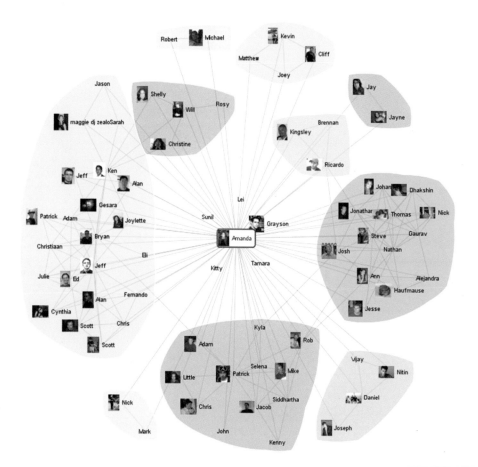

Figure 13.7. Created by Jeffrey Heer and Danah Boyd of the University of California, Berkeley, using *Vizster*.

The world is full of networks of all kinds. Employees are connected through email communications; research papers are connected by citations to one another's work; articles are connected through common topics; products are connected through common attributes. When these relationships are integral to the story that we're trying to uncover, network visualizations can play a critical role. When quantitative information is integrated into network visualizations, such as by varying the sizes of nodes that represent websites to show the amount of traffic they get and varying the thickness of the lines that connect them to show the number of links between them, we are dealing with a special form of quantitative analysis.

Intelligence and law enforcement agencies have considered network visualizations critical for several years, but their use for an expanding range of applications is now catching on. People who routinely do other types of quantitative analysis are now recognizing the potential of network visualizations, which is encouraging researchers and some software vendors to merge network visualizations and other quantitative visualizations into single products. For instance, the Human-Computer Interaction Lab (HCIL) at the University of Maryland is working on a project to better integrate these complementary visualizations and operations, which they describe in the following image:

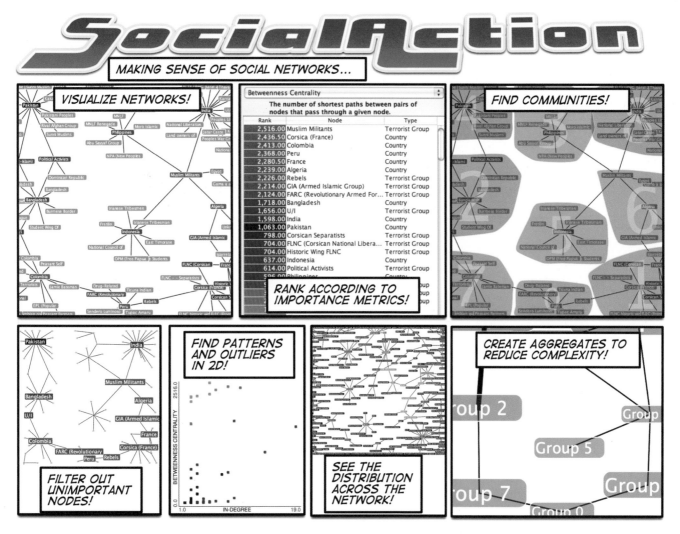

Imagine the ability to examine a network of connections to find significant relationships, then see how they have changed through time in a line graph, then put a few items into a bar graph to see how they relate to one another by rank, and finally pick a smaller subset so we can examine specific correlations in a scatterplot. As the best of network visualizations become an integral part of our analytical toolsets, over time they will become just another tool that we use as naturally as traditional graphs, and that's when their potential will be truly realized.

Figure 13.8. Created by Adam Perer of the Human-Computer Interaction Lab at the University of Maryland.

Integrated Support for Collaborative Analysis

As the old saying goes, sometimes two heads are better than one. Two heads (or more) are definitely better in data analysis, but few of the tools that we use for analysis support collaboration. This has recently begun to change as information visualization researchers are exploring the social aspects of data analysis. During the past few years, several researchers, inspired by the popularity of social networks on the Web, have focused on this promising venture. The best example of this work so far, called *Many Eyes*, was developed by Martin Wattenberg and Fernanda Viégas of *IBM Research* and is freely available for anyone to use.

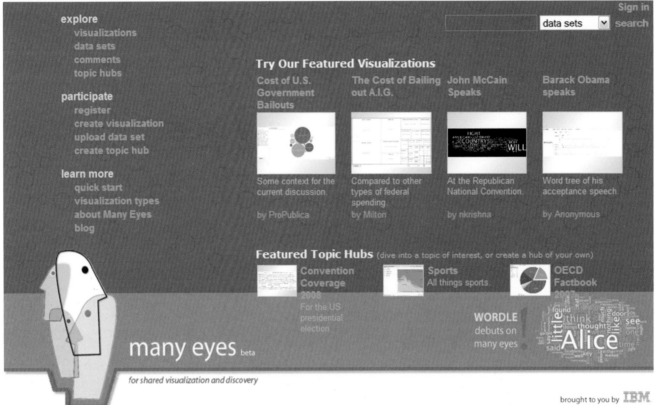

Figure 13.9. The home page of Many Eyes at www.many-eyes.com

It's clear that these folks love their work, care about visualization, and want to make it easier for people to think about important information by collaborating to deepen and broaden understanding. In their own words:

> *All of us…are passionate about the potential of data visualization to spark insight. It is that magical moment we live for: an unwieldy, unyielding data set is transformed into an image on the screen, and suddenly the user can perceive an unexpected pattern. As visualization designers we have witnessed and experienced many of those wondrous sparks. But in recent years, we have become acutely aware that the visualizations and the sparks they generate take on new value in a social setting. Visualization is a catalyst for discussion and collective insight about data.[1]*

1. From the "About Us" page at www.many-eyes.com

In a study that preceded the release of Many Eyes, Wattenberg and Viégas, working with Jeffrey Heer of the University of California, Berkeley, elaborated on their motives.

> *Information visualization leverages the human visual system to improve our ability to process large amounts of data…In practice, however, sensemaking is often also a social process. People may disagree on how to interpret the data and may contribute contextual knowledge that deepens understanding. As participants build consensus or make decisions they learn from their peers. Furthermore, some data sets are so large that thorough exploration by a single person is unlikely. This suggests that to fully support sensemaking, visualizations should also support social interaction.[2]*

In addition to a nice selection of well-designed visualizations, Many Eyes makes it easy for people to upload their own data to the site, organize and find displays on particular topics or based on popularity, filter data with ease, comment on one another's displays in blog-like fashion, and then add their own variation for others to view and respond to, perhaps featuring some other aspect of the data involving a different type of graph.

Here's the visualization that had the highest popularity rating on the Many Eyes website when I wrote this sentence:

2. Jeffrey Heer, Martin Wattenberg, and Fernanda Viégas, "Voyagers and Voyeurs: Supporting Asynchronous Collaborative Information Visualization," *Proc. ACM CHI*, Apr 2007. In this study they confirmed the usefulness of supporting collaborative analysis in the following ways:
- *Doubly linked discussion.* Means to post comments about a visualization as discussion threads
- *Graphical annotation.* Means to annotate specific parts of a visualization
- *Bookmark trails.* Means to embed links in comments to different versions of a visualization to enable narrative about the data
- *Comment listings and social navigation.* Means to search for particular comments that are of interest based either on topics or the people who posted them

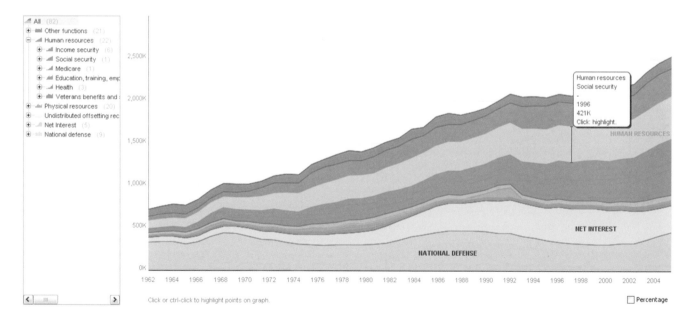

As you can see, people are interested in knowing how the federal government is spending our tax dollars. The legend on the left, which I clicked on to show the list of items that make up the human resources category of expenses, also functions as a filter control. The tooltip window near the right edge of the graph popped up when I hovered with the mouse over that particular item (Social Security expenses in the human resources category) at that particular point in time (the year 1996) to get the amount of social security expenses for that year

Figure 13.10. Example of a graph that was posted on the site www.many-eyes.com

($421K, which, because these values are being expressed in millions, actually equals $421 billion).

By the time that I captured this image from the site, 30 people had posted comments about various aspects of this information, many of whom created their own visualizations to highlight particular discoveries that they'd made or to pose questions. The first commenter added the following visualization to the discussion and asked "What is this spike in housing assistance?"

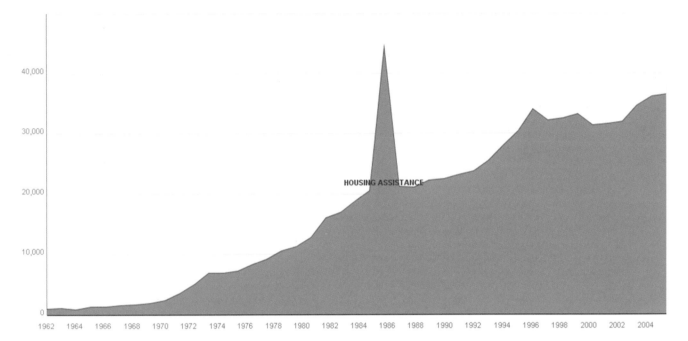

Figure 13.11. Example of a graph that was posted in response to the one in Figure 13.10 on the site www.many-eyes.com

We are only beginning to learn how collaborative analysis can be fostered through research projects such as Many Eyes. As we learn more and products add functionality to support better collaboration, I have no doubt that our efforts will be richly rewarded. Each of us benefits when our two eyes and one brain are complemented by the many eyes and brains of others, each adding unique perspectives and insights.

Many Eyes supports collaboration asynchronously, but at least one other effort has made it possible for people to analyze data collaboratively in real time. The software company *Viz* (formerly *Maya Viz*, before it was acquired by *General Dynamics*) developed a product named *CoMotion*, which is currently being used primarily by the U.S. military to manage field operations in Iraq and Afghanistan. Commanders and analysts are able, both individually and collaboratively, to view and analyze facts about military actions as these actions are happening. Individuals maintain their own views but also have the ability to share their views with others, which remain available for anyone to examine as needed. Anyone can get a sense of what others are thinking by looking at their views and can interact at any time, not only by speaking with the others, but also by annotating their shared views, just as they might do if they were standing around a map in a command post.

To effectively support this kind of analytical collaboration, technology must make it possible for people to share a common "cognitive space" (that is, a common mental model). For military operations, that shared model primarily revolves around a geographical display (that is, a map), which is supplemented as needed by other visualizations, such as line charts that show what's happening through time. As you can imagine, collaborative analytical technology of this sort could be used for many purposes other than military operations. Viz is currently reaching out to organizations of all types to help them apply this powerful and enriched approach to collaborative thinking and decision making. One example involves work that they're doing with pharmaceutical companies to help them manage the drug development process. In this case, rather than constructing a shared cognitive space around a map, a timeline visualization similar to a Gantt chart helps everyone from project managers to individual scientists feel as if they're standing around a huge project model together with plenty of blackboard space available to express and discuss their ideas, rather than being separated by thousands of miles.

A Gantt chart is commonly used by those who manage programs and projects to keep track of tasks and their relationships on a timeline.

Custom Analytical Applications

Not everyone whose job involves some degree of data analysis has the skills needed to tackle complex analytical challenges on their own. People who aren't highly-skilled analysts but are experts in their work and the information that informs it, however, can often handle complex analytics using prebuilt software applications that support the process in a simple, straightforward manner. Sophisticated analysts can work with subject matter experts to develop custom applications to support their analytical requirements—applications that the subject matter experts couldn't build by themselves but could easily use once they're built.

Many of the best visual analysis tools now provide the means for skilled analysts to build specialized analytical applications that ease the process for others by including only the required data, expressed in familiar terms, and involving a limited set of simple interactions. This opens the door for the expansion of analytical opportunities to a broader audience of people who could not and need not perform a wide range of analytical tasks, but who have no trouble making sense of their data when the right customized tools have been built for them.

In the example on the next page, routine sales analysis tasks have been delivered in a series of screens, which we can access in separate tabbed folders. Each screen provides us with instructions (shown on the left in the example), along with a set of customized visualizations (a scatterplot, map, and bar graph in this case) and only those filter controls that are needed for the task at hand.

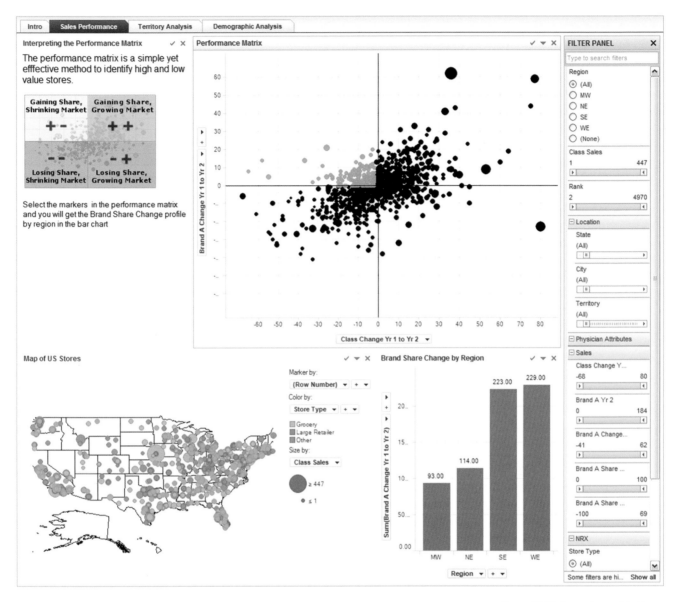

Figure 13.12. Example provided by Spotfire

This is a relatively simple example that wouldn't require a high-level of analytical skill to construct, but others can be quite complicated to design, perhaps involving sophisticated statistical models, but quite easy to use once they're put together.

Illuminating Predictive Models

In this book we've focused primarily on analysis that attempts to uncover and understand the meanings that reside in existing information, a record of the past. This kind of analysis is called *descriptive analysis* (a.k.a. *descriptive statistics*). The greatest benefits of data analysis, however, often come from using what we have learned of the past to predict the future. This is called *predictive analysis* (a.k.a. *predictive statistics*) or in some cases *"what-if" analysis*. If we understand the past well enough to describe it clearly and accurately, we can often build a model that we can use to predict what will likely happen as a result of particular conditions, events, or decisions in the future.

This interest in prediction is a preoccupation of statistics, and for good reason. When supported by good visualizations, statistical analysis comes alive in a way that not only helps statisticians but makes it easier for a broad audience to make good decisions with greater certainty about the outcomes.

The goal of predictive analysis is not to produce certainty about the future, but to reduce uncertainty to a degree that enables us to make better decisions. To reduce uncertainty about the future, statisticians build models. Don't let the terms *statistical model* or *predictive model* throw you. In concept, they're quite simple, just like more familiar models of other types. Generally speaking, models are representations of things or events, which we use to examine and understand those things or events when it isn't possible or practical to observe or interact with them directly. Statistical models represent mathematical relationships between the parts that make up the thing or event. Predictive models are those that we can interact with to investigate the results of hypothetical conditions, such as by changing the values of particular variables. A model must capture the essence of the thing it represents, finding the right balance between too much information and too little. To build an effective model, you must understand the thing being modeled well enough to pick out the important parts and ignore the others, and to represent only the aspects of those important parts that are relevant to the task.

Most of the applications that I've seen marketed by business intelligence software vendors for predictive analysis allow data to be entered on one end (inputs) and then results (outputs) pop out the other; what goes on in between remains hidden in a black box. Unfortunately, without seeing what goes on in that black box, our brains aren't fully engaged in the process and too much is missed. Visualizations help us see more of what's going on, allowing us to reason about relationships—how variables interact with one another to produce particular results. I call these *transparent* predictive models. This level of involvement in the analytical process takes advantage of our brains in a way that throws open the windows to insights we might never otherwise experience.

I developed the following example to illustrate how a predictive model can be built to reveal the relationships within using *JMP*, a product from SAS.

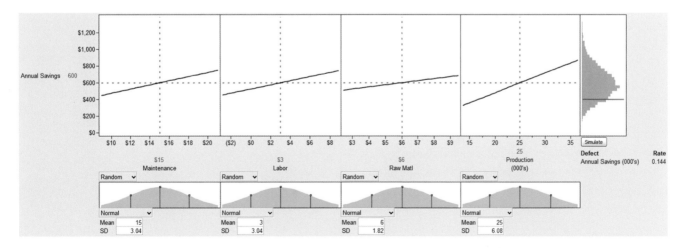

Figure 13.13. Created using the "Profiler" in JMP

This relatively simple model was designed to predict the risk associated with leasing a piece of manufacturing equipment for $400,000 per year. It involves four independent variables—maintenance savings, labor savings, raw material savings, and production volume (the number of items manufactured)—that can be manipulated by entering various values to estimate the amount of annual savings (the dependent variable) that will result. Each of the four square-shaped graphs along the top shows the relationship between one of the independent variables, with a quantitative scale on the X-axis (for example, maintenance savings on the far left with a dollar scale ranging from $10 to $20), and the dependent variable, annual savings, with its dollar scale (in thousands) ranging from $0 to $1,200,000 on the Y-axis. The vertical red dashed line can be moved left or right to change the input value for the independent variable and watch how that change would likely affect annual savings. Unlike many predictive models, this one allows us to not only immediately see the effect of changes to independent variables on the dependent variable, but also the effect that changes to one independent variable has on the other independent variables. Within a few seconds of playing with this model, changing the value of one variable to watch the effect on others, I noticed that labor savings and raw material savings had relatively little effect on annual savings and that an effort to increase maintenance savings and production volume would yield the best results.

In addition to testing "what-if" scenarios, JMP made it easy to run more sophisticated and revealing *Monte Carlo simulations* to assess the risk that annual savings would fail to meet or exceed the $400,000 annual cost of the lease. Monte Carlo simulations generate random values for the independent variables within ranges of likely values (for example, an expert estimate that 90% of the time maintenance savings would range between $10 and $20 per unit) and instructions about how the distribution of a full set of random values should be shaped (such as the shown in the bottom row of graphs in the example above, each of which was set up as a normal, bell-shaped distribution). After defining these parameters for the randomly generated values, I simply asked JMP to run 5,000 Monte Carlo simulations. In less than a second I was informed by the green histogram on the right with the red reference line marking the $400,000 savings threshold that the risk of saving less money than the cost of the lease was only 14.4% (the defect rate below the histogram).

My purpose here isn't to teach you how to build predictive models or to run Monte Carlo simulations, but simply to demonstrate that if we have good tools to build models like this, even if we don't know how to build the model, any one of us could easily use it once it's built to do predictive analysis. When a model is built like this to make good use of our eyes for pattern detection and to engage our minds by revealing relationships among all the variables, we have the means to reason analytically about the future, rather than to simply trust the answer that the model spits out, with no means to judge its merits.

I derived this risk assessment scenario from a wonderful book by Douglas W. Hubbard entitled *How to Measure Anything: Finding the Value of Intangibles in Business*, John Wiley and Sons, Inc., Hoboken NJ, 2007.

Integrated Data Mining

Data mining is one of those terms that people often use imprecisely, often erroneously as a synonym for data analysis. Data mining involves computer-based processes that search for and discover potentially meaningful relationships in our data that we don't already know are there, and for which we might have not even thought to look. With the right algorithms, computers can search through huge databases to find anomalies and potentially interesting connections at a speed and in a manner that we could never match with our eyes. Computers often can't explain the relationships that they find, nor can they spot some of the patterns we can easily discern with our eyes when represented visually. Why not marry the processing power of computers to the complementary abilities of our eyes and brains? This seems like such an obvious thing to do, but relatively few products have done this so far. I suspect that this is because an unfortunate rift exists between experts in data mining and experts in other forms of data analysis, including information visualization, which has undermined collaboration between these camps. A few vendors, however, are trying to bring them together.

One such product that I've worked with—*Advizor Analyst*—combines data mining's potential for discovery with data visualization's ability to examine patterns and make sense of them. It allows us to begin by selecting a variable as our target of interest (dependent variable)—usually a quantitative measure, such as profit margin. It then helps us discover what influences the target variable's behavior by setting the data mining algorithm loose in search of those variables that affect it most. This results in a display in the form of a bar graph that we can use to compare the influence of each independent variable on the target variable. But the real value of data mining resides not solely in what I've described so far—data mining alone—but in what emerges when it and visualization are seamlessly integrated. We can attain much greater levels of insight by using information visualization to confirm data mining's results and learn what they mean. I hope that in the next few years more software vendors will find ways to marry data mining and visualization in ways that leverage the strengths of each. It's time for these two powerful tools shake hands and begin working together.

Improved Human-Computer Interface Devices

A couple of years ago I watched a video on the Web of Jeff Han, founder of *Perceptive Pixel*, demonstrating his new multi-touch computer interface. It was more like watching a magician than an engineer. Like many others who've seen Han doing demonstrations, I began drooling within a few seconds for an interface like that of my own.

Figure 13.14. Jeff Han (right) demonstrating the technology of his company Perceptive Pixel.

Multi-touch interfaces respond to simultaneous inputs from multiple fingers and even multiple people. Beyond the obvious coolness of being able to interact with a computer in this way, multitouch computing is potentially exciting because "simultaneous finger inputs allow more complex gestures than simple pointing and clicking, such as rotating or resizing a photo by grabbing two corners and pulling or navigating a map by pulling and twisting the image with your fingers." According to Han, "Multitouch gets most exciting when it's big. Up until now, computers have been all about you and the machine, but multi-touch is all about multiple people collaborating."[3] Similar to what Han is making available in large formats for multiple people to use at the same time, *Apple Computer* has given us in the small format of the *iPhone*. The extent to which multitouch interfaces will be useful is not yet clear. They produce an engaging demo, but we humans tend to use one hand at a time, and to produce complex gestures with our dominant hand only. New ways of interacting with information such as multi-touch interfaces probably won't replace the keyboard and mouse anytime soon, if ever, but they do seem to make it possible at times to do information visualization, especially in groups, with greater ease, speed, and agility.

Science fiction has been teasing us for years with possible ways to make the computer a more natural and seamless extension of our bodies and minds, and some of those glimpses into the future have found their way to the present. Virtual worlds, such as *Second Life*, suggest potential new ways to interact, not just with other people, but perhaps with visualizations of abstract data. So far, I haven't seen examples of information visualization in virtual worlds that seem useful (climbing around on a bar graph just isn't that enlightening), but who knows what might be born from the right collision of ideas. For now, I'm happy to see researchers applying multitouch computing to information visualization, but next year a whole new paradigm could emerge. When it does, I'll be there to put it to the test.

3. "Buzzword: Multitouch Computing", Glenn Derene, www.popularmechanics.com, February 20, 2007.

14 WISDOM IN THE AGE OF INFORMATION

Information can't always speak for itself. It relies on us to give it a voice. When we do, information can tell its story, which leads to understanding. Our ultimate goal, however, is not to just increase our understanding; it is to use our understanding wisely. Understanding becomes wisdom when it's used to do something good. Information has served its purpose and we have done our job only when we use what we know to make the world a better place.

> *Our networks are awash in data. A little of it is information. A smidgen of this shows up as knowledge. Combined with ideas, some of that is actually useful. Mix in experience, context, compassion, discipline, humor, tolerance, and humility, and perhaps knowledge becomes wisdom.*[1]

1. *Turning Numbers into Knowledge*, Jonathan G. Koomey, Analytics Press, Oakland CA, 2001, p. 5, quoting Clifford Stoll.

I could have ended the book without this final chapter, or I could have tucked it away in an epilogue that few would ever read, but what I'm trying to say here is too important to omit or downplay. As professionals who work with information, we bear a responsibility to use information wisely. If we take pride in our work, we want it to count for something. Granted, we can't control all the decisions that are made based on the understanding that we achieve and pass on to others, but we can do our best to make the truth known and understood and thereby give those we support what they need to choose wisely.

Of all the many parts that combine to produce an information system, none is more important than this final step of actually putting the information to good use. I love information, in part for the understanding that it offers; understanding in and of itself brings me pleasure. Mostly, though, I love it for what I can do with it to leave the world a little better off than I found it.

It's so easy in the flurry and fog of life to forget who we are and why we're here. We should heed the poet's warning:

> *O perpetual revolution of configured stars,*
> *O perpetual recurrence of determined seasons,*
> *O world of spring and autumn, birth and dying!*
>
> *The endless cycle of idea and action,*
> *Endless invention, endless experiment,*
> *Brings knowledge of motion, but not of stillness;*
> *Knowledge of speech, but not of silence;*
> *Knowledge of words, and ignorance of The Word.*
>
> *All our knowledge brings us nearer to our ignorance,*
> *All our ignorance brings us nearer to death,*
> *But nearness to death no nearer to God.*
>
> **Where is the Life we have lost in living?**
> **Where is the wisdom we have lost in knowledge?**
> **Where is the knowledge we have lost in information?**[2]

2. Excerpt from *The Rock*, T.S. Eliot, 1930 (emphasis mine).

We need not suffer so much loss. We can choose differently. The word "heresy" comes from the Greek word that means "to choose." The negative connotation that was attached to this word long ago was meant to mark heretics—those who chose something other than what was expected of them—as evildoers in a time when passive acceptance of what you were told was heralded as the height of goodness. That led to what we now call the dark ages. Those who made the rules and lived above them kept information to themselves. They understood that the Truth could set people free, but they feared what that freedom would bring if granted to anyone but themselves. Today, we live in the "information age." We dare not squander this opportunity to foster freedom for all. Each of us can make the world a better place by shining the light of truth on the shadows that surround us and by demonstrating a little wisdom. It's time for a little heresy.

APPENDIX A   EXPRESSING TIME AS A PERCENTAGE IN EXCEL

To compare two or more sets of time-series data with periods of different lengths, it is necessary to convert them to a uniform scale. The easiest way to do this is to convert the dates to percentages (0 for the beginning date through 100% for the end date) and use an XY (Scatter) graph with lines to display the data.

If the data set includes actual dates, such as "12 May 2007," follow these steps:

1. Sort the data so that the dates are ordered, with the earliest date at the top and the most recent at the bottom.

2. Copy all of the dates into a second column and format the cells of that new column. In the *Number* tab of the *Format Cells* menu, change the *Category* from *Date* to *General*. If the dates weren't already in the *Date* category, you might have to change their *Category* to *Date* first and then change them to *General*.

3. Now all of the dates in your second column should be converted to numbers. These numbers will probably all be around 40,000.

4. Calculate the range of these numbers by subtracting the smallest one (this should be the top-most date) from the largest one (this should be the bottom-most date).

5. Format the cells in the empty column to the right of the numbers as *Percentages*.

6. In this third column, create a calculation in the first row that subtracts the lowest number from the current number and then is divided by the range. Assuming the information has been sorted in ascending order, if the column of numbers begins at B1 and the range is located in the B20 cell, the formula would look like this: "=(B1-$B$1)/$B$20". The dollar signs indicate that when this formula is copied, the rows and columns that they precede should not change. However, because there are no dollars signs in the first "B1," this reference will change as the formula is applied to other cells.

7. Assuming everything went correctly, the third column should display a value of "0%". Copy and paste this value into all of the other cells to the right of the numbers. The bottom number should be 100%, and everything in between should be a number between 0% and 100%.

8. Repeat this process for all of the other data sets that you want to display.

9. Create an XY (Scatter) Graph with lines turned on and dots turned off. Create a separate data series for each line and use the percentage values that you calculated for the X values.

If the data set doesn't use full dates but instead uses only a month name or day of the week instead:

1. Put the dates in chronological order starting with the oldest.
2. In the cell next to the oldest date, put the number "0."
3. In the cell below the cell with the "0," put the following calculation: "=X+1" where X is the cell with the "0" (for instance B1).
4. The cell with the formula should display 1. If so, copy and paste that cell into every other cell that is located to the right of your dates. As you look down the column, each cell should increase in value by 1. Your final and highest number is also your range.
5. Format the cells in the empty column to the right of these numbers as *Percentages*.
6. In a third column, create a calculation that subtracts the current number from the lowest number and then is divided by the largest number (the range). If the column of numbers begins at B1 and the range is located in the B20 cell, the formula would look like this: "=(B1-$B$1)/$B$20." The dollar signs indicate that when this formula is copied, the rows and columns that they precede should not change. However, because there are no dollars signs in the first "B1," this reference will change as the formula is applied to other cells.
7. Assuming everything went correctly, the third column should display a value of "0%." Copy and paste this value into all of the other cells to the right of the numbers. The bottom number should be 100%, and everything in between should be a number between 0% and 100%.
8. Repeat this process for all of the other data sets that you want to display.
9. Create an XY (Scatter) Graph with lines turned on and dots turned off. Create a separate data series for each line and use the percentage values that you calculated for the X values.

APPENDIX B   ADJUSTING FOR INFLATION IN EXCEL

When the value of money decreases over time, we refer to this as *inflation*. In order to accurately compare dollars in the past to dollars today, we must express them using an equal measure of value. To do so, we must do one of the following:

- Convert past dollars to the amount that is equal in value to today's dollars,
- Convert today's dollars to the amount equal in value to dollars at the beginning of time period, or
- Convert both today's dollars and past dollars into the same measure of value as of some specified point in time (for example, dollars in the year 2000).

If you're not in the habit of doing this, don't get nervous. It takes a little extra work, but it's not difficult. The process requires the use of an *inflation index*. Several such indexes are available, but the two that are most commonly used in the United States are the *Consumer Price Index (CPI)*, published by the *Bureau of Labor Statistics (BLS)*, which is part of the *U.S. Department of Labor*, and the *Gross Domestic Product (GDP) deflator*, published by the *Bureau of Economic Analysis (BEA)*, which is part of the *U.S. Department of Commerce*. For the sake of illustration, we'll use the CPI, which represents a dollar's buying power relative to goods that are typically purchased by consumers (food, utilities, and so on). CPI values are researched and computed for a variety of representative people, places, and categories of consumer goods. Let's look at a version of the CPI that represents an average of *all classes of people* across *all U.S. cities* purchasing *all types of goods* for the years 1990 through 2002.

Year	Jan	Feb	Mar	Apr	May	Jun	Jul	Aug	Sep	Oct	Nov	Dec	Annual
1990	127.4	128.0	128.7	128.9	129.2	129.9	130.4	131.6	132.7	133.5	133.8	133.8	130.7
1991	134.6	134.8	135.0	135.2	135.6	136.0	136.2	136.6	137.2	137.4	137.8	137.9	136.2
1992	138.1	138.6	139.3	139.5	139.7	140.2	140.5	140.9	141.3	141.8	142.0	141.9	140.3
1993	142.6	143.1	143.6	144.0	144.2	144.4	144.4	144.8	145.1	145.7	145.8	145.8	144.5
1994	146.2	146.7	147.2	147.4	147.5	148.0	148.4	149.0	149.4	149.5	149.7	149.7	148.2
1995	150.3	150.9	151.4	151.9	152.2	152.5	152.5	152.9	153.2	153.7	153.6	153.5	152.4
1996	154.4	154.9	155.7	156.3	156.6	156.7	157.0	157.3	157.8	158.3	158.6	158.6	156.9
1997	159.1	159.6	160.0	160.2	160.1	160.3	160.5	160.8	161.2	161.6	161.5	161.3	160.5
1998	161.6	161.9	162.2	162.5	162.8	163.0	163.2	163.4	163.6	164.0	164.0	163.9	163.0
1999	164.3	164.5	165.0	166.2	166.2	166.2	166.7	167.1	167.9	168.2	168.3	168.3	166.6
2000	168.8	169.8	171.2	171.3	171.5	172.4	172.8	172.8	173.7	174.0	174.1	174.0	172.2
2001	175.1	175.8	176.2	176.9	177.7	178.0	177.5	177.5	178.3	177.7	177.4	176.7	177.1
2002	177.1	177.8	178.8	179.8	179.8	179.9	180.1	180.7	181.0	181.3	181.3	180.9	179.9

Figure B.1

If you prefer an index that focuses more directly on the value of money relative to the purchase of a specific type of item (for example, food), by a particular class of person (for example, clerical workers), or in a particular area of the country (for example, the San Francisco area), it is likely that these values are available. Simply access the *Bureau of Labor Statistics* website, and select what you need from the broad range of available data. It's easy to transfer the data from the website to your own computer as a Microsoft Excel file. In fact, I was able to get the information for the table above simply by electronically copying it from the website and pasting it into Excel.

Once you have an index in Excel, here's how to use it. The current version of the CPI uses the value of dollars from 1982 to 1984 as its baseline. Each value in the index represents the value of dollars at that time compared to their value during the period from 1982 to 1984. For instance, according to the above table, in January of 1990, the value of the dollar was 127.4% of its value in 1982 to 1984, and for the year 1990 as a whole, it was 130.7% of its value in 1982 to 1984. Typically, if you were comparing money across a range of time, you'd express everything according to a dollar's value at some point along that range, usually its value at when you're doing your analysis. If you're analyzing data in 2002, including values ranging from 1998 to 2002, you would likely want to convert all the values to their 2002 equivalent. Here's how you'd convert a year-1998 value of $100,000 into its year-2002 equivalent, assuming you're only dealing with one value per year, as opposed to monthly or quarterly values:

1. Find the index value for the year 2002, which is 179.9.
2. Find the index value for the year 1998, which is 163.0.
3. Divide the index value for 2002 by the index value for 1998, which results in 1.103681.
4. Multiply the dollar value for 1998, which is $100,000, by the results of step 3, which is 1.103681, which results in $110,368.10, which you can round to the nearest whole dollar, reaching the final result of $110,368.

Because the year-2002 dollars are already expressed as 2002 dollars, you don't have to convert them. If you're using spreadsheet software, setting up the formulas to convert money using an inflation index like the CPI is quite easy to do.

Whether you decide to express money across time using an inflation index to convert it to a common base or to use the actual values without adjusting them for inflation, you should always clearly indicate what you've done if you pass your findings on to others. Don't leave people guessing. As a communicator of important information, labeling the way that you've expressed the value of money is a practice that you should get into the habit of following. If you haven't adjusted for inflation, you can simply state somewhere on the report that you are using "Current U.S. Dollars." If you have adjusted for inflation, a statement such as "Adjusted to a base of year 2002 U.S. dollars" or "Adjusted according to the CPI using a baseline of year 2002."

For additional information on this topic, along with comprehensive instruction to the use of quantitative information, I recommend that you get a copy of Jonathan Koomey's excellent book *Turning Numbers into Knowledge*, published by Analytics Press.

BIBLIOGRAPHY

Anscombe, F. J., "Graphs in Statistical Analysis," *American Statistician*, Vol 27, Feb 1973.

Aris, Aleks, Ben Shneiderman, Catherine Plaisant, Galit Shmueli, and Wolfgang Jank, "Representing Unevenly-Spaced Time Series Data for Visualization and Interactive Exploration." *Proceedings of the International Conference on Human-Computer Interaction (INTERACT 2005)*, LNCS 3585, 2005.

Bertin, Jacques, *Semiology of Graphics*, translated by William J. Berg, The University of Wisconsin Press, Madison WI, 1983 (originally published as Sémiologie graphique in 1967).

Brewer, Cynthia A., *Designing Better Maps: A Guide for GIS Users*, ESRI Press, Redlands CA, 2005.

Card, Stuart K., Jock D. Mackinlay, and Ben Shneiderman, *Readings in Information Visualization: Using Vision to Think*, Academic Press, San Diego CA, 1999.

Chernoff, Herman, "Using faces to represent points in *k*-dimensional space," *Journal of the American Statistical Association*, 68, 1973.

Cleveland, William S., *The Elements of Graphing Data*, Hobart Press, Summit NJ, 1994.

Cleveland, William S., *Visualizing Data*, Hobart Press, Summit NJ, 1993.

Cleveland, William, Douglas Dunn, and Irma Terpenning, "The SABL Seasonal Analysis Package—Statistical and Graphical Procedures," Bell Laboratories, Murray Hill NJ, 1978.

Cleveland, W. S. and M. E. McGill, editors, *Dynamic Graphics for Statistics*, Wadsworth and Brooks/Cole, Pacific Grove CA, 1988.

Cleveland, W. S., R. A. Becker, and G. Weil, "The Use of Brushing and Rotation for Data Analysis," *First IASC World Conference on Computational Statistics and Data Analysis*, International Statistical Institute, Voorburg Netherlands,1988.

Derene, Glenn, "Buzzword: Multitouch Computing", www.popularmechanics.com, Feb 20 2007.

Eliot, T. S., *The Rock*, 1930.

Farquhar, A. B. and H. Farquhar, *Economic and Industrial Solutions*, B. Putnam's Sons, New York NY, 1891.

Gilbert, E. W., "Pioneer Maps of Health and Disease in England," *Geographical Journal*, 124, 1958.

Hartwig, Frederick with Brian E. Dearing, *Exploratory Data Analysis*, Sage Publications, Inc, Thousand Oaks CA, 1979.

Heer, Jeffrey and Maneesh Agrawala, "Multi-Scale Banking to 45°," *IEEE Transactions on Visualization and Computer Graphics*, Vol. 12, No. 5, Sept/Oct 2006.

Heer, Jeffrey, Fernanda Viégas, and Martin Wattenberg, "Voyagers and Voyeurs: Supporting Asynchronous Collaborative Information Visualization," *Proceedings of ACM CHI*, Apr 2007.

Heer, Jeffrey, Jock D. Mackinlay, Chris Stolte, and Maneesh Agrawala, "Graphical Histories for Visualization: Supporting Analysis, Communication, and Evaluation," *IEEE Transactions on Visualization and Computer Graphics*, Volume 14, Number 6, Nov/Dec 2008.

Hoaglin, Mosteller & Tukey, editors, *Understanding Robust and Exploratory Data Analysis*, John Wiley & Sons, New York NY, 1983.

Horn, Robert, *Visual Language: Global Communication for the 21st Century*, MacroVU, Inc., Bainbridge Island WA, 1998.

Hubbard, Douglas W., *How to Measure Anything: Finding the Value of Intangibles in Business*, John Wiley and Sons, Inc., Hoboken NJ, 2007.

Keogh, Eamonn, Harry Hochheiser, and Ben Shneiderman, "An Augmented Visual Query Mechanism for Finding Patterns in Time Series Data," *Proc. Fifth International Conference on Flexible Query Answering Systems*, Copenhagen Denmark, Oct 2002.

Kida, Thomas, *Don't Believe Everything You Think*, Prometheus Books, Amherst, New York NY, 2006.

Kocherlakota, Sarat M., Christopher G. Healey, "Summarization Techniques for Visualization of Large Multidimensional Datasets," Technical Report TR-2005-35, North Carolina State University, 2005.

Koomey, Jonathan G., *Turning Numbers into Knowledge*, Analytics Press, Oakland CA, 2001.

McGilvray, Danette, *Executing Data Quality Projects*, Morgan Kaufmann, Burlington MA, 2008.

Millay, Edna St. Vincent, *Huntsman, What Quarry?*, 1939

Niederman, Derrick and David Boyum, *What the Numbers Say: A Field Guide to Mastering Our Numerical World*, Broadway Books, New York NY, 2003.

Playfair, William, *The Commercial and Political Atlas*, 1786.

Rao, Ramana, "TableLens: A Clear Window for Viewing Multivariate Data," *Visual Business Intelligence Newsletter*, Perceptual Edge, Berkeley CA, Jul 2006.

Reynolds, Garr, *Presentation Zen*, New Riders, Berkeley CA, 2008.

Robbins, Naomi R., "Introduction to Cycle Plots," *Visual Business Intelligence Newsletter*, Perceptual Edge, Berkeley CA, 2008.

Robertson, George, Roland Fernandez, Danyel Fisher, Bongshin Lee, and John Stasko, "Effectiveness of Animation in Trend Visualization," *IEEE Transactions on Visualization and Computer Graphics*, Volume 14, Number 6, Nov/Dec 2008.

Shneiderman, Ben, "Dynamic Queries for Visual Information Seeking," *IEEE Software*, 11(6), 70-77, 1994.

Spence, Robert, *Information Visualization*, Addison-Wesley, Essex England, 2001.

Thaler, Richard H. and Cass R. Sunstein, *Nudge: Improving Decisions About Health, Wealth, and Happiness*, Yale University Press, New Haven CT, 2008.

Triola, Mario F., *Elementary Statistics*, Eighth Edition, Addison Wesley Longman, Inc., New York NY, 2001.

Tufte, Edward R., *The Visual Display of Quantitative Information*, Graphics Press, Cheshire CT, 1983.

Tufte, Edward R., *Beautiful Evidence*, Graphics Press, Cheshire CT, 2006.

Tukey, John W., *Exploratory Data Analysis*, Addison-Wesley, Reading MA, 1977.

Tukey, John W. and M. B. Wilk, *Proceedings of the Symposium on Information Processing in Sight Sensory Systems*, California Institute of Technology, Pasadena CA, 1965.

Wainer, Howard, *Discovery: A Trout in the Milk and Other Visual Adventures*, Princeton University Press, Princeton NJ, 2005.

Ware, Colin, *Information Visualization: Perception for Design*, Second Edition, Morgan Kaufmann Publishers, San Francisco CA, 2004.

Ware, Colin, "Visual Queries: The Foundation of Visual Thinking", *Knowledge and Information Visualization*, Sigmar-Olaf Tergan and Tanja Keller, Editors, Springer-Verlag, Berlin Heidelberg, 2005.

Wattenberg, Martin, "Sketching a Graph to Query a Time-Series Database", Dow Jones / SmartMoney.com, New York NY, 2001.

INDEX

ABOUT THE AUTHOR

Stephen Few has worked for over 25 years as teacher, writer, consultant, and innovator, primarily in the fields of business intelligence and information design. Today, as founder and principal of Perceptual Edge, Stephen focuses on helping people in a broad range of industries and professions—business, non-profit, and government alike—understand and present quantitative information. He publishes the monthly *Visual Business Intelligence Newsletter* and teaches in the MBA program at the University of California, Berkeley. Through years of observation, study, and painstaking trial and error, working to solve problems in the real world, he has learned to squeeze real value from information that cries out for attention but rarely get a chance to tell its story.

When he isn't working, he can normally be found in or around his home in Berkeley, California, lost in a good book, savoring a delightful wine, hiking the hills, instigating an animated discussion about the meaning of life with close friends, or simply basking in the warmth of his happy home with his wife Jayne, his dogs Mangia and Atticus, and his cat Tuna.